Developmental
MANAGEMENT

CHARTING THE CORPORATE MIND

B

Developmental Management

General Editor: Ronnie Lessem

Charting the Corporate Mind*
Charles Hampden-Turner

Managing in the Information Society
Yoneji Masuda

Developmental Management
Ronnie Lessem

Foundations of Business
Ivan Alexander

* This edition not available in the USA.

Developmental
MANAGEMENT

Charting the Corporate Mind

FROM DILEMMA TO STRATEGY

CHARLES HAMPDEN-TURNER

WITH A FOREWORD BY
RONNIE LESSEM

Copyright © The Free Press, A Division of Macmillan, Inc. 1990
Foreword © Ronnie Lessem 1990

First published 1990
First published in paperback 1994
Reprinted 1994 (twice)

Blackwell Publishers, the publishing imprint of
Basil Blackwell Ltd
108 Cowley Road
Oxford OX4 1JF, UK

Basil Blackwell Inc.
238 Main Street
Cambridge, Massachusetts 02142
USA

British Library Cataloguing in Publication Data

A CIP catalogue record for this book is available
from the British Library.

Library of Congress Cataloging in Publication Data

A CIP catalog record for this book is available
from the Library of Congress.

ISBN 0–631–19305–7 (pbk.)

Typeset in 11 on 13 pt Ehrhardt
by Hope Services (Abingdon) Ltd.
Printed and bound in Great Britain by
Hartnolls Limited, Bodmin, Cornwall

This book is printed on acid-free paper

Contents

Foreword: Existential Strategy

by Ronnie Lessem

Introduction – Radical Management

A European Management Philosopher

Charles Hampden-Turner is one of a select few European management philosophers who, like the illustrious Peter Drucker, while making America their home have retained an essential Europeanness in their managerial perspective. In fact both these Europeans have sought relentlessly to resolve the conflict between order and freedom in management. The Austrian Peter Drucker, on the one hand, has focused primarily on order and accountable management and only secondarily on freedom and enterprise. The Anglo-Saxon Hampden-Turner, on the other hand, has oriented his thinking more closely towards 'existentially' managed freedom than towards organizationally constrained order.

Existential Management

Hampden-Turner, having graduated from Trinity College, Cambridge, England, acquired a doctorate at Harvard Business School before going on to teach at the Harvard Medical School and the Kennedy Institute of Politics in Cambridge, Massachusetts. In 1970, while Drucker was focusing on *The Effective Executive*, Hampden-Turner published his pathbreaking first book on *Radical Man*.

Whereas Peter Drucker was essentially a political economist, Charles Hampden-Turner was, by education and training, a social psychologist. Charles was influenced, in America, by the humanistic psychologists Carl Rogers and Abraham Maslow and, in Europe, by the political philosopher Jean-Paul Sartre. In fact Hampden-Turner became the first 'existential' management thinker, thereby concerned with the lot of the individual, of his situation in the world and of his ultimate significance.

Existentialism, then, is focused on the problematic character of the human (and hence managerial) situation through which man is continually confronted with diverse possibilities or alternatives, among which he may choose and on the basis of which he may project his life. Existence, then, precedes essence in that modes of individual or managerial being are not inherently given. Rather these modes are simply possibilities from which man or manager may choose, and on the basis of which he may project himself.

The issue thus becomes one of 'individuating', in every concrete situation, the real possibilities offered to the individual person. Such a choice amongst possibilities involves not only acute dilemmas but also risk and renunciation. Among the risks attached, the greatest is that of individual degradation – from a person into a thing – by virtue of alienation from the physical or social reality in which the 'existant' is engaged.

Interestingly enough, this pan-European existentialist philosophy found a particular relevance during World War II when the Continent found itself threatened alternately by material and by spiritual destruction. Today, some fifty years thereafter, individual freedom in both America and Europe is being similarly threatened, but this time not by militant fascism but by the collective spirit and economic power of Japan. In his existentialist approach to strategy and organization, Hampden-Turner charts a dual path towards freedom and responsibility for managers in the West. Before I outline this path, however, I want to introduce you to his 'radical management'.

Radical Management

For Hampden-Turner the individual person or manager exists in relation to others who receive his communications and witness the investment of his personality in the human environment.

Managers exist freely, to begin with (figure 1), to the extent that their capacity for synthesizing, symbolizing and exploring frees them from being 'stimulus bound'. Such capacity, according to Hampden-Turner, permits them to rebel against the absurdity of atrophying cultures and empty forms and enables them to create new meaning

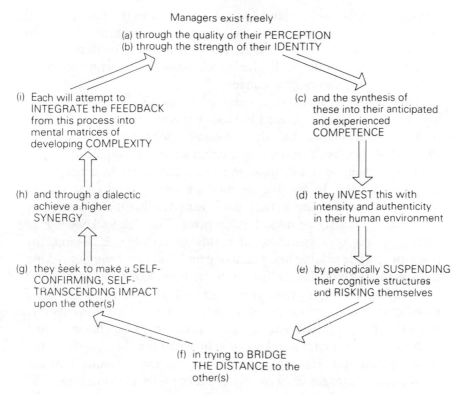

Managers exist freely
(a) through the quality of their PERCEPTION
(b) through the strength of their IDENTITY

(i) Each will attempt to
INTEGRATE the FEEDBACK
from this process into
mental matrices of
developing COMPLEXITY

(c) and the synthesis of
these into their anticipated
and experienced
COMPETENCE

(h) and through a dialectic
achieve a higher
SYNERGY

(d) they INVEST this with
intensity and authenticity
in their human environment

(g) they seek to make a SELF-
CONFIRMING, SELF-
TRANSCENDING IMPACT
upon the other(s)

(e) by periodically SUSPENDING
their cognitive structures
and RISKING themselves

(f) in trying to BRIDGE
THE DISTANCE to the
other(s)

Figure 1

and renew themselves in their environment. Through the *quality of their perception* (a), moreover, they are able to gaze upon absurdity while not permitting this nightmare to dull their sensitivity. In other words they retain their radical vision, notwithstanding the exigencies of the bottom line and the falling price points on the New York or London stock exchange. Finally, the *strength of their identity* (b) is reflected in their self-awareness, and in their self-acceptance, whereby they carve out a radical identity for themselves while deliberately fashioning it in dialogue with others.

Radical managers, then, take their perceptions along with their inner awareness and combine these into a personal sense of *anticipated goal-directed competence* (c). Such managerial competence is not merely self-centred but is *invested*, by existential managers, *with intensity and authenticity in their human environment* (d). 'While we begin to exist merely by perceiving and construing, we deepen our commitment and add significance to our being-in-the-world by projection into social (and economic) reality of our personal syntheses. The outside view sees freedom as residing in acts of investment, but the inner, existential view regards freedom as . . . inner conviction so that individuals feel compelled to act on the basis of the moral syntheses they conceive."[1]

When managers invest their personal syntheses, or competence, in others, they must be prepared to modify this competence in the light of external reactions, i.e. by *periodically suspending their cognitive structures and risking themselves* (e). Suppose, for example, that I am trying to convey to a colleague the value that I see in a revamped business strategy. In seeking to gain his support and trust I must temporarily suspend the structure of meanings that the new strategy has for me and imagine myself in his place. The risk I take is that of permitting my own structure of reality to crumble. I devalue my judgement while valuing his; I cannot gain his support without risking the loss of my credibility. In fact, in *trying to bridge the distance to others* (f), the dread that grips man or manager is that of finding nothing, of entering into a bottomless pit of unknown forces. What prevents me, as an Englishman, from reaching out to you, as a Frenchman, is just such a fear of the cultural unknown. The wider the abyss, such as that between American and Japanese, the greater the hesitancy that the conventional manager displays. Each sticks to his/her own guns. Yet the radical manager stretches every nerve to reach out to that radically unknown, to overcome the dichotomy between East and West, or between worker and management.

In so doing such managers *seek to make a self-confirming, self-transcending impact on others* (g). The more spectacular such an impact is, the more the other person will be propelled in the direction of his or her own growth, this force being harnessed to that of the investor. Since the other person, institution or society is unique, only a finely wrought synthesis could fashion an investment tailored to the other's needs.

Such a synthesis inevitably, according to Hampden-Turner, must be struggled for through *a dialectical process that seeks to reconcile apparent opposites* (h), *thereby achieving a higher synergy*. For if a manager's existence is highly creative, his vision, identity and competence radical, his risk-taking considerable and the distance he seeks to bridge wide, then he is unlikely to receive immediate confirmation from others. As a result weakly developed individuals or managers can withstand only small disagreements to win equally small synergy. The greater the force of contradiction, if it can be sustained, the more powerful the unity that can be created out of the diversity. For it is through a process of dialectic that one-dimensional managers confront one another to become two dimensional or better. For example a manager from Japan may extol the virtues of collective effort while a colleague from Sweden or the United States extols the virtues of individual enterprise.

Through a dialectical interaction between sufficiently developed managers, crossing the cultural and economic divide, a linking concept could emerge. Man should use his liberty to create a new relatedness, exercising his right to detach himself for more effective attachments. With this synthesis Eastern and Western managers could integrate into an expanding managerial consciousness much of the other's thought. Each would thereby *integrate the feedback from this process into mental matrices of developing complexity* (i).

Radical managers, in summary, whom we shall soon meet in the guise of arch resolvers of strategic dilemmas, project their own moral and creative synthesis into the world:

1 keeping open their *perception* of poverty and injustice, without yielding in their determination to transform both;
2 fashioning periodically new and daring facets to their *identity* which they examine and understand;
3 seeking for ever fresh and greater *competence*;
4 *investing* and committing *themselves* to others, authentically and intensely;
5 *risking themselves* by deliberately suspending their assumptions and exposing their undefended selves to others;
6 *bridging* great *distances* to reach foreign cultures, minority groups and competitive enterprises, to make contact, to bring compassion and to discover differences;
7 *transcending* their own personalities by entering into the consciousnesses of communities at large;
8 forming cooperative relationships of higher *synergy* but only after a desperate dialectical struggle to understand;
9 *integrating* these experiences by using the radical and unifying concepts that emerge from the consciousness-expanding dialectic.

It is upon these psychological and social foundations, laid down in the late 1960s, that Hampden-Turner built his distinctive organizational and strategic edifice, in the 1970s and 1980s.

From Dilemma to Strategy

The International Learning Race

As far as Hampden-Turner is concerned we are all, now, in an economic race to learn. The wealth-creating capacities of a nation are no longer contained in their physical resources nor even in their comparative economic advantages, but in 'the innovativeness and learning of their culture'. Translating such a general learning orientation into his particularly existential frame of reference, Hampden-Turner argues that 'we have no choice but to choose – and the freedom to which we find ourselves condemned consists of constantly elaborating and redesigning skeins of information into new configurations'.

Meanwhile, as a historically aware European, Hampden-Turner takes us back to the ancient Greeks. For the capacity to learn, he says, is 'heroic' in the tradition of Greek humanism, where virtue lay in the facing and surviving of catastrophe and in enduring the extremes of good and bad fortune. Similarly, the capacity to learn and the propensity to be human reinforce one another. 'How products are made and designed must, in the end, depend on how the social systems creating those products are made and designed. Lonely, ugly and adversarial relationships will result in badly fitting assemblies of junk that shake apart when used – not a bad description of certain American and British automobiles in the recent period of decline.'

Adding value to products and services, then, requires of managers that they resolve dilemmas, between profit and people, between supply and demand. Moreover, if creating value requires us to resolve such dilemmas, then every aspect of the corporation – its culture and strategy, its manufacturing and marketing – needs the *wā*, or harmony, that is the chief axiom of Japanese commercial practices. All need to perceive, confront and transcend those tensions which if they crack the social system will also flaw the products and services it supplies.

Charting Dilemmas and Steering Strategically

What Hampden-Turner has done, in effect, is to draw on the features of a Western culture, most particularly the 'existential' ones, that parallel those aspects of Japanese management which have recently proved to be so effective. In bringing individual and managerial dilemmas, and their resolution, into an organizational and commercial frame of reference, he has essentially transformed strategy formulation from a competitive undertaking into an existential one. 'A corporation must either create a premium product or be a low-cost producer. Any attempt to achieve both could trap the company in conflict. Michael Porter is entirely correct about the dangers of this dilemma, but wrong, we submit, in not seeing the power of reconciliation, of creating a premium product at lower comparable cost. Many managerial choices are not either–or, but both–and.'

Genuine reconciliation, moreover, only occurs among genuine differences. In that sense Hampden-Turner and his fellow Anglo-American, Mary Parker Follett, are at one. True unity can only be created out of proliferating variety.[2] Where there is no initial dilemma there is no gain from designing a solution. This applies as much to the design of washing machines as to the development of viable organization structures, or indeed of successful corporate strategies. In the final analysis, the greater the generalized ability to recognize and to reconcile dilemmas, the more finely tuned will be the overall organizational learning.

Steps to Reconciliation

Hampden-Turner roams the field from white goods to motor insurance, from television sets to personal computers, from Europe to America, and from West to East, to examine how strategic dilemmas are best resolved. The steps that he arrives at are not the conventionally acknowledged ones of environmental assessment, SWOT analysis or scenario building but those of

1 eliciting response through *humour*, to enable the dilemmas to surface;
2 *mapping* or charting the dilemmas, normally on two axes which serve to indicate polarities, for example between cost effectiveness and value added;
3 *processing* dilemmas to form intricate patterns that are mutually modifying;
4 *framing* the dilemmas within a context in which opposites can be reconciled;

5 *timing* the reconciliation of dilemmas, appropriately, in the sense of both analysing sequentially and synthesizing simultaneously;

6 *waving* dilemmas into wave-forms, whereby emergent strategies rather than competitive strategies take shape;

7 *synergizing* dilemmas by combining all elements so that they work together (the Greek *syn-ergo*) and are duly reconciled.

As we can see Hampden-Turner combines Western style confrontation of opposing forces with Easter style harmony between such forces. He often portrays this combination as a virtuous, as opposed to a vicious, circle (figure 2).

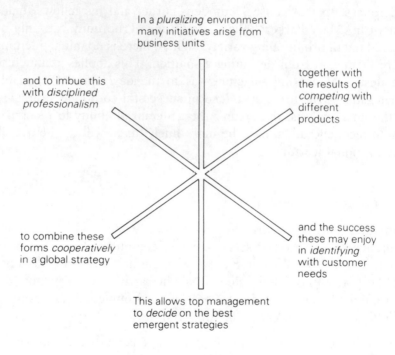

In a *pluralizing* environment
many initiatives arise from
business units

and to imbue this
with *disciplined*
professionalism

together with
the results of
competing with
different
products

to combine these
forms *cooperatively*
in a global strategy

and the success
these may enjoy
in *identifying*
with customer
needs

This allows top management
to *decide* on the best
emergent strategies

Figure 2

As we can see from the above, the existential strategist successfully steers between the centre and the periphery, between internal and external requirements and between competitive and cooperative world views. It is in this way alone that he is able to combat the strategic threat from the East.

Culture and Strategy in the Pacific Rim

Hampden-Turner explicitly states that his dilemma methodology is geared to loosen knots in the Occidental mind-set. Generally speaking Asians, he says, neither see separate atoms as we do nor stubborn antagonisms among these, but are sensitized to complementarities. Neither in judo nor in business do the Japanese clash head on, despite alternative Western preconceptions. Rather they create from that struggle a more elegant and efficient combination of forces than they had before. 'Nothing better illustrates our total incomprehension of Asian strategy than the imputation that they are "picking winners". This vision of a horse race or a demolition derby with every product [or company] racing against every other product is how we think, in bits and pieces, and in aggregations of individualists. Unlike us, *they* look out upon a world of complementarities and connections. For them [as for any truly developmentally minded manager] the economy is a whole organism.'

Similarly, the more knowledge that is organized into a particular product the less likely it is that you will have many competitors. This is because the skills and learning necessary to create product configurations of rich complexity are scarce. Just as complexity in human thought goes up the abstraction ladder, so there are products and meta-products. It is obvious, for example, to the Japanese that, if your machine tools are the best in the world, then most of the other goods you manufacture will benefit. Cross-fertilize microchips and electronics with machine tools, for instance, and you get numerically controlled machine tools in which Japan now leads the world. So complementarity and cooperation between people – *kaisha* – is matched by the same family perspective towards things.

Conclusion – A Critique of Pure Profit

In conclusion, and having duly praised the Japanese for placing profit in an appropriately subordinate position to human being, Hampden-Turner launches into a critique of pure profit as a one-dimensional measure of business growth and development. He has nine major objections to his so-called 'unicorn' of profit:

1 profit comes too late to steer by;
2 motivationally the desire for profit is too narrow to learn from;
3 profit conflicts with values of equal importance yet higher priority;
4 putting profitability first makes business strategies too predictable and too easy to defeat;
5 profiting is a 'text' which needs a context to support it;
6 profitability is an organic not a mechanical attribute;
7 profiting may not apply to all the units within a strategic alliance;
8 when initiated by factions and persons within the corporation, profiting becomes suboptimal;
9 it cannot deal with societal and environmental 'addictions'.

'Profit', Hampden-Turner maintains, 'is neither good nor bad in itself. Rather it is strategically ineffective unless it is woven into a larger configuration of reconciled values. It is not profits or people but both, not merit or participation but both, not competition or cooperation but both.' The most successful economies of our day are neither exclusively capitalist nor socialist. Rather the Japanese, the Swedes and the West Germans manage best to reconcile those opposites to which Hampden-Turner alludes.

Business, he says, is on the verge of a virtual renaissance which will make the ethos of early philistine industrialists and the doctrines of Grantham grocers' daughters into vestiges of the past! To reduce these extensive skeins of knowledge into measures of more or less money paid to persons not even present in the organization and not, for the most part, known as individuals with recognizable faces is to reduce a culture to an abstraction and a community to a set of accounts. This will produce not only a diminution of the energy and creativity with which we work but also a loss in the potential of all of us to find meaning in our lives. 'The hunt for the unicorn is a doomed quest. No pure, unambiguous essence of business virtue exists. We are all like jugglers with more and more balls in the air, who will drop them if we all get fixated on one.'

Existentialist first and last, Hampden-Turner has a radical vision of business and organization which he has daringly fashioned over his adult lifetime. For ever seeking fresh and greater competence for himself – as community developer and technological forecaster, as organization developer and business strategist – he has committed himself intensely to social and economic transformation. Suspending his anti-business assumptions in midlife he has since turned to business as the revolutionary force in contemporary society. In the process Hampden-Turner has bridged the gap between radical man and conservative businessman, investing new meaning into economic endeavours.

Having confronted head on the dialectic between people and profit, between socialism and capitalism, he has come up with a new synthesis, centred upon an existentially based strategy, focused upon the reconciliation of dilemmas. Integrating his own geographically, academically and institutionally diverse experiences Hampden-Turner has emerged with a unifying strategic concept that not only draws on his Western heritage but also encompasses his Eastern world view. Such an approach, true to developmental form, is destined to chart an auspicious path for progressive managers to follow, well into the twenty-first century.

Ronnie Lessem
London, 1990

Notes

1 Hampden-Turner, Charles M., *Radical Man: Towards a Theory of Psychosocial Development*. Schenkman, 1970, p. 41.
2 Graham, Pauline, *Unity in Variety*. Oxford: Basil Blackwell, 1991.

Acknowledgements

Several persons helped to make this book possible. I am most grateful of all to Arie de Geus, until recently Coordinator of Group Planning of Shell International Petroleum Co., the first major figure in international business to grasp what I was trying to say. He not only put up with me for three years in planning, but he also arranged for Shell to offer me support for three further years at the Centre for Business Strategy at the London Business School.

Through Arie I was introduced to Bill O'Brien of Hanover Insurance, who features in chapter 4 of this book, and to Peter Senge of MIT, whose network of CEOs and outstanding leaders has proved an invaluable resource. Bill helped to dispel any lingering doubts that personal integrity was the key to leadership.

Great scholarly encouragement was also given to me by Charles Baden-Fuller, a colleague at the Centre for Business Strategy and now a professor at the University of Bath. Charles helped me to write chapter 3 when it was a working paper, and I discovered a common ground with someone trained in economics, a bridge I had long feared was impassable. To Charles and to John Stopford I owe both my coming to CBS and my introduction to their mature industries project, which gave me access to the domestic appliance industry. I practised a lot of these ideas at the Niagara Institute in Canada and owe much to the support of Doug Bowie, Doug Ure and Ken Shephard.

The Centre for Business Strategy provided a stimulating if sceptical environment which helped to test my concepts. I am grateful to David Sainsbury for support during 1987–8 and to Shell Planning for support in 1984–7. Great personal encouragement came from Henry Mintzberg at McGill, Iain Mitroff and Warren Bennis at the University of Southern California, Chris Argyris and Bob Reich at Harvard, Don Schon at MIT, and Paul Ryan at INSEAD. I am

ACKNOWLEDGEMENTS

grateful for the continuing support of the Global Business Network, especially Napier Collyns, Stewart Brand, Peter Schwartz and Jay Ogilvy.

Many people at Shell have helped me. I am especially indebted to Kees van der Heijden, Tim Kenny, Jeremy Russell and Jap Leemhuis. If Bob Wallace of The Free Press had not heard me speak at a strategy conference in Amsterdam and tamed my compulsion to tell everything I know, this book would not have transpired.

Finally, let me come full circle to those whose ideas are always with me: the late Gregory Bateson and Rollo May are the two mentors who influenced me fundamentally and who shape the way I think. I hope this application of their ideas to business does them no dishonour. Since business of some kind is what most people do with most of their lives, it needs the enlightenment they provided.

Charles Hampden-Turner

Introduction:

The International Learning Race

In their recent best-seller, *In Search of Excellence*, Tom Peters and Bob Waterman inveighed against 'the rational model' and appear to have touched a chord. They extolled other ways of managing which were anecdotally well illustrated if rather vaguely described. Preferred practices involved 'managing values' rather than people, creating strong cultures, being tight and loose simultaneously, 'holding two opposed ideas in your mind at the same time' (the quote is Scott Fitzgerald's), managing by wandering about, by-passing bureaucracies with 'skunk groups', and keeping close to customers in order to learn from them.

But if these activities are not 'rational', then what are they? It hardly promotes their use to imply that they are irrational or non-rational. If there are categories of intelligent action which are 'beyond the rational model' then these have yet to be carefully described. We all know that much of management is an art and relies on personal judgement, intuition, flair, character and creativity, yet resorting to such terms only deepens the mystery of what is going on in the minds of outstandingly successful leaders. And can we learn from them: are there thought processes which distinguish the more successful from the less, and can these be untangled and described? I believe so.

What we cannot do is simply invoke being 'creative' or 'managing values' as explanatory principles, as if repeating these words could conjure up the results we wanted. Celebrating the indefinable qualities of greater leaders and falling about ourselves in enthusiasm will not suffice. I have sincere admiration for many of the executives described in this book, but I think I know why their strategies worked. I am not content simply to repeat their ideas and slogans in the hope that these have sufficient generality to be used in other contexts.

Management-by-slogans will not do. It merely causes us to rush precipitously from one end of a values continuum to another, from our own 'rationality' to embracing the customer and then back again. We shall need another sensational book a few years hence to signal that reason is okay. It is back in fashion. Are we to be condemned to this raising and lowering of corporate hemlines, this permission to hide or to reveal bits of corporate anatomy which were there all the time?

So, my aim here is to *broaden the definition* of intelligent corporate thinking and action to include more than technical rationality, which, I agree, is but one of the important skills available to managers. By technical rationality I mean a calculus made before the manager acts, which tries to identify the most logical and efficient means to achieving the goals set for the organization. These goals, in turn, must have a demonstrable effect in advancing the interests of the organization and its shareholders. The ideal is to develop forms of precalculation that allow one to predict and control successful outcomes and to discover quickly any errors of calculation so as to substitute a superior calculus.

Now there are several reasons why this ideal is rarely approximated in practice: because managers must usually act before all the information has been collected; because making mistakes and correcting these may be quicker and more profitable than the time taken to get it right first time; and because there is not, in fact, a consensus on the goals of the organization, so no shared premise exists on which a logical calculation can be based – rather, various factions are trying to manipulate 'logical means' for different ends. The rational ideal is further eroded because what customers want may not be 'rational' according to premises of the supplier but still they want it, because the environment is changing so fast that today's perfect calculus will not last the month and because those responsible for acting on instructions may not relish implementing to the letter a rational policy passed down to them but will seek to qualify this with their own preferences. Finally, formal rationality *cannot deal with the conflicts between different values*.

It is this last objection that epitomizes the whole list. We cannot achieve our ends by technical means unless we *know* what it is that various stakeholders want. It is this weighing of contending sets of values and choosing the right combination which remains the mystery at the heart of good leadership. So excellent companies 'manage values'. All right, but *how* do they do this and can the better management of values be separated from the worse? Do we have to surrender our 'reason' to grasp this process and learn some secret rites?

Rationality means only that there are reasons, ratios and criteria for what we decide. It does not decree the number of these reasons nor their form. So let me describe an alternative reasoning process, which we can call *encompassing* reason because it is circular, or *substantive* reason because it deals with issues of substance and meaning to people. This is a *binary* logic because values are really differences or contrasts. If a Chief Executive Officer engages in *risking*, we immediately understand, without having to be told, that this contrasts with *securing* behaviour or security. Now companies do not take risks for the hell of it. The purpose of risking is to *secure for that company a better future*. We can therefore inquire as to how effectively a leader is managing the two values on the continuum of risking and securing. Over time, if he manages these values well, the company should be *more* secure enabling it to take *higher* risks which feed back to enhance security still further. The two values develop together. There may be tension between those who enjoy hazards and those who seek more safety, but, in the end, both may achieve more of what they seek.

The method of inquiry consists of interviewing some outstanding managers or content-analysing their writings, while paying special attention to metaphors, symbols, slogans, visions and figures of speech, as well as hard plans and declared policies and strategies, along with the means designed to gain these ends. No attempt is made to disturb the managers' train of thought. Consider a slogan used by Steve Jobs at Apple Inc., adopted by John Sculley, its current President, and used by Steve at Next and which is also the title of his recent book: *The Journey is the Reward*.

There are various ways of interpreting this reference to operating in the computer industry. Do the speakers mean that the *process* of making the product is becoming more important than the *product* itself, since the process goes on to the 'next' product and the next. Do they mean that what you *learn* on the journey towards developing your product stays in your mind and in the memory of the corporation, while the *profits* from making it must fade with the obsolescence of technology? Do they perhaps mean that the personal fulfilment to be found in the discovery and development of innovative technologies has greater *intrinsic* satisfactions than any *extrinsic* satisfactions of money or status which the company could confer? Do they mean all of these and more? We do not have to guess, we can ask them or read them.

We can go on from there to locate graphically where the leader stands on the 'map coordinates', or value axes, of product versus process, learning versus profit and intrinsic versus extrinsic rewards. Is the leader trying to shift the balance from one value to another while retaining the influence of both? What are the consequences?

Now it does not matter to such an investigation whether the leader reasoned *before* he spoke or whether it was subsequent reflections on what he said, or whether it was what employees interpreted him as saying. The point of charting the shifts in the balance of values over time is that you can give form to intuitions and inspired hunches and clarify what seemed ambiguous at the time in the light of how it was heard and received.

There are good reasons for being ambiguous and using images with multiple meanings. It allows employees to interpret the image in the light of their own motives and so *participate in the creation of shared meanings*. 'The journey is the reward' means what employees *want* it to mean. They may agree that there is not enough money in the computer industry to match the sheer exhilaration of inventing and creating, in which case the value of intrinsic motivation has been consensually evolved between leaders and led, or they could suspect an argument designed to pay them less!

It is *not* the point of this book that we should henceforth draw charts carefully before making key decisions or issuing statements. There is no alternative to thinking on your feet and some of the wisest judgements are probably intuitive and quite unmediated by conscious deliberation. The point is that we can check from time to time where we are on charts drawn from our own values, and that reflecting on past judgements and intuitions need not slow these down or impede them but make them wiser in future by recording their consequences. Like navigators, we can steer by our judgement, while periodically checking our position on the charts. That is all the graphic representations in this book aim to do. They are aids to judgement, not substitutes for it. If a leader misjudges risks and leaves the company less secure, no map drawn from these very misjudgements can avail him. But if his judgements are adequate, then checking the charts periodically could assist him and improve his judgement.

The charts can help to make the company's values explicit to all those responsible for steering and to those capable of causing drift.

They can become frameworks and contexts for group discussion, records of where the company has been and visions of where it should now head. Charts are ways of checking the mental models in the minds of senior managers with each other to gauge their consistency or discrepancies, since the use of the same words can often mask widely varying interpretations. Charts can guide the combination of values so that risking and securing, process and product, learning and profit, intrinsic and extrinsic sources of reward can be reconciled to good effect. And, of course, charts allow you to test collective judgements against the harder, if later, verdicts arising from the market-place.

While technical or formal rationality is linear, you reason, you act, you achieve accordingly; encompassing reason is circular and iterative. You probe, discover something interesting, reflect, cogitate and probe again. The manager acts with whatever degree of forethought is appropriate but carefully examines the feedback and, through a cybernetic process, rethinks and acts again, learning along the way.

For learning is, in the end, what this book is mostly about. To say that business is about profits, market share, pleasing customers, assuming total quality, creating wealth, is to speak about ports of call and passing destinations. All these are necessary to the journey, all are vital in maintaining supplies, all are places of absorbing interest, but still they are stations upon a voyage that never ends. But this journey has a direction, towards an ever richer synthesis of values, towards mounting complexity, towards packages of knowledge more intensely and aesthetically organized, and, in the case of the computer industry, towards the expansion of mind itself.

For the contemporary reality is that we are in an international learning race where the stakes are very high – the relative rise and fall of nations and whole regions of the world. What was once accomplished by war is now done by commerce, as the losers in World War II seem to have discovered before the winners awoke to this reality. William James once called upon the human race to discover 'a moral equivalent for war', some activity with war's excitements and heroics but without its lethal legacies. James would probably have shuddered at the idea that commerce could ever supply this equivalence; was it not about prosaic things? Or, as Masefield put it, 'road-rail, pig-lead, firewood, ironware and cheap tin trays'.

Of course, business can still be trivial and boring. The war of colas and uncolas will continue yet a while, as our TV sets display the acceptable ass of capitalism cavorting. . . . But we must not let ourselves be fooled by our own beguilements. Business grows more difficult and demanding by the day. The highest quality innovation, development and distribution in the knowledge society will stretch us to the utmost, asking for every ounce of our potentials and more. Those unprepared to live creatively and dynamically will not be good enough, and those unprepared to keep learning all their lives long will be by-passed. Nations unable or unwilling to educate their children to the highest attainable standards will find that business, so far from being beneath them, is far, far above their capacities to contribute.

But no learning is worth the candle unless it includes the values at the centre of our aspirations and our visions. It is for those searching for the elusive meanings of their working lives that this book is written.

How Value is Created: Two Forms of Choice

Those who would lead others in the process of 'adding value' should be clear as to what this entails. Presumably a pair of jeans with buttons, a belt and reinforced knees and seat is more valuable than jeans without these, so we add such features, one by one, and sell the garment for more than the cost of the materials and the labour. Each incremental feature is an added piece of value.

But let us consider a rather more complex product – say, an automobile. When we try to make this more valuable, we encounter the problem that many values are not simply additive. For example, can we simply *add* the high performance of a car to its low cost? Can the vehicle be safe if customers want it to be sporty and dashing?[1] Suppose the dreams and aspirations of those who designed and produced the car cannot simply add themselves to the preferences of customers since these are not the same? What if the value of 'great reliability' does not add itself to the value of 'replacement purchasing'? If we standardize the car so as to produce it cheaply on a large scale, how on earth can it also be distinctive, come in many variations and be customized? Can the car be compact or subcompact with good mileage and also have plenty of room?

In practice, this is highly problematic because most of the values listed above are, to some degree, resistant or even opposed to one another. Instead of adding to each other, they subtract. If, for example, an automobile performs very well, this typically raises the cost and must be paid for. No less an authority than Michael Porter has assured us that a business must *either* compete on some quality that earns a premium price *or* be a 'low-cost' competitor.[2] Selling a brilliantly performing car cheaply can cost you the profits you could otherwise have gained. Super-reliability can adversely affect a car's replacement cycle. The economies of scale, by which Henry Ford first excelled, are the antitheses of the economies of flexibility. A car is *either* a compact/subcompact *or* it has plenty of room. The two don't add up.

We have a conventional way of handling these conflicts which is to cry 'choose!' Do you want a 'man-sized' car or a compact, a car much like the one driven by other people or something more distinctive? The pluralistic society will cater to a thousand tastes, including uniformity. Allied to this general approach is the vision of the leader as a dauntless decision-maker choosing between the life and death of the organization, agonizing at the lonely pinnacles of power before 'cutting off' (*decido*) all options but the fateful chosen path. He 'stands at cross-roads'; 'the buck stops' at his desk. He can't please everyone.

But before we get carried away with the heroic nature of choice, we should be sure what we mean by this. If values are somehow added to one another, then brandishing a mental sword which 'cuts off' this value in preference to that, chooses 'man-sized' cars instead of compacts, chooses variety over standardization and a strategy emphasizing premium cars over one emphasizing low costs, then have we not sacrificed a priceless opportunity, if not to 'add' then somehow to combine values? Are these values-in-tension really alternatives, one of which must be chopped off by the 'sword of decision'?

For there is a second way in which we choose. We choose to combine values in particular configurations, despite the fact that these values may initially clash and resist one another. In short, there are *two forms of choice*, choice as *either–or* and choice as a *chosen configuration* of values, not simply 'added' like buttons and bows but *reconciled*.

Now this second kind of choosing takes us beyond mere taste and subjective preferences. Whether a customer likes a red or blue interior to his/her car is a matter of subjective choice and no one could possibly assert that one choice was inherently superior to the other. But the choice to *combine*, say, low comparative costs with high performance and a very reliable car with innovations, exciting enough for owners to want to replace it with the latest model, is to 'choose' all four values rather than 'choosing' just two values in preference to two alternatives.

Once we admit that values can be reconciled, we have entered a different world from the one we were taught at school. Secular authorities have insisted that values were merely a question of subjective preference, a kind of consenting relationship in private with our own taste-buds. Whether a customer likes a red or blue interior to his/her car is a matter of subjective choice and no one could possibly assert that one colour or choice was inherently superior to the other. The only objective characteristics of contending values is the price they fetch on the market. 'Pushpin is as good as poetry', Jeremy Bentham insisted, if the market price of each was the same.

But is this so? Must capitalism and philistinism cohabit, or is their long association over?

There is good reason to believe that *combinations* of two, four, six, eight, ten or twelve values etc. *are inherently superior* to a simple series of paired alternatives because customers simply have *more* values when these are combined than when they are separated or polarized. Moreover, a product combining a large variety of values is likely to attract nearly everyone, even if their reasons differ. Although the driver of a sporty and dashing car is likely to be uninterested in its safety, his wife, children, insurers, community and other road users may prefer this value. The car then is more valuable as a whole and to all concerned if both dash and safety have been emphasized in its design.[3]

This is not to suggest that a product which attempts to reconcile many sources of value is in any way guaranteed to succeed, or has a worth that is independent of the verdicts of consumers. What we are concerned with here are the *potentials* of various products. The more values the product attempts to resolve, the greater is its potential value and the more complex is the task of creating its value.

The theme of this book is that, just as 'choice' hides within it two contrasting ideas, that of separating and that of combining values, so all values are really contrasts among which there are necessarily dilemmas. *Di-lemma* is from Greek meaning 'two propositions'. When we try to create wealth there are always contrasting and hence dual propositions laying claim to our allegiance. These seemingly 'opposed' propositions are converging upon us simultaneously. If we give exclusive attention to either one in the pair, the other is likely to impale us. For example, if we give our exclusive attention to larger, more profitable, gas-guzzling, premium-priced automobiles at a time when gasoline is scarce and expensive, then we leave ourselves open, as did the American automobile industry, to massive import penetration by compact and subcompact vehicles with lower prices and better mileage. It was a grievous error, I submit, to think of these characteristics as alternatives, and to choose one set in preference to another.

Value, then, is less 'added' than 'reconciled'. Value creation lies in the capacity of acknowledging those dilemmas which arise from competing and contrasting claims, and of combining both 'horns' of the dilemmas in a resolution which enhances all values in contention. What we offer to customers are solutions or, more precisely, resolutions. We offer coherent systems of satisfactions in which a large number of values have been designed into the product and thus reconciled.[4]

In the case of our automobile, it would perform outstandingly and yet be priced below other offerings that were not even its equivalent. It could be sporty and dashing and yet engineered to withstand collisions and protect its occupants, thereby commanding lower insurance premiums. It would represent the finest aspirations of those who designed and produced it and would arouse the enthusiasm of customers. Although highly reliable and fetching a premium price on the used-car market, it would be traded in for a newer model because constant innovations and improvements made recent models more attractive. Great economies of scale could be realized through the standardization of components, yet the finished car, thanks to the techniques of flexible manufacturing, could appear in many varieties with customized special features.

But what of the choice between compact and subcompact cars compared with those with more room and comfort? Isn't this, surely, an alternative choice pure and simple? In one sense, yes, the customer either buys a smaller car or a larger one. But from the point of view of the supplying organization, the resolution of this dilemma may still be the better strategy. Subcompacts offer the greatest engineering challenges by forcing the producer to save space and reduce component size. They also mount the greatest challenge to fitting the human body to the car's mechanism like a hand to a glove. Surmount this challenge and your roomier cars will have more room than those who never met and never solved the dilemmas of how human and mechanical systems can closely interact. Besides, you can price your luxury cars at levels which reflect the massive contribution of your volume car business to total overheads. Why choose between values when you can choose to have them all?

These remarks are not, of course, confined to automobiles, as subsequent chapters will demonstrate. They apply, at the very least, to all 'high commitment purchasing', i.e. decisions to make and to buy which involve the manufacturers' and the consumers' personal convictions and integrities. This point should not be overstated. We do not have insurance, personal computers, VCRs or cameras in the place of our souls. Yet such products *do* play a crucial part in how we organize our lives and our values. If I trust a personal computer to do my banking, then its operations are a part of the integrity of my financial dealings, much as insurance is the way I discharge responsibilities to those who depend on .me, and my camera is entrusted with how I see the world.[5]

If we ask why videotape won consumer allegiance rather than videodiscs, then the conventional explanation will hardly do. Discs were lighter, potentially cheaper, easier to clean, easier to store, iridescent, akin to long-playing records or compact discs, and with sleeves containing more information or illustration. Yet they failed two tests of vital importance to users. Fewer films were available to consumers to play, and the discs could not record off the airwaves. If we assume that human beings are the orchestrators of their own values' synthesis, then the videotapes, more than the videodiscs, turned each user into an 'impresario' or a minor movie-house proprietor.

If, then, the processes of value creation involve filling a product-and-service with as many resolved satisfactions as possible, and then placing the consumer on a 'podium' from which he or she can 'conduct this orchestra', where do these resolutions come from? They come from the organization itself, its values and the way these are managed and led. To return to our automobile example, you are not going to combine high engine performance with low costs unless the cost accountants and the performance engineers establish harmony between them.

The relationship between sportiness and dash on the one hand and safety on the other can only be as good as the human relations between designers and safety engineers. If producers are going to supply what customers want, then the closeness of this fit will be pre-figured in how well manufacturing and marketing work together and how completely the views of customers have been internalized by the organization.

How the economies derived from scale and volume are combined with the economies of changing tools rapidly depends on how well the versatile members of a production team are led so as to deploy and redeploy their powers, using standardized components in great numbers, yet turning these into a variety of different combinations. There is no escaping the underlying theme that the product or service can be no better, no more sensitive, subtle, aesthetic, congruent or intelligent than are relationships and the communications among those who create the product. If creating value requires us to resolve dilemmas, then every aspect of the corporation – its planning, strategy, employee relations, its incentive, culture, research and development, its manufacturing, marketing and distribution all need the Japanese *wā* (or harmony) which is the chief cultural axiom of Asian commercial practices. All need to sense those tensions which, if they crack the social system, will also flaw the products and services it supplies.

Western traditions are full of the pessimism that has dubbed economics 'the dismal science'. We are told that scarcity is endemic, labour inevitably alienated, that bureaucrats are creatures with copying fluid in their veins, that organization men are alternately bland and other-directed or superrational and faceless role-players.[6] Business success is regarded as a Darwinian struggle where the weakest go to the wall for the greater good of the rest of us. All this may have had its uses in helping the business class to defy their pre-industrial overlords, but it describes at best a retreating phase of capitalism and is ludicrously inappropriate, even damaging, to the dynamics of value creation in a knowledge-intensive economy where organizations must race to learn.

Wasting the lives of 'manual' workers in repetitive and humdrum tasks was always wrong and regarding them as so many 'hands' to make movements which managers had planned for them was always to diminish their humanity. The difference is that today it must also be regarded as stupid, because diminished persons will make diminished products, and the industry will fall behind its competitors. The machinery which once gave the West so decisive an edge that poor labour relations could be regarded as the merest nuisance in comparison is now in the hands of our competitors. We are left with the people we allowed those machines to alienate and dehumanize, so that we face both serious levels of unemployment/underemployment *and* a growing skills famine. How products are made and designed must, in the end, depend on how the social systems creating those products are made and designed. Lonely, ugly and adversarial relationships will result in badly fitting assemblies of junk that shake apart when used – not a bad description of certain British and American automobiles in the recent period of their decline.[7]

Of course, resolving values in potential conflict is not easy. If you cling just to some political ideology which tells you that workers are (a) our saviours, possessing a redemptive form of superior cooperative consciousness, or (b) agents of subversion, undermining sacred 'rights to work', then resolution will prove impossible. Political ideologies are the enemies of learning as we shall see.[8]

Capitalism as a system actually foundered in large parts of the world on the dilemma of how much wealth was owed to working people and how much to the owners of capital. The dispute still scars us. Dilemmas not resolved live on as semipermanent social schisms and ideological conflicts in which rival groups of partisans celebrate their own preferred 'horn'. This book will not pretend that resolving dilemmas is easy. If left too late, dilemmas tear apart those rash enough to stand between them. When two horns compete for your attention and the one ignored impales you, then the prospects for leadership are not good. Yet, resolving dilemmas to create greater value combinations is a process that can be learned and is one in which the author has instructed many corporations and multinationals. It has a logic, ways of estimating progress and demonstrable consequences on the financial performance of the company. Upon such logics of value creation the wealth of people, organizations and nations now depend.

Let me summarize the important points in the chapter.

Values are less 'added' to products than *reconciled into* products-plus-services. This is because many values resist and oppose each other, unless carefully reconciled into one overall design.

Hence there are really two forms of 'choosing'. We can choose *between* values or we can *reconcile* values into 'choice combinations'. In practice we do both, offering the consumer a *choice between combinations*.

More potential value is created when a product and/or service combines many values which are also sources of satisfaction to the consumer.

This 'reconciling capacity' is a form of integrity or inner harmony, which suppliers not only attempt to personify through their corporations, but which they seek to transfer to consumers. In the case of complex products to which the purchaser is highly committed, these products may themselves form subsystems of the purchaser's integrity, shaping the way he/she thinks (computers), controls risks (insurance), entertains (VCRs) and makes images (cameras).

The quality of resolution among the values constituting a product-plus-service can be no better than the mutuality and harmony among those who make and market that product.

While all of us need to reconcile value dilemmas as a part of daily living, those who lead groups or organizations are beset by many dilemmas, stemming from the opposing demands and claims made upon them. Confronting dilemmas is both dangerous and potentially rewarding. Opposing values 'crucify' the psyche and threaten to disintegrate both leader and organization. Yet to resolve these same tensions enables the organization to create wealth and outperform competitors. If you duck the dilemma you also miss the resolution. There is no cheap grace.

Notes

1 A current commercial for Volvo has the 'rule book' being thrown out of an upstairs window. Safe cars are now also imposing and dramatic.
2 Michael E. Porter, *Competitive Strategy: Techniques for Analyzing Industries and Competitors*. New York: Free Press, 1980.
3 This theme is explored in Charles Hampden-Turner and Franklin Carlisle, *Lifestyle Marketing*. Menlo Park, Calif.: SRI International Leading Edge Publications, 1986.
4 My views are much influenced by Gregory Bateson who held that information was 'news of differences'. It follows that a product with more differences would be more informative; see *Steps to an Ecology of Mind*. New York: Ballantine, 1975.
5 Hampden-Turner and Carlisle, *Lifestyle Marketing*.
6 Alvin Gouldner called this tradition 'metaphysical pathos'; see 'Metaphysical Pathos and the Theory of Bureaucracy', *American Political Science Review*, 49, 1955, pp. 496–507.
7 See David Halberstam, *The Reckoning*. New York: Avon, 1986.
8 'Ideology and Catastrophe', ch. 11 of Charles Hampden-Turner, *Gentlemen and Tradesmen: the Values of Economic Catastrophe*. London: Routledge and Kegan Paul, 1983.

2

Standing at the Helm

If the 'corporate mind' is to plan a successful strategy it must learn to steer in the direction chosen. Apart from the need to create value, a business organization has patterns and dynamics of its own.

Kubernetes is the Greek word meaning 'helmsman' or 'steersman' and from this we get cybernetics as a field of study. If we want to understand leadership we need to consider what it means to take the helm. Let us consider the very simple circle in figure 2.1. This figure is known as a cybernetic loop or a recursive system. It goes endlessly around, yet changes all the time because every gust or pull of the tide calls for a different response from the helmsman. There are also

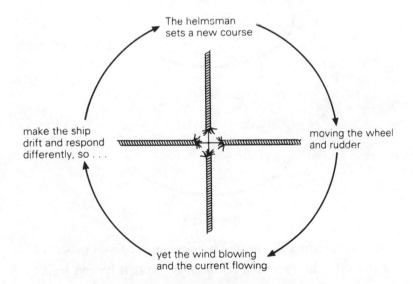

Figure 2.1

within this circle at least two tensions or dilemmas, indicated by the painfully stretched ropes crossing at the centre. The tensions occur because the course steered by the helmsman is resisted by the wind and current which pull in other directions, while the direction in which the wheel points is in tension with, and is different from, the drift of the ship as caused by the elements.

Between 12 o'clock and 6 o'clock on this circle and between 3 o'clock and 9 o'clock are two related dilemmas. The helmsman must be simultaneously aware of the course being steered and the deviations occurring and must keep on correcting his course. The skill of the helmsman or that of anyone who tries to lead a group or organization is to resolve these tensions or dilemmas, in this case to use wind and current together with wheel and rudder to bring the ship to its destination. Depending on the helmsman's skill, the wind and tide, despite their seeming opposition, can be used in ways that further, and combine with, the course that has been charted.

In fact, there are many more dilemmas present in any basic loop, and to make this clearer let us empty the figure of content and make it even simpler: figure 2.2.

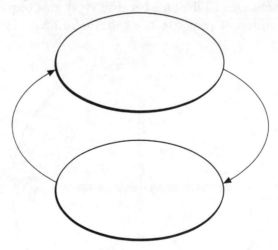

Figure 2.2

From the helmsman's viewpoint he is engaged in a process of
- *leading* so that he can *learn* and *learning* so that he can lead.
His ship keeps
- *erring* so that it must be *corrected*.

Steering this ship involves
- maintaining *continuity* in the midst of *change*.

In holding to his course he is both
- the *cause* of the ship's position, yet *affected* by it.

Each element in the system, i.e. wind, rudder etc., is
- *independent* of the other, yet *dependent* on it.

All elements in the system can be
- *analysed* as *parts*, yet they *combine* as a *whole*.

And how would we recognize excellence in a helmsman? Surely the outstanding skipper spots an error fast and corrects it, can change course rapidly while maintaining the continuity of his/her purpose and is the cause of his craft's superior performance because he/she takes every disturbance into account in determining the course of action. He/she knows the independent influence of each element and how the ship depends on each and all of these, and he/she can analyse any problem quickly to yield a better performance from the whole enterprise.

What makes the nautical metaphor particularly apt is that the 'seas' of international commerce have become more and more turbulent of late. Time was when the only waves were made by large, mostly American, corporations, but today there are so many actors plying so busy a trade that every craft must navigate the choppy waters created by the unpredictable combinations of half a dozen bow-waves and all manner of mutual adjustments must be made to avoid destructive collisions, especially head on.

But there is another reason why cybernetic thinking cannot be avoided by even the most determined leader ready to defy the elements. An organization, its markets, employees and customers are living systems; that means that several elements in that system have their own energy, purpose and direction. You can drop-kick a football made with leather from a dead bull. But you cannot drop-kick a live bull because it has its own preferences and will prefer that you be the one to fly through the air. No sooner do we introduce another living system or human organism into a cybernetic loop than these will go their own ways, like the wind and the current, and we at once face the dilemma of resolving at least two directions in tension with one another.[1]

If we assume that our ship is a living system then there are dilemmas which arise from this reality as well.

- Any biological or social system is *differentiated* in its function, yet these need to be *integrated* if the whole is to develop
- Its members must have some local *freedom* and *discretion*, yet all remain subject to the captain's *authority* and *command*
- Orders must go from the *top down*, yet these cannot maintain their quality unless information goes from the *bottom up* to educate decision-makers
- The captain *empowers* his subordinates to make certain judgements and decisions, yet expects their exercise of such responsibility to confirm his *own power* and influence in the ship
- All crew members may legitimately *compete* with each other to achieve the skills of seamanship but all must *cooperate* in furthering the effectiveness of the ship itself.

We could multiply such tensions indefinitely.

Virtuous and Vicious Circles

But not all cybernetic systems are benign and not all result in leaders' or organizations' learning. Systems can grow 'virtuously' or they can regress 'viciously' and it can mean life itself to recognize the difference. In a vicious circle the tensions between opposing 'sides' of the circle (or horns of the dilemmas) become so severe that 'the rope snaps'. In other words, the mutually constraining influence of values-in-tension is lost and the system 'runs away'.[2] Let us return to our nautical metaphor and consider the case of Captain Queeg on the bridge of the USS *Caine* at the height of the typhoon, described in Herman Wouk's *The Caine Mutiny*. Because the storm is clearly in charge of the situation I have begun with the unruly elements (figure 2.3).

Note what happens when the 'tensions snap'. The Captain no longer responds to the typhoon, and the ship's course no longer responds to the danger of capsizing. Yet the arrows feeding *around* the circle continue their vortex of mutual intensification. The more the storm rages, the more the Captain is immobilized, and the more the ship is inundated by the waves, the more rigidly the Captain repeats 'Fleet course is 110°!' Each opposed element is escalating the

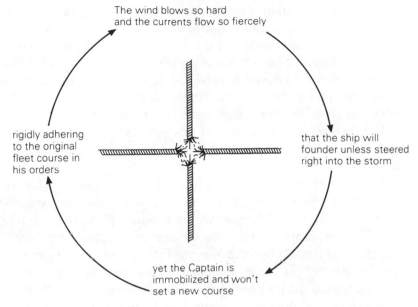

The wind blows so hard
and the currents flow so fiercely

rigidly adhering
to the original
fleet course in
his orders

that the ship will
founder unless steered
right into the storm

yet the Captain is
immobilized and won't
set a new course

Figure 2.3

force of its opposition. The storm and the ship's increasing danger is immobilizing and rigidifying the Captain, while the latter's rigidity is increasing the peril of his ship and the dire effects of the storm, with a vicious circle resulting.

The anthropologist Gregory Bateson called the process *schismogenesis*, 'a growing split in the structure of ideas'. In this example 'the wind blowing' gets *split apart from* 'how the Captain should steer the ship', and the ship's 'imminent foundering' gets split apart from 'the best direction to steer'. The splitting in this story occurred within the paranoid mind of the captain. The Navy dealt with this split by court-martialling the officers who relieved him but finding them innocent.

Note that only an organization that *heals its split* can learn as the US Navy learned in this story. Split systems 'run away' until they autodestruct. This is what would have happened to the *Caine* had not Lieutenant Maryk relieved Captain Queeg and then headed the ship into the wind so as to give its screw some purchase in the water. This action reconnected the snapped nerves of the ship's social system and it survived.

Vicious circles are not usually the products of a psychotic break within a leader or the disintegration of his/her mind. It is more common for leaders to prevent their own disintegration by siding with one clique or faction against the others. In this way they 'save' themselves, yet the organization is severed. Whether or not a leader has personally contributed to the 'growing split in the structure of ideas', the dynamic has a momentum of its own, and the leader may be as one 'tied between wild horses' and is pulled apart psychologically by the 'snapping ropes' at the centre of the vicious circle. Because dilemma is so painful, many managers prefer to rend the system rather than rend themselves, yet this will blind the managers to the polarity they have rejected and may fatally cripple the organization's capacity to learn.

Splitting, then, which precipitates a vicious circle, is an often inadvertent response to painful stress and anxiety from which the individual flees to find support within a clique. This can happen in all kinds of corporate conflict. As we saw in chapter 1, automobiles designed and made by even the most dedicated producers will not necessarily delight their intended customers. Workers will not necessarily see the purpose of the organization as identical with their own purposes. Rather than assume a unanimity which is not there, or an ideological antagonism which is everlasting, why not recognize a dilemma whose pain must be endured so that it can be resolved? Resolve means to solve again and again. Just as the helmsman keeps noting errors and correcting them, so dilemmas do not go away but perpetually re-present themselves in changing forms and varieties. Employees may develop (or regress) in their levels of skill. Shareholders may prefer the bid of a corporate raider. Customers may change their tastes or grow more sophisticated with the help of your product. The environment may suddenly deteriorate, the community clamour, the government interfere. The struggle to resolve the claims of different stakeholders in the organization never ends.

Yet, the cybernetic 'virtuous circle' presented here is above all else a form of organizational learning which can accelerate to help us win the learning race or can lag and lose us a prosperous and creative future. It is not just leaders or helmsmen who learn. The whole 'ship' can organize its experience to perform more effectively. Some lessons can be automated, much as a stabilizer corrects for disturbance or a compass shows the course that must now be steered if the original destination is to be attained. But other types of learning are relational, as when the crew of a racing yacht learns to act as one.

The rest of this book will show how producers can learn to combine their aspirations with those of customers, how workers, despite the fact that their goals are different from those of managers, can learn – with management's help – how to design congruence between differing priorities. We shall see how branches who seek autonomy can resolve this value with corporate headquarters seeking to exercise their authority and how learning and business objectives can combine. It is possible to plan yet remain spontaneous and flexible, and to enjoy the economies of both scale and scope.

In chapter 3, 'Charting Dilemmas and Steering Strategically', we see how dilemma methodologies can be used to steer an organization as between a rock and whirlpool. In a study of the British domestic appliance industry, it was found that you can 'chart' a company's progress on a 'map', using as cross-coordinates the economies of scale and the economies of flexibility. Professor Charles Baden-Fuller and I were able to discover from managers the extent to which this dilemma and eight others had either been reconciled or were still in opposition. Estimates made by the senior managers in each of the companies of how well they had reconciled these dilemmas correlated significantly and consistently with their later financial performances. The better reconcilers had better returns on investments, better returns on capital employed and higher profits.

Chapter 4 describes the extraordinary comeback of Hanover Insurance from near bankruptcy twenty years earlier to become an acknowledged leader of the US insurance industry today. The feat was achieved by a company philosophy of integrity which literally 'integrated' a large number of conflicting values which plague the insurance industry. Although spurious and even fraudulent claims are common, Hanover trained its adjusters for 'fast, fair and friendly' service, thereby constantly seeking collaborative relationships with the claimant in place of adversarial ones.

Hanover is of great interest because the company has been consciously conceived and designed as a learning system, wherein the headquarters acts as the mentor, the score-keeper, the resource-provider and the cheer-leader of its own branches who enjoy very high degrees of local autonomy with which to explore America's highly heterogeneous and locally diverse insurance markets.

Chapter 5, 'Odysseus in Silicon Valley', takes the personal testimony of John Sculley of Apple Computer Inc. and shows how his diagnosis and his turnaround of Apple grew from a unique understanding that computers use a 'contrarian' language. The new world of information is then one of dilemmas and their resolution.

This chapter was originally commissioned by Apple University as a 'template' to organize their thinking and to systematize the ideas of their Chief Executive Officer in a format that could be used in teaching. It shows how Sculley's thinking evolved from a style suitable to PepsiCo, a 'second wave' company, to a style suitable to a 'third wave' company which is engaged in designing a 'Knowledge Navigator' to explore oceans of information.

In chapter 6, 'Seven Steps to Reconciling Dilemmas Strategically', the author goes through an exercise he conducted initially with the forty most senior leaders of the Shell International Petroleum Company. Initial interviews elicited eight major dilemmas which were fed back to the group, who accepted ownership of five of these, arguing that the other three were true but derivatives. Because the contents of these interviews were confidential, the chapter shows how the same methodology was employed with several major chemical companies.

Chapter 7, 'Efficiency and Effectiveness', describes an intervention by the author in a situation of growing tension between the manufacturing function and the local refineries of the Canadian Oil Company (CANO), headquartered in Western Ontario. CANO's celebrated engineering experts, educated largely at the University of Waterloo, championed a *technological reasoning process* through which the best ways of refining a mix of products and of operating a refinery could be calculated in advance and codified as a set of procedures.

The refineries, on the other hand, faced by a sudden buyers' market for their products and serious overcapacity, used an *error-correcting logic*. For them, the patterns of demand were arbitrary if not haywire. Success depended on finding what was and what was not in demand and correcting the mix of refined products as speedily as possible. The author created a cybernetic system in which technological reasoning was corrected by feedback from the environment and the whole network learned to resolve their logics rather than resist each other's calculus.

In chapter 8, 'Strategically Outclassed', the author draws conclusions from a three-year study of how the Japanese think strategically, compared with Western forms of strategy. The West is trapped into the dichotomous thought structure: 'either earn a premium through quality or go for least-cost structure'. The Japanese, following their own martial arts tradition, know how to utilize the strength of their opponents or customers and how to ride on market forces as on favourable winds and tides. Using the concepts of harmony among potentially opposing forces, they simultaneously resolve their own dilemma while imposing that same dilemma on their opponents.

Nothing is more vital than that our educational institutions and our industries learn to work together, pouring knowledge into needed products and services. In chapter 9, 'The Shotgun Wedding', the author describes a conference between Canadian industrialists and the deans of Ontario universities in which, on the final day, he tried to resolve the polarized positions of each side of the dispute, an exercise reminiscent of a warning once uttered by Dean Swift, 'Hell hath no fury as when a friend of both parties tactfully intervenes'. For all that, some valuable opportunities emerged and several groups are now at work.

In chapter 10, 'The Hunt for the Unicorn', the book asks its toughest and most controversial question. Is the West's unquestioned pursuit of 'the bottom line' its Achilles' heel? Of course, profitability must be one objective of an organization, but should it be *the only* one, or is not profitability one horn of several dilemmas? In that case, are we sacrificing the values necessary to the learning race to short-term profitability? If it is *long-term* profitability we seek, what are the mediating values which will assure us getting it?

Notes

1 Gregory Bateson likened such dilemmas to the croquet party in *Alice in Wonderland* in which Alice had to use a live flamingo as a mallet, hedgehogs as balls and men stooping as hoops. The consequence of using live creatures as instruments was chaotic; see *Steps to an Ecology of Mind*. New York: Ballantine, 1975, p. 256.
2 A good description of systems dynamics is in Draper L. Kauffman, *Systems 1: An Introduction to Systems Thinking*. Minneapolis, Minn.: Future Systems, 1980. A writer who takes 'paradox' very seriously is Robert E. Quinn; see *Beyond Rational Management*. San Francisco, Calif.: Jossey-Bass, 1988.

3

Charting Dilemmas and Steering Strategically

Popular legend on decision-making has heroes standing at crossroads, nailing themselves to decision-trees and making inexorable life-and-death decisions at the lonely heights of the organization. Typical of this style is the Boston Consulting Group which consigns companies to exclusive categories with *Untermenschen* labels, like 'dogs' and 'cash cows', which can lead inexorably to their divestiture or sale.

But, as we saw in chapters 1 and 2, choice includes *combining* values, not simply dividing them. Reconciling value dilemmas is much more than a private mental logic for creating value or for steering the organizational 'ship'. The 'horns' of a dilemma can be used like the cross-coordinates on a chart, allowing an organization to navigate and to plot its progress. Dilemmas are twin perils which you steer between.

The Rock and the Whirlpool

In early Greek mythology those sailors who tried to navigate the straits of Messina were said to encounter a rock and a whirlpool. If you were too intent upon avoiding the rock you could be sucked into the whirlpool. If you skirted the whirlpool by too wide a margin you could strike the rock. These twin perils had markedly contrasting natures: the first was hard, solid, static, visible, definite, asymmetrical and an object; the second was soft, liquid, dynamic, hidden, indefinite, symmetrical and a process.

Now anyone with a bias towards regarding either peril as 'more important' puts lives and ship in danger. The notion that only rocks matter 'because they can be easily seen and touched' is as perilous as believing that one's feel for the pull of the whirlpool is of paramount importance. Leaders who seek to steer organizations must somehow give due weight to evidences of a quite different order. The degree of danger is a function neither of the clarity of the threat nor of its sinister ambiguity.

Not all dilemmas are of such contrasting forms, but many are, and many pit discipline against discipline or one political ideology against another. This has led at least one prominent strategist, Michael Porter, to speak of exclusive aims and generic strategies. In his view, a corporation must either create a premium product or be a low-cost producer. Any attempt to achieve both could trap the company in conflict, muddle and compromise. Porter is entirely correct about the dangers of this dilemma, but wrong, we submit, in not seeing the power of reconciliation, of creating a premium product at lower comparable cost than competitors. The purpose of the charts that follow is to show that many managerial choices *are not either–or, but both–and*. The 'horns' of the dilemmas can be steered between and it is possible to navigate in the direction of, say, 'higher quality at lower cost', while avoiding *both* the rock of relentless cost cutting and the whirlpool of ineffable and fathomless quality.

The Companies in the British Domestic Appliance Industry

As part of a major study of the European domestic appliance industry, undertaken by the Centre for Business Strategy at the London Business School, Professor Charles Baden-Fuller, now at Bath University, and the author conducted extensive and open-ended interviews with the senior managers of three British companies in the 'white goods' industry. Hotpoint, Creda and Thorn were (at that time) owned by GEC, Tube Investments and Thorn-EMI respectively. We chose the companies for their widely differing levels of success in an otherwise mature industry. Hotpoint, led by Chaim Schreiber and later by Jeoff Sampson, had been extraordinarily successful. Creda was moderately so, while Thorn had fared disastrously, losing £10 million in 1987, when it was sold off to Electrolux.

Surfacing Dilemmas – the Methodology

We interviewed the top decision-makers in all three companies – eighteen in all. Most were interviewed more than once. The initial interviews were individual and open ended. The clients were encouraged to follow their own trains of thought, to say how they perceived their challenges, what they sought to achieve, their own sense of success or failure and the reasons they adduced. Thus far, the word dilemma was not mentioned. Interviewers did, however, respond with greater than usual interest to signs of ambivalence, ambiguity, perplexity or inner conflict. This is not an emphasis on the negative. In our view it takes moral courage and great integrity to let organizational conflicts pull you different ways. We showed the respect we felt.

Where respondents put themselves on one side of a factional conflict, we simply echoed the speaker's sentiments. 'Those production people are *really* rigid. . . .' We found the respondent would often swing back and explain production's side of the dilemma. We ended up with several dilemmas and/or conflicts in the organization where the respondent felt that both sides had a case.

Metaphors as Clues to Charting

The occurrence of a metaphor or simile can be an important clue to the presence of a dilemma. Levi Strauss once described a metaphor as 'the likeness of unlike categories'. So persons pulled between categories will frequently resort to metaphors to describe this feeling. 'Between a rock and a hard place', 'between the Devil and the deep blue sea' are well-known expressions, as is 'between Scylla and Charydbis' (the rock and the whirlpool). But the key metaphors are those specific to corporate dilemmas.

For example, Don Patterson, the works manager at Creda, referred to the factory as having 'islands of excellence in a sea of chaos'. Despite some excellent individual machines, the logistics of the plant as a whole were incoherent. Our procedure is to take such colourful metaphors and to 'frame' these with the constructs the speaker appears to have assumed. Here he has assumed that machines taken singly can be excellent or otherwise, while the plant may vary from coherent to chaotic. Other remarks he made attributed the 'chaos' to the refusal of the parent company to invest the requested funds. This assumes a construct of parental support/non-support.

Sample Cross Axes

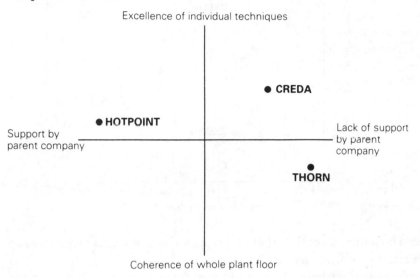

Hence we drew Sample Cross Axes and asked respondents, including Hotpoint and Thorn, to *separate* or *polarize* the quality of 'individual techniques' with the quality of 'overall coherence', and 'support from parent company' with 'lack of support'. After this was done, we showed respondents the Sample Dual Axis which allows respondents to report that these axes remain polarized, but *also allows them to report the integration or reconciliation of the two axes*. These dual axes are far more important to us because they show degrees of dilemma resolution. The reason for showing the cross axes to respondents first is that *genuine reconciliation only occurs among genuine differences*. Where there is no initial dilemma there is no gain from designing a solution. Besides, we need to interrupt at intervals the 'synthesizing response set' where the easy answer to all alternatives is 'both'.

If we look at Creda's score on the two sets of axes we can see what Patterson was telling us. His plant was good on individual techniques but poor on coherence, and this is a consequence of non-support by the parent company. We located Patterson's metaphor on both charts to check whether we had framed it accurately. He agreed that we had,

Sample Dual Axis

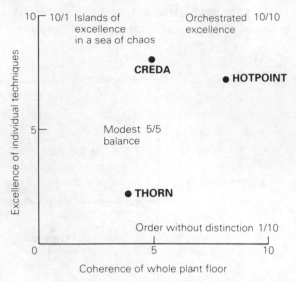

and only then were the other companies asked to locate themselves on 'Patterson's dilemma'.

Note that we have added additional metaphors at bottom right and top right of the Sample Dual Axis, because these were not forthcoming from respondents. In any event, they represent the antithesis and synthesis of the original Patterson thesis. All respondents, when interviewed a second time, where possible in a group, were invited to amend or improve the charts before locating their positions.

We can see that Hotpoint, Creda and Thorn located themselves in quite different places, sometimes after argument among the managers within the companies. (If there was no consensus, verdicts were aggregated, but this was rare.) Of particular interest is the fact that Creda managers located themselves in the region of 8/5, slightly short of excellence and well short of chaos. Patterson's colourful metaphor was an *exaggeration* – as colourful language usually is – being an attempt to entertain as well as to inform. Charting the position of one's corporation is therefore a more carefully considered act of judgement than talking about it, although the talk supplies the coordinates.

The Fallibility of Judgements

But is not our method built upon highly subjective and fallible judgements? Yes, in some respects, but a company whose collective strategic judgements are all wrong is not going to succeed *with or without our charts*. Charting records judgements and allows these to be compared with the harder results and consequences that follow. If more objective estimates of the quality of individual techniques and overall coherence are needed, these can be devised.

Even when disagreement is rife, as it was at Thorn, this usually concerns arguments as to whether one horn of the dilemma or the other horn is too dominant. Both factions will readily agree that they are a *long way from being reconciled*. Since dilemma theory holds that we can *oscillate* from horn to horn, the actual location of a quarrelling company is of less concern than the quarrelling itself.

Pure and Practical Dilemmas

The two 'horns' of individually excellent techniques and coherence are dilemmas in the sense of being mutually impeding. *Every time a new technique is added the balance of the whole is liable to be disturbed.* We can only avoid this by giving careful attention to both aims. By dilemma we do not mean a bind invented by philosophers or academics to perplex students in perpetuity. Nor do we mean an act of fascistic oppression in the sense of Churchill's phrase 'Everyone believes that if he feeds the crocodile, the crocodile will eat him last'. These are 'pure dilemmas', designed to be insoluble. We are here concerned with *practical dilemmas*. It is not easy to get excellent techniques into coherent order, but it is possible. Creating value consists of reconciling practical dilemmas.

Measurement

The Sample Dual Axis allows respondents to locate their companies in terms of *distance* from the top right-hand corner, or reconciliation point. We infer, from how companies position themselves on such charts, how well they have been coping with their own key dilemmas or whether they have been pursuing singular objectives to the detriment of the other 'horn'. As will be seen, executives were remarkably frank in admitting to low levels of reconciliation, yet not one objected to reconciliation as a goal, once the charts had been presented to him. Only two doubted whether colleagues would support one specific reconciliation. We were greatly encouraged by the alacrity with which integrated goals were accepted as desirable. There was almost no argument.

A position close to 10/1 on our Sample Dual Axis suggests that improving individual techniques has been chosen as a goal *over* the need to make the plant floor coherent. A position close to 1/10 means that no new techniques of whatever merit are being allowed to disturb a pre-established coherence. A position close to 5/5 suggests that one objective has blunted the other, with neither first-rate techniques nor a really coherent system.

The genuine reconciliation of the dilemma (10/10) means that a potential conflict between objectives has been reconciled, so that both courses of action contribute positively to the other, i.e. the excellence of each technique contributes to coherence, while coherence makes possible the highest contribution by each technique, resulting in orchestrated excellence. We believe we have not only a valid method of *ranking* companies (an ordinal measure) but a valid measure of *scoring* companies (a cardinal measure), both achieved by measuring the distance to the reconciliation point (10/10).

In practice, these dual objectives are achieved in *sequence*, with corporate helmsmen steering a *winding course between objectives*, first assembling and improving the techniques, then rendering them all coherent, then adding and improving further, and then re-establishing coherence once more (figure 3.1). The charts that follow are usable by corporations to plot their own courses.

Reducing Dilemmas to Manageable Numbers

The penultimate stage of the research methodology is to whittle down the number of dilemmas uncovered to a manageable number. For research purposes this could be eight or more, since we wish to illustrate variety. For management purposes four to six dilemmas are the most that one group can track without straining itself.

Dilemmas are reduced by distinguishing 'key dilemmas' from

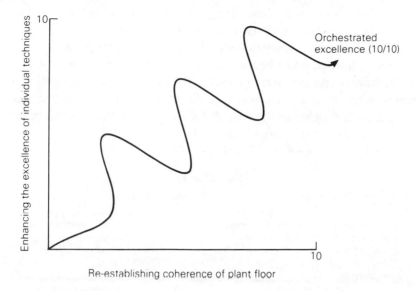

Figure 3.1

'derivative dilemmas'. The second are subsets of the first and will reconcile themselves automatically when the key dilemmas are reconciled. Our sample dilemma fell victim to this rule, since it was argued that the inability to make the plant floor more coherent had nothing to do with Patterson's failings but was entirely the result of poor communications with Tube Investments, the parent company. Reconcile *that* dilemma and the plant floor would right itself. The parent dilemma held Patterson's dilemma in its thrall. (The problem did, in fact, cure itself after Creda was sold to GEC.)

The Eight Key Dilemmas

We whittled down a dozen dilemmas to eight key ones. Few of these are new, in the sense of being without precedent in research on management, but this is not our concern. What concerns us is *which* dilemmas assail particular industries at this time and how managers themselves, not researchers, experience such dilemmas and name them. We have no suppositions as to the *content* of dilemmas. This is surely the sovereign right of those who have spent years rather than weeks in an industry. We do have ideas about the *form* in which potentially conflicting aims are expressed, and we try to help managers see these conflicts in a new way.

It is up to the managers, and the managers alone, to say what manner of horned beast bears down upon them. In Exhibit 3.1 we list the managers' descriptions of their dilemmas on the left, while the nearest equivalent we know of in the literature of management studies is listed on the right. In the case of Dilemma 3.1 some managers had

---

Exhibit 3.1

Managers' Description	Nearest Equivalent
3.1 The extent to which departments of the organization having divided labours and functions can also be coordinated	(3.1) Differentiation and integration in organizations, also autonomy versus interdependence (Lawrence and Lorsch[1], Kotter and Lawrence[2])
3.2 The extent to which registering, rather than buffering, the turbulence of the environment can enable an organization to respond fast	(3.2) The value of planning versus allowing strategies to emerge (Mintzberg[3])
3.3 The extent to which 'economies of scale' are compatible with 'economies of flexibility'	(3.3) A low-cost position versus a premium earned by flexibility and variety (Porter [4], Abegglen and Stalk[5])
3.4 The extent to which one can aim rationally for a large mass market and still discover, attack or defend particular niches	(3.4) Mass marketing versus niche marketing (Takeuchi and Porter[6])
3.5 Can the subsidiary to a parent company be both a means to making a profit for that parent *and* an end itself?	(3.5) The designation of companies in a portfolio as cash cows versus stars etc. (Hedley[7])
3.6 The extent to which the necessary introduction of new technology can be combined with the effective reorganization of working relations around that technology	(3.6) The effectiveness with which the technical system and the social system has been redesigned into a 'sociotechnical system' (Emery and Trist[8])
3.7 The extent to which workers, while adapting their demands to exigencies of the market, still feel themselves to be justly treated and consulted	(3.7) The quality of participation by workers in the competitive challenges faced by the corporation and the 'felt fairness' of pay (Lawler[9], Jaques[10])
3.8 The extent to which suppliers can create sufficient value for retailers, so that the latter do not resort to discounting at the supplier's expense	(3.8) The dilemma in bargaining, cooperation or conflict (Rapaport[11], Axelrod[12])

read Lawrence and Lorsch's work and so we adopted their terms, but this was an exception.

Nor should we assume that one dilemma is reducible to another. In fact, they never recur in quite the same way. As any matador can tell you, when you have fought one bull you have *not* fought them all, however similar their horns. The smallest difference can prove lethal if it catches you unawares. A detailed account of the dilemmas follows.

3.1   Functional Integration

Discovering the Dilemma

All companies gave us essentially similar histories of the 'bad old days' when the sales departments were in luxury offices and display rooms in the West End of London, while factories were located in the North and the Midlands. Effective coordination was minimal.

Creda executives attributed much of their success to their decision to locate all functions and three departments at their single Staffordshire site and 'to camp out on each others' doorsteps'. Creda had 'Chiefs acting like Indians'. Every senior executive chaired cross-functional committees and scheduled and rescheduled operations in the light of unpredictable changes in the market.

When Chaim Schreiber came to Hotpoint in 1974 he found a marketing department so much a law unto itself that it knew less about its retail outlets than Schreiber, after a brief tour, knew himself. Even worse, they knew little of the rest of the organization. The service department engineers who were paid by the number of calls they made on customers were calling an average of three times for each repair, and were telling the design engineers nothing that might disturb their profitable little business in correctable faults. The design engineers were also in a world of their own, screened off by technical obfuscation. Schreiber axed the whole marketing department, cut design staff by 60 per cent and had the service department brief the design engineers on what was functioning well or poorly. He flattened the hierarchy, eliminating whole levels of management, increased the number of face-to-face meetings, campaigned against obfuscating memoranda and launched his partnership philosophy, about which more will be heard later. He closed outlying facilities in Dundee and Liverpool, dropped unprofitable lines, de-emphasized exports and consolidated operations wherever possible.[13] 'Today our level of integration is good', says Jeoff Sampson, Hotpoint's chief since 1983, 'but it's still a struggle to remind Service that it's not a profit centre . . . We've eliminated geographical distance between interdependent functions as much as possible.'

Thorn faced very similar problems but has been far less successful in surmounting them. A doctoral dissertation written in the mid-1980s noted: 'Thorn has been struggling to find a new means to integrate its disparate parts. Its growth has been by acquisitions and the five main sites have never really come together into a unified entity.' In the late 1970s and early 1980s marketing was located too far from the other functions and was unable to influence them. In two crucial decisions, the switch to microwave ovens, in which Korean and Japanese competition became fierce, and the refusal to match foreign trends towards 'slip-in' ovens, the advice of marketing was overridden and the interests of production engineers in 'cooking by light' won the day. A brave attempt by Thorn to integrate the gas and electric cooker marketing departments foundered on the historic antipathy between their two major retail distributors, the Gas Boards and the Electricity Boards, each of whom refused to confide in a marketing department in league with 'the enemy'. The merger had to be abandoned. When the Small Appliance Division was split from the Medium-sized Appliance Division they quickly became known as SAD and MAD.[14]

Until recently, the managing directors with responsibility for Birmingham and Sperrymoor, in Yorkshire, lived in London while research and development were located on the south coast. Selling was centralized as was design, but marketing was decentralized to the different production units, so that central sales and decentralized marketing were obliged to do a little of their own marketing and selling respectively. 'We were seriously over-differentiated both in style and organization,' explained the then head of the domestic appliance division. 'The integration was largely through accounting practices. . . . We tried to organize around a single brand, Kenwood, changed our minds and organized around Thorn instead. It was a muddle.'

Defining the Dilemma

Because two of our respondents had read the work of Paul Lawrence and Jay Lorsch on differentiation and integration, we adopted these terms, which seemed readily understood by all.[15] We were also concerned about unbalanced influence among functions, stemming from the Thorn interview. Accordingly, we devised the following dilemma concerning functional coordination.

Dilemma 3.1: Functional Coordination

Given the pressure for ever more differentiated functions to pursue their own criteria of specialized excellence, is it also possible to integrate these divisions of labour at equally high levels of coordination and balance?

Locating the Positions of the Companies

At this point we invited the top managers in each company to locate their company at a particular point on Cross Axes 3.1 and Dual Axis 3.1 and to make any comments they wished in the process. Their verdicts are recorded below. Both Creda and Hotpoint regarded themselves as well integrated and well balanced. Thorn saw itself as highly differentiated and unbalanced.

Cross Axes 3.1

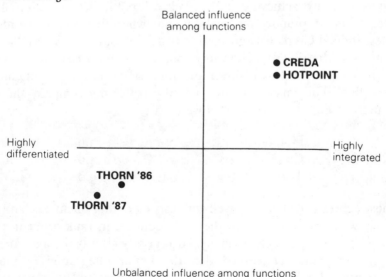

On Dual Axis 3.1, the companies having gauged the cross-pressures are asked whether and to what extent they have reconciled these tensions. Are they 'coming apart at the seams' (10/1) through

Dual Axis 3.1

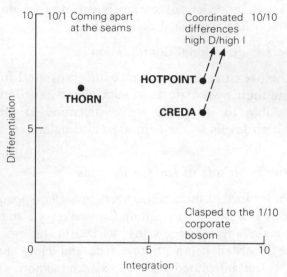

being overly differentiated, or are they 'clasped to the corporate bosom' (1/10) by being overly integrated? Or have they 'coordinated differences' by achieving high levels of both differentiation and integration? In practice they will be somewhere between these ideal types. Indeed Creda located itself at 6/8, Hotpoint at 7/8 and Thorn at 8/1.5. What is crucial to our hypothesis is the distance between where a company locates itself and the 10/10 position of dilemma resolution. The smaller the distance the better the company should be performing. These distances were

Hotpoint	3.6
Creda	4.6
Thorn	9.0

These scores correlate very well with those of other dilemmas, and as we show in the next section they are identical in rank order to the financial results of each company. Also gratifying was the agreement by all companies concerned that the better integration of more differentiated subsystems *was* their strategic goal and that our axes had clarified this for them. Creda and Hotpoint themselves drew in the dotted arrows to indicate their goal.

3.2   Responding Fast to Turbulent Environments

The second dilemma found among our interviews was related to the first is an important way. The advantage of a highly integrated, highly differentiated company is in its capacity to respond faster to any turbulence in the environment. Outsiders might be forgiven for believing that domestic appliances are a mature market: its sales are mostly for replacement, overall growth in the market is low and the basic product has changed little in twenty years. Insiders felt differently, and here we are concerned with managers' perceptions, not those of outsiders.

Discovering the Dilemma

Creda described itself as 'a fast number 2'. By this it meant that other companies were allowed to do the dangerous task of innovating and bearing the brunt of miscalculation. Creda was sufficiently fast on its feet to move swiftly once the market had responded favourably. The market for domestic appliances, it claimed, defied prediction or control. The factory was loaded every four weeks on the basis of the latest fluctuations. 'We compete with everything – holidays, entertainment, theatres, restaurants, automobiles, VCRs. . . . You get a wet summer and tumble dryers jump, or a cold spell and storage heaters soar.'

Jeoff Sampson of Hotpoint explained that he refuses long-term contracts or orders for months in advance. This is because the customer will often renege on the deal if demand falls while Hotpoint will lose if it rises. 'We make five-year plans but we don't believe years 2 to 5.' The planning is there as a context to highlight the sudden changes.

There are other reasons for reacting fast. 'Faulty design needing service is a potential nightmare,' Sampson explained. 'It's not like an automobile that can be taken into a garage. You have to go to *them*.' Huge expense can be saved by early detection of faults and rapid redesign, preferably when the product is still with the dealer and before it reaches the consumer.

Creda had a problem with its washer and was able to tell dealers before they had discovered this themselves. Repairs were made in the pipeline. Both Hotpoint and Creda had top managers immersed in the details of demand and scheduling. Like ships with stabilizers they could ride the rough waters. We were particularly concerned whether turbulence *registered* with the companies concerned. There are ways of buffering against turbulence, but many of them such as using inventories can be very costly.

In the early 1980s Thorn had buffered itself with inventories, but later when it became aware of turbulence it complained of an extended inability to respond appropriately. It had tried to fight import penetration by lobbying the government about 'unfair competition'. 'You can't push this business from the factory floor, or even the research lab.' 'We've responded very slowly, almost blinded by our own internal problems and complications.' 'We were slow reacting to the market and far too cautious, yet we were almost reckless with the extent of our internal changes and the way we decimated the "old guard", who, whatever their failings, *knew* the white-goods market.' 'For too long we were manufacturing driven. It saved us in the sixties when others couldn't keep up with the sheer demand, but it's hurt us as the markets changed. In the traditional Thorn culture if you weren't running around hitting bits of iron with hammers or wielding a spanner, then you weren't a *man.*'

Defining the Dilemma

Had any of the three companies *buffered turbulence to good effect*, i.e. had they found a category of 'random turbulence' which could be safely ignored, or had they set their sights on a long-term market trend and simply ignored shorter-term fluctuations, then our dilemma would have been written differently. As it happened *all three* found the market entirely fickle, but only two had learned to chase each unpredictable twist or turn. Hence the dilemma was framed as follows.

Dilemma 3.2

Given the high costs of buffering against a turbulence that cannot be predicted, is it still possible to gain an advantage over competitors by responding faster to unforeseeable events?

Locating the Positions of the Companies

All three companies located themselves on Cross Axes 3.2 and Dual Axis 3.2. There was little difference as of 1987 in the degree to which each group of managers registered the level of turbulence. All three

Cross Axes 3.2

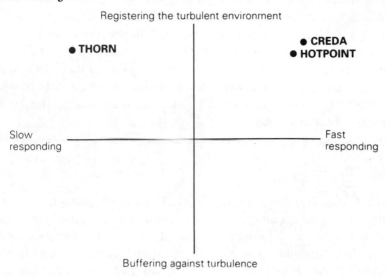

Dual Axis 3.2

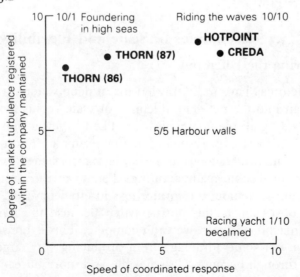

had allowed these levels to disturb them rather than buffering themselves. Both Hotpoint and Creda rated themselves as coming close to 'riding the waves'. Creda was marginally ahead of the larger Hotpoint, and was acknowledged even by Hotpoint to have 'managed in depth', i.e. senior managers had very detailed knowledge of operations. Thorn claimed to have made rapid progress since 1986 but as of 1987 was still 'foundering in high seas', although working hard on its 'response time'. Thus on Dual Axis 3.2 Creda put itself at 8.2/7.4 and Hotpoint, who felt that its turbulence was a shade higher, at 8.7/6. Thorn had moved from 7/1 in 1986 to 7.5/3 in 1987 and aimed to reach 8/6 by 1988, but had not yet achieved this. Once again all three agreed that a reconciliation of turbulence with fast response was their aim. This gives us the following distances to the 10/10 ideal, as of summer 1987:

Creda	3.3
Hotpoint	4.2
Thorn	7.7

Again these are close to the overall financial results, with the qualification that on this particular dilemma Creda is just ahead. But what is to prevent all companies simply increasing the speed with which they respond to market fluctuations? One problem is that production has a logic of its own to do with the sheer scale of operations and the need to derive economics therefrom. To that issue we now turn.

3.3 Economies of Scale and Flexibility

Discovering the Dilemma

Some dilemmas have to be trawled for in deep waters, while others jump clean into the net. The dilemma of scale versus flexibility was volunteered by all the companies we talked to, even those who had made little progress in resolving it. For example, Thorn managers told us, 'The white goods industry is right at the centre of the revolution in flexible manufacturing. Today we can produce wider product ranges without the former loss in efficiency. . . . There has been an obsession in this business that because the Italians make 600,000 machines a year, we can't compete. This is nonsense. Even where you get some advantage from producing very large runs you lose this through becoming less flexible and more bureaucratic.'

Hotpoint explained to us how flexibility in production was vital to a market-led, fast-responding company. 'To me flexible manufacturing is the policy whereby production is sufficiently flexible to produce what marketing needs, as opposed to producing for stock or producing because the labour is there. Despite this, we plan the longest runs we can. There is still a learning curve for long runs and we schedule major changeovers and retooling for weekends.'

But the usual way of combining the economics of flexibility and scale was to produce a standardized shape in large quantities and then add the variations on top. 'We produce a standard carcass robotically in forty-five seconds; then we use human labour to add the variety and flexibility,' Creda told us. Another source of flexibility was frequent rescheduling. 'The factory is programmed every four weeks for twelve weeks on a twenty-four week shadow,' they explained. 'We often change our schedules at two weeks' notice,' said Hotpoint. 'We've achieved both economies of scale and of flexibility.' A fourth source of scale-with-flexibility is machines whose operations can be altered automatically. Creda had recently installed a flexible manufacturing line of reprogrammable machines where down-time was minimized.

While all our informants urged the need for both kinds of economy, Thorn acknowledged greater difficulties in switching over from its 1960s' policy of maximum scale. In those days it was a feat to stay abreast of demand and Thorn had managed this better than others. The virtues of this policy had been over-learned, driven by the historic dominance of the production engineers.

Defining the Dilemma

Defining the dilemma was relatively easy, but we were concerned that the meaning of the word 'flexible' would vary with the range of products, and so we decided to check on product range independently while holding it constant with the dilemma as formulated.

Dilemma 3.3

Given the continued need to derive low costs from economies of scale and specialization, to what extent is it also possible to incorporate variety and flexibility into the production process, thereby extending product range and absorbing fluctuations in demand?

Locating the Positions of the Companies

The differences in estimates of product range turned out to be small. Creda insisted that its 'walls were bulging' and its range of over 350 products was wide. Hotpoint and Thorn questioned Creda's self-estimate but, since the disagreement was minor while ways of counting separate products differed, we left the personal judgements as they were. As we see in Cross Axes 3.3, Thorn's and Creda's ranges were the widest, but Hotpoint was close behind. However, differences in the emphasis upon the economies of flexibility were major, largely eclipsing the more traditional concern with scale. Perhaps this is because flexibility can be defined so as to *include* scale.

Cross Axes 3.3

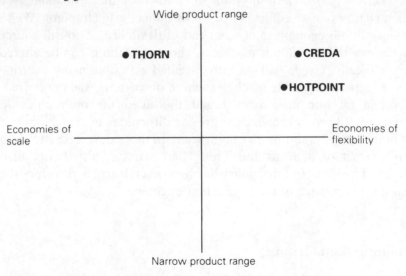

This seems to emerge from an examination of Dual Axis 3.3 where both Hotpoint and Creda crowd into the top right-hand corner of the high scale, high flexibility, with Hotpoint scoring 9/7.3 and Creda 7.3/6. The seeming discrepancy between the two charts, with Hotpoint and Creda giving more conscious emphasis to flexibility and less to scale, is not as strange as it seems. Not only does flexibility include scale, but its achievement is more complex and requires greater conscious effort. All three companies were trying hard to make the scales they had already achieved as flexible as possible –

Dual Axis 3.3

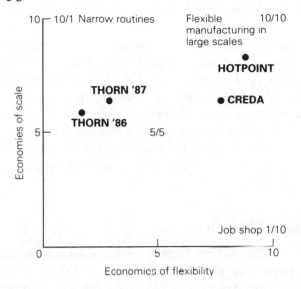

hence the heavier loadings on flexibility. However, Thorn admitted to far less success. Although moving quite determinedly from its dismal 1986 standing at 6.8/2.1 to a 1987 position of 7.2/3.6, this still put it well behind its rivals and much closer to the 'narrow routines' position on Dual Axis 3.3.

This gives us the following distances from the ideal 10/10 position:

Hotpoint	3.0
Creda	4.8
Thorn	7.0

Once again this correlates highly with overall financial performance, while also allowing us to see how well-integrated fast-responding organizations manage 'to ride the waves' of a turbulent market. They do it by manufacturing flexibly, using basic components and subassemblies on a large scale. But flexibility is not only constrained by the need to produce in scale. What if a company has a long-term strategy in which it seeks to persist? What if the rewards for a particular policy are delayed so that short-term fluctuations are a distraction from underlying trends? Is there a world market for certain domestic appliances which is visible beneath the vagaries caused by British weather? We now turn to these issues.

3.4   Mass Marketers and Niche Players

In the broader spectrum of European competition companies tend to divide between those who go for the mass market, such as Electrolux, Zanussi (before the former acquired it), Rolls (before it went bankrupt), Bosch-Siemens, Philips and Merloni, and those who infiltrate and defend niches, such as Hotpoint, Creda, Lec, Thomson-Brandt and Thorn.[16] The British companies which concern us in this study have been chiefly on the defensive against European 'invaders'. Recently, that defence has been more profitable, while invasion has been more costly.

Discovering the Dilemma

We divided our respondents between those who spoke as if they knew *before* they acted what the result would be, and those whose actions were tentative and exploratory. We called the former *rationalist* and the latter *empiricist*. We also distinguished 'attackers' from 'defenders', and those going after the *mass* market with its *universal* values from those going after *niche* markets whose values were *particular*.

For example, Creda described to us how well they had done out of storage heaters, a particular British niche, on account of the low cost of night-time electricity. Likewise, they were successful selling stand-alone tumble-dryers, since European invaders did not appreciate the wetness of British summers.

Yet there were strong elements of rationality in all the companies as well. Thorn had switched over to elaborate planning after its merger with EMI and had tried to think its way rationally out of its problems. Its attempted answer was that a vital competitive edge lay in superior design, not just of the product itself but of the 'Kitchen of the Future', with coherently designed families of appliances which would make the kitchen the new aesthetic 'work-centre of the home'. This new consciousness had come hot on the heels of Thorn's earlier 'empiricist' slogan 'I steer by the seat of my pants'. The company was plunged back from rationalism to empiricism with the takeover by Electrolux in 1987 which largely abandoned the design concept. Of this era one Thorn manager commented, 'I refuse to believe that one centre, however excellent, can tell us what consumers will buy.'

Hotpoint had made a famous decision in 1981 to switch to pre-painted steel which needs especially careful handling if the paint is not to crack. This allows variety of colour at no extra cost. Hotpoint also plans its products and its capacity over five years, not because it believes its own forecasts, but so that empirical changes are quickly drawn to its attention. It was in the statements of Jeoff Sampson that we found our first clues that rationalism and empiricism were being combined, a rational 'ground' upon which empirical changes 'figure'.

We had decided that Hotpoint was a niche player, but they had resisted this suggestion when an earlier interviewer had made it. We found out why. They saw numerous niches gradually configuring themselves into a mass and had no intention of neglecting any aspect of the market that could be profitably included.

[handwritten margin note: planning without believing but in order to notice deviation]

Defining the Dilemma

Accordingly we formulated these issues as follows.

Dilemma 3.4

Given the need to plan rationally for the largest attainable mass market, is it also possible to discover empirically and to aim for, attack or defend particular known niches?

Locating the Positions of the Companies

We used two Cross Axes 3.4(a) and 3.4(b) to locate our companies. Cross Axes 3.4(a) contrast attackers with defenders and universalists with particularists. Zanussi was a typical European attacker.[17] (Its score was attributed by its British rivals but is consistent with Zanussi's top manager's views.) Hotpoint attacked in the particularist British market. Creda was a particularist defender, as was Thorn, although under its new management (Electrolux) it is being geared up to attack – hence the arrow pointing top left.

Cross Axes 3.4(b) contrast a focus on niches with that on mass markets and divides rationalists from empiricists. Again Zanussi is the rationalist mass marketer, both historically and currently. Hotpoint leans slightly towards niches and even more slightly towards rationalism. Creda is the archetypal niche empiricist, a venerable Oedipus walking on 'three legs' (i.e. tapping the ground with a stick). Thorn described itself as *oscillating*, lost in an empirical mass market

Cross Axes 3.4(a)

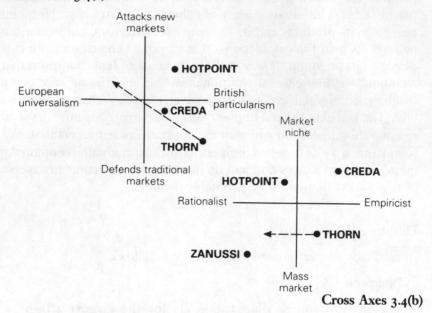

Cross Axes 3.4(b)

in 1986, but pushed over by the rationalist design policy and now by Electrolux's European strategy. It felt dizzy.

Dual Axis 3.4 clarifies the picture. Here empiricism has been attached to niche-finding, while rationalism aims at a larger target,

Dual Axis 3.4

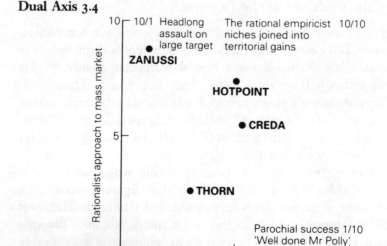

the mass market. To Zanussi is attributed (stereotypically) a headlong assault on the ineffable at a point near 10/1. Thorn modestly rated itself at 2.7/3.5, more empirical than rational, and torn between the mass market (to which rationalism was more appropriate) and the niche market (for which it had more capacity but did not aim). In contrast, Creda at 5.3/7 is taking the empirical niche-capturing route to the top right-hand corner, while Hotpoint at 7.3/6.5 is taking a more rationalist approach. Both these leading companies *see the mass market as a configuration of niches* and are busy combining islands into solid pieces of territory. By looking at the 'mass' through a microscope, as it were, they see details joined into themes, rather than some uniform mass.

This yields the following distances between the points at which each of the companies located itself and the top right-hand position:

Hotpoint	4.4
Creda	5.6
Thorn	9.7

Thorn's policy now that it has been acquired by Electrolux is of special interest, because the latter is *not* aiming at the 10/10 position of the rational empiricist but at the rationally perceived mass market. This was one of the very few occasions when our informants told us (with regret) that the company was not aiming at a resolution of the dilemma but at the maximization of one 'horn' or axis. They believed this was mistaken, but the parent was in charge. This raises the issue of the relationship of our three companies to their parent companies. To what extent are policies constrained by the demands and expectations of owners? It is to the dilemmas of this relationship that we now turn.

3.5 On Cows, Dogs and Stars

We live in an age when Grand Acquisitors stalk Western economies, and companies are bought and sold with labels reminiscent of livestock. All three of our companies were units in the portfolio of a conglomerate and we were just concluding our research when two of the three were acquired. Creda was sold by Tube Investments to GEC. Thorn-EMI sold its domestic appliance division to Electrolux.

We were interested to discover the effect of this traffic on 'the properties'.

Discovering the Dilemma

All three companies had at one time reported difficulties with their owners. All were comparatively 'low tech' and unexciting compared with the knowledge intensiveness and research orientation of their parent companies. Hence if they were profitable they risked being milked like 'cash cows' to feed faster-growing less mature businesses, closer to the enthusiasms of their owners. If they were unprofitable 'dogs' they risked neglect and divestiture. Chaim Schreiber of Hotpoint had to fight hard with GEC to invest during a recession. Had he not brandished his own minority shares, Hotpoint might not have been in the strong position it occupies today.

Creda prepared a video to argue its case for new investment but was turned down by Tube Investments. The chairman of Thorn, Ivor Owen, resigned in March 1987 when it became clear to him that EMI was not going to invest in Thorn the funds he believed were necessary. 'I'm constantly battling to get GEC to think longer term,' Jeoff Sampson told us. 'The merger with EMI was very diverting,' said a Thorn executive. 'The core businesses were not attended to. We were nothing compared to electronics and entertainment.'

Relationships to parent companies are not easy to assess because there is a fair amount of rhetoric belied by actual experience. Arnold Weinstock of GEC is notoriously 'tough' to deal with and plays the part of a sceptic to all requests for investment funds. He was a critic of Chaim Schreiber's family-type culture. 'Don't try to do good or save the world,' Weinstock told the incoming CEO, 'just concentrate on making money.' But in the end Weinstock leaves his managers to manage, a sensible precaution since Hotpoint and Creda perform considerably above the average GEC portfolio. Sampson has never had a request turned down and even Schreiber before him had his own way eventually.

Defining the Dilemma

We were concerned with the *quality* of the parent–business unit relationship and we judged this by how each had behaved towards the other rather than by any warmth in the atmosphere. The dilemma we posed was the following.

Dilemma 3.5

Given the right of the parent company to use its subsidiary as a means to generate profit, can it also view that subsidiary as a valued end in itself, which invests in its own future?

Locating the Positions of the Companies

On Cross Axes 3.5(a) we map the pressure for profits against the long-term versus short-term orientation of the parent company. Creda and Hotpoint both experienced high pressure, but Hotpoint has been marginally more successful at persuading its parent to think longer term. Thorn felt it was the victim of extreme short-termism with low pressure for profits increasing somewhat up to 1987, and markedly under its new owners Electrolux. Cross Axes 3.5(b) find Hotpoint in the fortunate position of being viewed as an end itself and allowed (if not encouraged) to invest in its own future. Creda (until

Cross Axes 3.5(a)

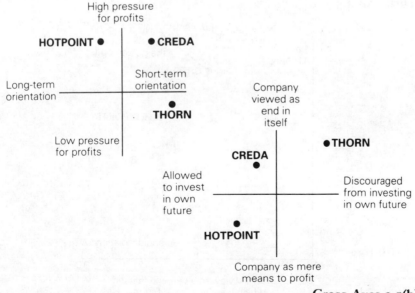

Cross Axes 3.5(b)

GEC took it over) felt it was regarded merely as a means to Tube Investment's profitability. It had been allowed to invest in its own future, but only to a limited extent. Thorn's domestic appliance division had been actively prevented from investing in its own future and felt that Thorn-EMI saw it only as a means.

These moral strictures on parent companies are significant, not in pointing to culpability as much as in indicating strained relationships. The Appliance Division's continuing losses made it very difficult for Thorn-EMI to sanction further investment in Thorn. Tube Investment's decision to sell Creda probably accounted for its hesitation to invest as much as was requested. Assigning responsibility for the breakdown of relationships is a task we leave to moralists or, better, to the individuals concerned.

What *does* concern us are the consequences to the organization of strained relations and these are seen most clearly in Dual Axis 3.5. Thorn's appliances virtually vanished into the top left-hand corner with a score of 9/0.5. It felt like a cow, dehydrated of its cash, like a mere means to Thorn-EMI whose creature *should* be making money but could not. So totally preoccupying to both companies were Thorn's losses that nothing Thorn said about its own aspiration to revolutionize design was heard by its parent company. However,

Dual Axis 3.5

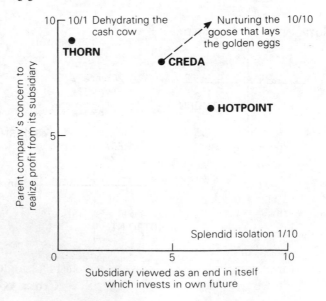

under Electrolux this relationship is improving. In contrast, Hotpoint located itself at 6/6. It was not easy to influence GEC but it was possible, and a certain rough justice had been achieved. Creda, in 1987, was still smarting from the rejection of a recent request to invest in the logistics of its plant floor and rated itself a cash cow at 8/3. However, its request was approved by its new owners, GEC, and hence the arrow is moving right.

The locations yield the following gap to the ideal in which the parent company would, with far greater appreciation than was recorded here, 'nurture the goose that laid the golden eggs':

Hotpoint	5.6
Creda	7.3
Thorn	9.6

But the quality of the relationship with the parent company is only one of a network of crucial relationships, the successes of which are interdependent. All things being equal, a company's relationship to its parent depends on how successfully it has related to its own work-force, its suppliers and retailers.

3.6, 3.7   Relationships to the Work-force

Discovering the Dilemma

We should recall that not all dilemmas are contemporary. There are corporate sagas about the slaying of the two-horned monsters of the past. Time was when Hotpoint would provoke a strike when its stocks of unsold appliances were backing up. In those days, absenteeism was chronic and even sabotage was experienced. All this ended in 1978 with Chaim Schreiber's 'partnership philosophy', originally imposed on a sceptical work-force but quickly gaining acceptance and participation. The plan, unprecedented in the British domestic appliance industry, distributed 10 per cent of annual profits among the work-force and provided retirement benefits and a voluntary sick-pay scheme. Works councils ruled on whether absentees should be paid. Their numbers shrank.

Clocking on and off was ended. Piecework was abolished in favour of group performance. The whole company moved to a 'single status' system. Gone were the reserved parking spaces, the directors' dining rooms, the drinks cabinets for senior staff and the myriad symbols of status.

'Our profit sharing scheme is absolutely vital for motivation and for our wide concern with quality,' Jeoff Sampson explained. 'We use pre-painted steel and unless it's handled carefully it flakes and scuffs. We found we had a 2.0 per cent delivery damage rate. We focused on that problem and it's down to 0.9 per cent and falling.'

There were several references to how the work-force responded to new ideas, new technology and the consequent rearrangement of work stations. 'The shop floor is very receptive to new ideas . . .' Hotpoint managers told us. 'The building of Kimberly itself required some totally new procedures, but they helped us work them out.' 'But we are very concerned to maintain morale,' Sampson told us. 'We agonized long and hard before putting on a second shift here. We wanted to be sure the shift was permanent. Time was when we'd work short time during March, because sales were low and we didn't want to build up stocks. But I'd rather re-plan all the phases of production to eliminate short-time working or lay-offs, because nothing is so destructive as dropping people and then trying to pick them up again. You lose the best because they won't be treated that way.' 'You could say we've become more caring but we expect them to confront realities . . . to see that we can all do better.'

Creda expressed great admiration for Hotpoint's profit-sharing scheme and was planning to adopt it. Known as 'friendly Creda' and 'honest Creda' it had come through the recent recession with no major job losses, partly owing to its 'cushion' of part-time seasonal workers. Its extensive use of small groups organized around oval work stations and interdependent tasks further contributed to high morale.

However, its personnel director, Warren Bradley, was concerned that workers were insufficiently realistic and that Creda's charmed life during the recent recession had made them complacent. There had been a history of collusion between the previous managing director and the chief shop steward, who had conferred as strike deadlines approached and emerged with last-minute deals. Such procedures fostered immaturity. There had recently been trouble in comparabilities between a large number of different jobs. But these were being negotiated by a joint management–union bargaining committee.

Thorn-EMI's labour relations could not withstand its sliding fortunes. It idled 1,200 workers when closing its gas cooker site in

London, endured a four-month strike in 1986 after slimming its work-force by 1,500 and was struck twice in 1987. Major concessions had been made to politicized shop stewards in the early 1970s with the result that rationalization was resisted until it was too late to cut without mutilation. Labour relations lurched from cosy delusions of security to drastic cutbacks as the company's financial position deteriorated. Even the new plant at Spennymoor with its potted palms, carpets and restful lighting was soured by 'the cardigan revolt', when workers were forbidden to wear cardigans.

Defining the Dilemma

Labour relations were such a tangle of contrasting forces that it was necessary to distinguish two dilemmas, 3.6 and 3.7. These were as follows.

Dilemma 3.6

Given the necessity for workers to disrupt their relationships periodically and reorganize themselves constructively around new procedures and technologies, can renewal of their social bonds and attention to the morale of the workforce facilitate such changes?

Dilemma 3.7

Given the need for workers to adapt their wage demands and working practices willingly to the exigencies of a competitive market, can the resulting work bargains still be experienced as just and consensual?

In both these dilemmas workers voluntarily alter procedures and agreements which have helped cement their social organization, and in return expect managers to assist them in achieving new arrangements at least as satisfactory as the earlier ones. Where management is not trusted and protection has been hard won, the resistance to new technology will be high, and cooperation in making the company more competitive will be blocked by a defensive solidarity.

Locating the Positions of the Companies

Cross Axes 3.6 asked companies to what extent the introduction of new technology was rapid and unimpeded, or slow and impeded, and

Cross Axes 3.6

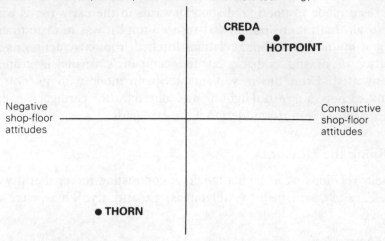

Rapid unimpeded introduction of new technology

CREDA

HOTPOINT

Negative shop-floor attitudes — Constructive shop-floor attitudes

● THORN

Slow impeded introduction of new technology

whether shop-floor attitudes were constructive or negative. Creda and Hotpoint both achieved the rapid and constructive quartile. As of 1987, Thorn reported negative attitudes and slow impeded attempts to introduce new technology, which were now rapidly improving under the auspices of Electrolux. On Dual Axis 3.6 Hotpoint located

Dual Axis 3.6

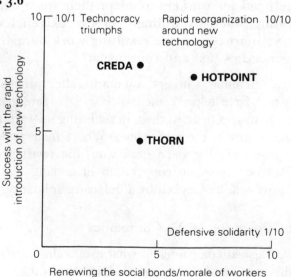

10 ⌐ 10/1 Technocracy triumphs   Rapid reorganization 10/10 around new technology

CREDA ●

● HOTPOINT

Success with the rapid introduction of new technology

5 ⊢

● THORN

Defensive solidarity 1/10

0   5   10

Renewing the social bonds/morale of workers

itself at 7.2/7, Creda at 7.6/5 and Thorn at 4.2/5; all three were steering their way between technocracy triumphs and defensive solidarity, with Thorn still suffering from residues of the latter. The ideal is to reorganize rapidly around new technology, renewing and improving one's social bonds in the process. The distances between this 10/10 position and where each company located itself were as follows:

Hotpoint	4.0
Creda	5.4
Thorn	7.7

The dynamics around Dilemma 3.7 required two cross axes, 3.7(a) and 3.7(b). In Cross Axes 3.7(a) we were interested in how friendly or hostile, realistic or complacent the work-force was seen to be by management. Creda was very friendly but, as we had been warned, a shade complacent. Hotpoint was realistic and friendly. Thorn had recently moved from a hostile complacency in 1986 to a realistic hostility in 1987; arguably their anger was justified even if it did not help. In Cross Axes 3.7(b) we were interested in the perceived fairness of the pay structure and whether solutions to any unfairness were typically negotiated or imposed. Both Creda and Thorn were

Cross Axes 3.7(a)

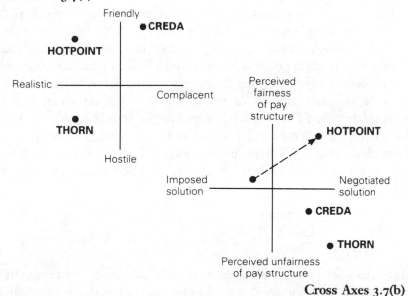

Cross Axes 3.7(b)

negotiating changes to structures perceived to be less than fair. Schreiber at Hotpoint had, ironically, imposed his partnership philosophy, yet it had been perceived as fair and was now regularly negotiated – hence the arrow moving left to right.

Dual Axis 3.7

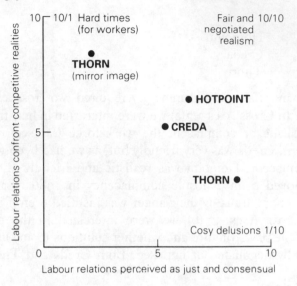

Dual Axis 3.7 registers to what extent the capacity of workers to confront the competitive realities of their industry has been reconciled to relationships with management perceived to be just and consensual. These vary from the cosy delusions which Thorn managers believed their workers to be suffering from, to the hard times suffered by the many who were laid off or fired. Thorn managers located their workers at 2/8. (The workers' view, had we sought it, was likely to have been the 'mirror image' 8/2.) Creda scored itself at 5.6/4.6 and Hotpoint at 6.4/6. All three felt they were still some distance from the fair and negotiated realism they sought. Their distances were as follows:

Hotpoint	4.0
Creda	5.5
Thorn	7.7

But relationships with workers were only one aspect of Hotpoint's partnership philosophy. Just as important, and perhaps more of a competitive edge, were its relationships with its retail distributors. To these we now turn.

3.8   Over-mighty Retailers and Maintaining Margins

On one subject there was much unanimity between our three companies and much dismay. The days of resale price maintenance had gone for ever. 'Today it's the retailer who calls the shots.'

Discovering the Dilemma

The problem was that the manufacturer had lost his former power to decree the terms of sale. A Thorn executive commented: 'The changing face of distribution is that greater and greater power is falling into fewer hands, so that a whim on their part [the chain stores] about sourcing has a dramatic impact on our lines.'

The rise of such chains as Dixons, Rumbelows, Curry and Comet meant that retailers' margins were falling and this induced pressure on suppliers' margins. Manufacturers' products could have their retail or wholesale prices slashed, especially if they were moving slowly or were subject to extensive competition. If this happened, smaller independent retailers would complain to the manufacturer and seek matching discounts. There could be a general erosion of retailers' and manufacturers' margins in all outlets, with no form of legal recourse.

Hotpoint's solution to this problem has been to give its retailers several benefits via its partnership philosophy and withdraw these if requests to maintain margins and maintain a full range of appliances were not heeded. For example it organizes a Hotpoint Centre within all its retail outlets with catalogues and point of sale material. Because 11.0 per cent of Hotpoint's sales are through its own mail-order catalogues it has considerable market intelligence to share with retailers. Moreover 40 per cent of customers visiting Hotpoint dealers have seen these catalogues in advance.

Hotpoint offers its dealers a £2 for £1 subsidy to advertise its products and uses its clout with the mass media to obtain preferential rates. It guarantees two deliveries a week to all stores that promise not to sell display models, and will make direct deliveries to the customers of larger retailers. It offers a five-year parts guarantee. In exchange, all Hotpoint Centres must include the full twenty-six products in its range and not discount them.

As Thorn complained to us, this policy squeezes rival appliances out of the shop. Nothing else that Hotpoint does is so devastatingly effective in the eyes of its competitors. It gains retailer allegiance without sacrificing profits. Creda also reported a long and close relationship with its retailers, especially the Electricity Boards to whose long-term strategies it was privy, with Creda demonstrators even helping out in the Boards' shops. Thanks to this relationship Creda stuck with storage heaters after Hotpoint had abandoned them, and launched with considerable success their new slim-line storage heaters. There remains, however, the problem that Electricity and Gas Board showrooms are losing market share to the multi-fuel chain stores.

Thorn has been caught and badly squeezed in the discount wars. Its microwave ovens, challenged by Japanese and Korean imports, were unable to hold their margin, and many of their slower moving lines were discounted. For Hotpoint, in contrast, the defence of margins was a never-ending priority. 'I kill up to six new products a year,' Sampson told us, 'because I don't believe we could make the margin at the prices we are going in at.'

Defining the Dilemma

This led us to pose the following dilemma and assess its degrees of resolution.

Dilemma 3.8

Given the considerable power in the hands of retailers to increase volume and turnover by heavy discounting at the expense of suppliers' profitability, is it still possible for suppliers to exercise strong influence so as to display their full range and maintain their margins?

Locating the Positions of the Companies

On Cross Axes 3.8 we set out to discover to what extent retail prices for the same appliance were similar or dissimilar and to what extent the supplier sought to maintain margins or sought to increase sales volume. Hotpoint had an emphasis on maintaining margins and

Cross Axes 3.8

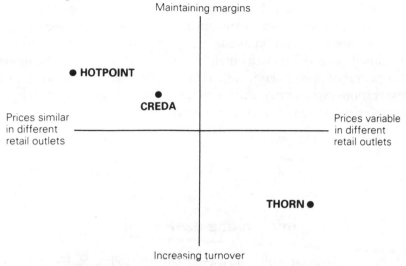

consistent prices across the board. Creda's special relationship with Electricity Boards put it under less pressure, but it located itself in the same quartile as Hotpoint, although less emphatically so. Thorn had found that its products were heavily discounted by retailers chasing volume, although 1987 had been better in this respect than 1986.

Hotpoint's unusually strong position can be seen in Dual Axis 3.8, where it had largely reconciled the retailers' power to increase turnover

Dual Axis 3.8

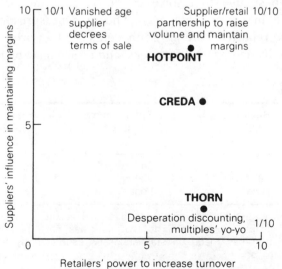

with its own influence upon retailers to maintain margins. With a score of 8/7 it achieved the goals of its partnership philosophy, to combine high volume with strong margins. As Sampson reminded us, 'Volume does actually generate margins. No one is going to cut margins if turnover remains high.' Creda is not far behind Hotpoint at a score of 6/7.5. However, Thorn saw itself as the victim of desperation discounting and at 1.4/8 it was close to becoming a multiples' yo-yo. Scores were as follows:

Hotpoint	4.3
Creda	5.3
Thorn	9.0

Interpreting the Findings

There was a remarkable consistency in the ability of Hotpoint to resolve dilemmas better than either Creda or Thorn and in the inability of Thorn to resolve any dilemma. This consistency of managerial behaviour can be seen by examining Exhibit 3.2. Hotpoint was ranked first in seven of eight dilemmas, scoring between 3.0 and 5.6; Thorn ranked last in all eight, scoring between 7.0 and 9.7. Creda was clearly closer to Hotpoint than Thorn in resolving dilemmas, scoring between 3.3 and 7.3.

Examining the recent financial performance of the firms revealed that those best able to resolve dilemmas gave the best financial performance in 1987 (table 3.1). The two measures of financial performance reported here are return on sales (net profit before tax and interest divided by total revenues) and return on capital employed

Table 3.1

Company	Return on sales (1987) (%)	Return on capital employed (1987) (%)	Average distance to 10/10 position (cm)
Hotpoint	12.5	34.7	3.9
Creda	9.1	23.1	5.2
Thorn	Loss	Loss	8.5

Source: Hotpoint and Creda from audited annual accounts; Thorn does not publish detailed figures but confirms that its sales have been about £100 million and that it has made substantial losses estimated by the *Financial Times* at £10 million.

Exhibit 3.2

Rank ordering the companies against the eight dilemmas (with scores in parentheses)

3.1   Given the pressure for ever more differentiated functions to pursue their own criteria of specialized excellence, is it also possible to integrate these divisions of labour at equally high levels of coordination and balance? (Hotpoint, 3.6; Creda, 4.6; Thorn, 9.0)

3.2   Given the high costs of buffering against a turbulence that cannot be predicted, is it still possible to gain an advantage over competitors by responding faster to unforeseeable events? (Creda, 3.3; Hotpoint, 4.2; Thorn, 7.7)

3.3   Given the continued need to derive low costs from economies of scale and specialization, to what extent is it also possible to incorporate variety and flexibility into the production process, thereby extending product range and absorbing fluctuations in demand? (Hotpoint, 3.0; Creda, 4.8; Thorn, 7.0)

3.4   Given the need to plan rationally for the largest attainable mass market, is it also possible to discover empirically and to aim for, attack or defend particular known niches? (Hotpoint, 4.4; Creda, 5.6; Thorn, 9.7)

3.5   Given the right of a parent company to use its subsidiary as a means to generate profit, can it also view that subsidiary as a valued end in itself which invests in its own future? (Hotpoint, 5.6; Creda, 7.3; Thorn, 9.6)

3.6   Given the necessity for workers to disrupt their relationships periodically and reorganize themselves constructively around new procedures and technologies, can renewal of their social bonds and attention to the morale of the work-force facilitate such changes? (Hotpoint, 4.0; Creda, 5.4; Thorn, 7.7)

3.7   Given the need for workers to adapt their wage demands and working practices willingly to the exigencies of a competitive market, can the resulting work bargains still be experienced as just and consensual? (Hotpoint, 4.0; Creda, 5.5; Thorn, 7.7)

3.8   Given the considerable power in the hands of retailers to increase volume and turnover by heavy discounting, is it still possible for suppliers to exercise strong influence so as to display their full range and maintain their margins? (Hotpoint, 4.3; Creda, 5.3; Thorn, 9.0)

(net profit before tax and interest divided by capital employed). These measures are, of course, for the division and are recognized by the industry as important indicators of success. It can be seen that Hotpoint's performance was better than Creda's and both were far better than Thorn's. Until the mid-1980s, Hotpoint was not doing as well as Creda, but it went ahead in 1985. Thorn's demise has been long and slow.

For anyone used to teasing weak relationships out of masses of social science data such results are suspiciously strong. Where, we might ask, is the flaw in this methodology? How did we cheat? The answer is obvious: all our work is an attempt to measure multiple dimensions of a single phenomenon, not multiple phenomena.

The Problem of Measuring Holistic Phenomena

An organization, its working assumptions and its strategies constitute a whole mental and cultural pattern. We can try to analyse the whole into discrete dilemmas, but these are not in fact discrete or separate. All dilemmas are connected weakly or strongly to all other dilemmas. All solutions or near solutions make the other dilemmas easier to reconcile. All failures or near failures to resolve a dilemma make the other dilemmas harder to reconcile. When we measure eight attempts to reconcile dilemmas, we are in a sense measuring the same theme or pattern eight times, and it is no surprise that those who are better at reconciling dilemmas are the better performers.

How, then, are dilemmas connected? We shall first consider *what* connects them and then *how* they are connected. One obvious answer to the 'what' is by the money resources which these attempted reconciliations generate, or fail to generate. If, for example, Hotpoint combines high volume with strong margins (Dilemma 3.8), then the funds so generated make relationships with the work-force more effective (Dilemmas 3.6 and 3.7) since there are now profits to share. Moreover, the parent company is now more likely to treat its prospering subsidiary with respect (Dilemma 3.5). Any failure would similarly redound. In the absence of strong margins, there might be no profits to share, and a parent company eager to divest its 'dog'.

These dilemmas are also connected by a *generalized skill* in the capacity to reconcile dilemmas, akin to steering a ship skilfully. Moreover, such skills are learned not simply by individuals but by whole groups and organizations, so that the reconciliation of several dilemmas is mediated by *organizational learning*, i.e. by routinized ways of combining the needs and the claims of different groups both inside and outside the organization.

If we ask how the dilemmas are combined, then we must draw upon the cybernetic processes outlined in chapter 2. Consider first a

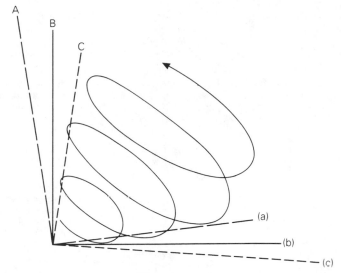

Figure 3.2

'six-horned' dilemma, created by combining Dilemmas 3.1, 3.2 and
3.3. What we have in figure 3.2 is a three-dimensional depiction of
our first three dilemmas. A cycle, or more precisely, a helix, shows
development on all three dilemmas sequentially. Such a cybernetic
loop could read as in figure 3.3. As the helix developed the
corporations concerned would become steadily more differentiated
yet better integrated, and encounter greater turbulence to which they
responded even faster to achieve even greater economies of scale,
supported by increased flexibility and versatility. From such learning
circles the corporations would develop as wholes.

As we shall discuss in later chapters, there is nothing fixed about
the order of these dilemmas. Figure 3.3 'starts' at point A, but
managers talking policy or strategy could start *anywhere* on this circle
and place the dilemmas in *any* sequence they chose. The possible
permutations of our eight dilemmas run to thousands. But, however
such circular sentences are expressed, all elements in the circle must
develop together if the corporation is to learn.

Yet we must not allow an enthusiasm for wholeness to obscure the
details. Good organizational performance requires us to break down
value creation into its components and chart our progress on the
separate planes or strategic maps. By concentrating on key dilemmas
we discover which issues and which reconciliations are crucial to
better performance.

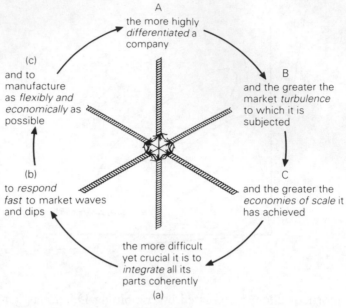

A
the more highly *differentiated* a company

(c)
and to manufacture as *flexibly and economically* as possible

B
and the greater the market *turbulence* to which it is subjected

(b)
to *respond fast* to market waves and dips

C
and the greater the *economies of scale* it has achieved

the more difficult yet crucial it is to *integrate* all its parts coherently
(a)

Figure 3.3

Conclusions

So what are the lessons of this chapter?

- In any mental conflict the 'two propositions' (*di-lemma*) may be of a very different order and clarity. Several of our 'horns' had 'rock-like' characteristics, i.e. hard, solid, definite, separated and visible. These have included individual techniques, differentiation, fast response, economies of scale, new technologies and competitive realities. But opposed 'horns' have had 'whirlpool' characteristics, i.e. soft, liquid, indefinite, whole and hidden. These included coherence, interaction, turbulence, economies of flexibility, the morale of workers and consensual just relationships.

- Those who insist on high clarity and easy measurement may be asking for greater precision than 'whirlpool' phenomena can permit. These persons could finish up chasing single horns of a dilemma and courting catastrophe.

- Shown an opportunity to combine two policies in tension with each other over 95 per cent of decision-makers accepted the desirability of this strategy.

- Successful strategy includes charting a course *between* 'hard' and 'soft' options in a way that achieves both and avoids either–or thinking.
- Reconciling the eight dilemmas in this chapter consistently anticipated superior financial performance.
- Researchers and academics cannot ignore, by-pass or escape the fact that managers exercise personal judgement in conditions of uncertainty. If these are charted and recorded as consensually validated estimates, *then* it is possible to learn how good those estimates were and to correct them quickly in the light of further experience.
- Reconciling dilemmas is a way in which the whole organization can learn to create value.
- Different dilemmas are multiple dimensions of one overall organizational pattern. There is no unilateral 'cause' or 'effect', only points of intervention. The relationship among variables is cybernetic and, where learning occurs, helical.

Notes

1 See Paul R. Lawrence and Jay W. Lorsch, *Organization and Environment.* Boston, Mass.: Harvard Division of Research, 1967. I am also indebted to personal communication with Paul R. Lawrence.
2 The theme is repeated in a study of more or less successful big city mayors; see John P. Kotter and Paul R. Lawrence, *Mayors in Action.* New York: Wiley, 1974.
3 See Henry Mintzberg, 'Crafting Strategy', *Harvard Business Review*, March/April 1987, pp. 66–75.
4 Michael E. Porter, *Competitive Strategy, Techniques for Analyzing Industries and Competitors.* New York: Free Press, 1980, ch. 2.
5 James C. Abegglen and George Stalk Jr, *Kaisha: The Japanese Corporation.* New York: Basic Books, 1985.
6 H. Takeuchi and Michael E. Porter, 'Three Roles of International Marketing in Global Strategy', in Michael E. Porter (ed.), *Competition in Global Industries.* Boston, Mass.: Harvard Business School Press, 1987.
7 Barry Hedley, 'Strategy and the Business Portfolio', *Journal of Long-Range Planning*, February 1977.
8 Fred Emery and Eric Trist, *Towards a Social Ecology.* London: Plenum, 1973.
9 Edward E. Lawler, *High Involvement Management.* San Francisco, Calif.: Jossey-Bass, 1986.
10 Elliot Jaques, *Requisite Organization: The CEO's Guide to Creative Structure and Leadership.* Arlington, Va.: Cason Hall, 1989.

11 Anatol Rapaport, *Strategy and Conscience*. Boston, Mass.: Houghton Mifflin, 1963.
12 Robert Axelrod, *The Evolution of Cooporation*. New York: Basic Books, 1984.
13 I am indebted to Sebastian Green for some of this information; see his 'The Hotpoint Story', *London Business School Case Studies*, No. 3, 1987.
14 Graig Wood, 'The Hotpoint Story, 1921–1981', Master's Thesis, Warwick University, 1983 (mimeo).
15 Lawrence and Lorsch, *Organization and Environment*.
16 I am indebted here and throughout this chapter to Charles Baden-Fuller who co-wrote with me 'Strategy and Dilemma', *Centre of Business Strategy Working Paper No. 51*, 1988; also to John Stopford who, with Charles, ran the Mature Industries Project at the London Business School, which gave me access to all three companies.
17 Personal communication between Charles Baden-Fuller and Zanussi. Charles also showed these maps to Thomson, the French white goods manufacturer, who filled them out without difficulty.

4

Lean and Local:
the Integrity of Hanover Insurance

The three companies charted in the last chapter had originally guided themselves by their own judgement, intuition and plans (albeit tentative). We mapped their successes and failures *after the fact*, and although they approved the maps and located themselves upon them, generally endorsing them as good representations of their progress or lack of it, we detected no vows to steer by these coordinates henceforth. This did not surprise us. We were researchers, not consultants, and were not trying to sell our way of thinking.

It was a quite different case with Hanover Insurance. Its president, Bill O'Brien, had been told of the author's work by Arie de Geus, coordinator of planning at the Shell International Petroleum Co. Before Bill and I had even met, Bill had identified two key dilemmas at the heart of his enterprise. But Hanover's major claim to distinction is its *conscious design as a system intending to learn from its environment more rapidly than its competitors*, or what de Geus has called 'accelerated corporate learning'.[1]

The headquarters of Hanover in Worcester, Mass., acts not as a director – or commander – of operations but as *coach* and *mentor* to the initiatives and performances of its branches and as a score-keeper registering their achievements. All this is part of a corporate philosophy written by Bill and explained in a dozen or more blue pamphlets, which are widely disseminated to branches, customers and agents.[2] It is a philosophy of unusual sophistication, influenced in part by the contributions of two earlier consultants, Chris Argyris of Harvard and Peter Senge and his Systems Dynamics Group at MIT. Among my challenges was demonstrating the relevance of the contributions made by these considerable scholars to Hanover's key dilemmas.

Hanover's Extraordinary Recovery

Hanover was founded in New York more than a century ago. By 1968 the company was losing $1.2 million a year on sales of $109 million. Using Best's data of insurance companies, Hanover was tied for last place. Its stock value was $38 million. Today, its profits stand at $65 million. It is rated consistently among the top ten of all US insurance companies. It stock value has multiplied fourteen times to $660 million, and its growth has exceeded many times the growth average of the industry as a whole. The comparison of Hanover with the rest of the industry is set out in figures 4.1 and 4.2.

This recovery was initially achieved by Jack Adams, but for the last ten years Bill O'Brien has been steering the company through a period of phenomenal achievement. Bill, like John Sculley of Apple discussed in the next chapter, is an example of how outstanding leaders employ a cybernetic reasoning process which is intuitive rather than formalized and exhibits a rare sense of the vital balance of objectives. We shall first examine O'Brien's philosophy on its own terms before revealing the dilemma structure which Bill immediately recognized as the underpinning of his philosophy. Then I shall describe my own research with the branches and my attempt to assist Hanover's new strategist, John Kittel, to develop charts of branch achievements and progress as well as modelling the crucial tensions between headquarters and the field.

O'Brien's more important values' configurations include *leanness, localness, openness* in a *merit environment, the customer* and *advanced maturity.* I shall describe these in Bill's own terms, touching on the influence of consultants where this is seminal. 'The credit', Bill reminded me, 'belongs as much to the General and District Managers and employees as it does to me. The philosophy is about what employees have actually *done*, not about my inventions. They perform. I write about it and help keep score. You must get our relative contributions in perspective.

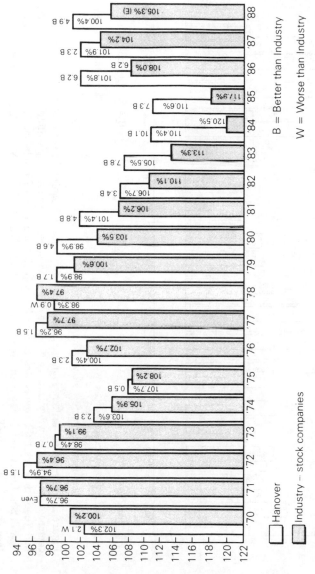

Figure 4.1 Combined ratios: Hanover versus industry, stock companies. The degree of Hanover's betterment in underwriting performance in comparison with the industry is depicted at the left. In sixteen of the last nineteen years Hanover has bettered the industry combined ratio. The combined ratios include the loss ratio, the expense ratio and the policy holders' dividend ratio. Where this is over 100, the industry is paying out more than it takes in. However, investment income can be used to turn a profit. *Source:* Annual Report Hanover Insurance Company, 1988

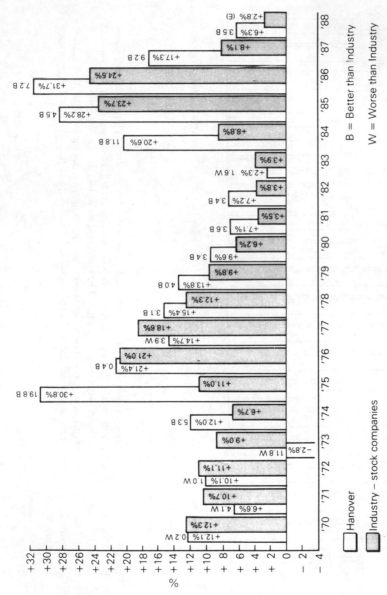

Figure 4.2 Premiums written: Hanover versus industry, stock companies. In the early years of Hanover's comeback, premium growth was de-emphasized while they stressed needed underwriting improvement. In the mid-1970s they reset their objectives to achieving superior underwriting results and bettering the industry growth rate. In eleven of the last fourteen years they achieved this dual objective. *Source*: Annual Report Hanover Insurance Company, 1988

Leanness

Leanness, as Bill describes it, is a 'value for all seasons'. His concern is with two seasons in particular, the good times and the bad times of the business cycle. Companies behave either like eggs or like tennis balls: both go down in a recession but only the tennis ball comes back since the egg stays smashed. Leanness then is the capacity to stay fit in boom times when others are indulging themselves and wasting resources. Hence leanness is also the capacity to survive a squeeze. 'Though the poor practices occur in good times, the penalty does not strike until bad times.'

Leanness escapes being cheap, shoddy or mean in its salary structure by always marrying itself to quality. Cutting the expenses of doing business is not simply a question of efficiency, rationalization or sacrifice, it is a question of ingenuity and creativity, of making a single act serve more ends and of redesigning work to avoid waste and duplication. Leanness pays off in competitiveness and by adding to the quality of work-life. What is fashionably called 'restructuring' is the butchery that follows five to ten years of folly. Leanness contributes to personal growth through voluntary self-discipline and foresight. The metaphor is deliberately chosen to combine nutrients with exercise and diet. Leanness is an aesthetic value which eliminates the spurious, the excessive, the self-indulgent, the ostentations and the defensive. It prunes operations to their spare essentials. Nothing that contributes to health and energy is omitted. Nothing that pads the profile of the organization is tolerated.

Leanness goes down to the grass-roots where employee task-groups rack their brains to cut duplication, combine tasks, simplify processes. The Atlanta office had saved 22 per cent of their annual budget for travel by centralizing their bookings and using cheaper flights, free air miles and discounted hotel rooms and car hire. The secretaries discovered several duplicate files and eliminated these. 'I always thought that cutting costs was misery,' the convener of the task force told me, 'but actually it's fun, and our people get control of their own work procedures.'

Localism

But it is O'Brien's concept of localism that is crucial to virtually every corporation discussed in this book and where his ideas are particularly inventive. Localism means first and foremost that decisions are made locally – in Florida, Texas, California or Georgia – wherever Hanover has branches and not, save in certain circumstances, at headquarters. This is, in part, a selective adaptation to environments which differ widely from state to state. The insurance market is heterogeneous in the extreme. But it is also a crucial part of Hanover philosophy that people grow, fulfil their potentials and learn through making decisions and taking responsibility for the outcomes. The idea is to move the freedom to be creative and to act on the 'fair, fast and friendly' aspects of the company's philosophy to every branch office employee and all who interface with customers.

It is important to grasp what localness is *not*. It is not a power grab by branches at the expense of the national office. It is not a simple moving out of functions, including those more economically performed centrally. It is not being 'cut off' or 'put on one's own'. Above all, it is not an abdication by national office of the authority and responsibility placed upon it by shareholders. Yet it is profoundly different from the traditional, hierarchical, top–down organization. How so?

Here is where the concept of 'mentoring' or 'coaching' comes in. Headquarters as coach is ultimately responsible to the board and shareholders for the quality of each branch's performance. But high quality performance is evoked by devolving on the branches the freedom and the initiative to perform as well as they can in highly diverse environments and learn at first hand from the feedback. Each branch is a 'family' with the cohesion, intimacy and independence of which families are capable, yet each branch can call on the resources of the entire organization to inform its judgements or help analyse its data.

But the most telling difference between Hanover and traditional hierarchies is that in normal operation the branches *pro-act while the headquarters react*. This is crucial to rapid learning because those in the field can exercise initiative, learn directly from the feedback and be assisted in their reflection by a 'scoreboard' that registers their hits and their misses, 'and be fair and visible to everyone'. The coach retains authority in vital respects while devolving the freedom to learn from experience upon the branches.

For example, the coach still retains the right to define and redefine the meanings of achievement and of excellent performance, still retains the right to evaluate branches in the light of such definitions and reward them appropriately, still retains the right to intervene in local decision-making if the system as a whole is threatened by adverse ratios or if a particular adverse trend needs emergency aid, still acts as a 'brain' for the whole organization in processing and distributing information. But interventions are the exception and are kept to a minimum. The key task of headquarters is what O'Brien calls 'business and insurance scholarship'. By comparing and evaluating the strategies of different branches a total vision or meta-strategy can be created. The lessons learned by one or two branches can be incorporated into the vision offered to all.

'It is possible', O'Brien writes, 'to delegate total authority and responsibility to someone else, and yet retain full authority and responsibility.' How can such a seeming contradiction be explained? It is explicable by grasping that the two sets of authority and responsibility are for different processes. The branch has responsibility for providing specific customers with a service superior to that obtainable from competitors at a better price. Headquarters has responsibility for trusting the branch to do that job, evaluating it fairly on the quality of its work and coaching it to do even better.

Localism recognizes that virtue in operating an insurance service involves creating custom-made syntheses of various kinds of expertise particular to the situation. The claims experts at headquarters, the actuaries, underwriters, marketers and researchers may have brought their separate functions to the summits of sophistication, but only the judgement of locals can bring the relevant parts of this knowledge into a unique combination suitable to a particular case. Such judgements cannot be exercised unless those dealing with agents and customers have the power to take advice or leave it, and to qualify each function's idea of best practice. You cannot have the responsibility in the front line unless the judgement is there as well.

Openness in a Merit Environment

The value of openness can only work if there is something to be open to and some purpose to be open for. For Bill O'Brien that thing and purpose is merit. A bureaucratic environment is one that follows rules and procedures. Its value is conformity to a pre-established routine, not the achievement of the organization's purpose, nor inquiry into that purpose. A political environment is in some way the antithesis of the bureaucratic one. It focuses not on the 'what' but on the 'who': who wins, who gets their way, who has the power, who 'makes it' at whose expense? This environment is competitive in the sense of rivalrous. People rarely work together and the organization, treated as mere arena for conflict, suffers.

'A merit environment is one where the conclusions, decisions and rewards focus on the attainment of the organization's purpose and vision in a way that is consistent with its values.' Merit does not imply that there is a right answer, it implies only that of the many interpretations and creative initiatives attempted some will succeed better than others in advancing Hanover's purposes, and that all employees are engaged in a never ending search for, and inquiry into, these more effective actions. Such a quest is more important than who wins and is a good test of whether a particular rule is still needed.

It is in this search for merit that openness becomes crucial. Here Hanover's philosophy and Bill's leadership is strongly influenced by the consultancy of Chris Argyris[3] and Lee Bolman,[4] to whose approach Donald Schon[5] has also contributed significantly. O'Brien writes, 'Openness – even when not practiced perfectly – encourages us to express our ideas and gives us access to the ideas of others. It lets us know what is happening, why it is happening, and the thinking behind what is happening. It results in decisions which incorporate many viewpoints and experiences. It enhances our personal as well as our business relationships. It is a powerful contributor to a merit environment – one in which the search for the best solution takes precedent over other considerations.'

According to Argyris and Schon, the chief limitation on openness is what they call 'model I behaviour'. This is close to O'Brien's concept of office politics. In model I you set out to use human relations in a way designed to attain the objectives you had before the discussion began. The objectives themselves may be selfish or charitable, criminal or benign. What defines model I is less the ends sought than the process of attainment. In this behaviour the protagonist advocates his/her position in an attempt to manipulate the consent of others. In this endeavour all manner of skills may be employed, 'listening with rapt attention', 'invitations to participate' and the utmost sensitivity to the feelings of others. But none of these stratagems alter the advocate's central purpose which is to win through and to have his/her way with others.

It takes heightened levels of self-awareness to admit that, although one's *espoused theory* is full of 'listening' and 'participation', one's theory-in-use employs such techniques to sell one's original conviction and that one is not genuinely open, even while advocating this value!

Openness requires model II behaviour, where the manager advocates his/her position as before but does this in *a way which invites inquiry into it*. Openness reconciles advocacy with inquiry, and listens with a genuine willingness to qualify what is advocated in a shared quest for the solution of greatest merit.

Lack of openness may involve an authentic reluctance to hurt the feelings of another – say a subordinate being supervised – but the damage to the merit environment is serious nonetheless. You cannot learn to perform better if managers are too squeamish to contrast a mediocre performance with a higher standard. The standard itself may lose touch with the organizational reality it supposedly measures if the discrepancies are evaded and *defensive routines* are employed to ease embarrassment.

Argyris and Schon argue that *double-loop learning* will occur where an organization both advocates positions and invites inquiry into these. Single-loop learning occurs when a standard is set and the employee learns to meet that standard.[6] But a second loop comes into play where the organization *inquires into the adequacy of that standard itself*. Hence double-loop learning asks two questions in perpetual alternation: 'How has the employee performed in relation to the values and standards of the organization? Are the values and standards of the organization adequate measures of the real potentials of employees and of the changing business environment?'

In any discussion between supervisors and supervisees, both must be open to the discovery of a discrepancy between standards and performance and both must be open to changing this in two contrasting ways: by improving the performance, by modifying the standard or by both. Only model II behaviour can accomplish this.

The Claim Philosophy

If Hanover was a naive or sentimental organization it could not survive the veritable jungle of insurance claiming. If it believed that the customer was 'basically honest', the sheer number of shocks to its system would be shattering. There are some honest claimants who expect to be fairly reimbursed contractually, but this is the far end of the spectrum. At the other end are the outright crooks, those who see their chance to make a 'killing', those who want to make 'accepted' extra dollars, and those who want 'fair' reimbursement regardless of the contract. For these persons the insurer is a handy scapegoat in their misfortunes, someone to suffer vicariously for them.

Hanover faces formidable obstacles. There is a massive erosion of moral standards on many sides of the insurance business. All concerned have a dismal public reputation. In Massachusetts, auto insurance has long been a political football, with 60 per cent of policies assigned by the State to carriers from a pool, the murky depths of which hold drivers who menace life and limb and combustible vehicles without lights or brakes. Above this mess there circle, vulture-like, some of the most litigious trial-lawyers in the country. This mess cost Hanover $30 million last year. The company has no illusions about human behaviour in adversarial conditions.

Which is why Hanover's policy is not to let that adversarialism develop. If clients claim too little, the adjuster will say so. Decent clients are identified and hoarded like precious metal on the grounds that honest customers have a genuine rapport with an honest insurer and will save him millions in litigation expense. If the reader thinks this is propaganda, I should testify that Bill told me to raise my consulting fee, an attitude that would certainly pay off were I ever to claim from his company.

The only way to withstand the great tide of spurious claims is to be 'fast, fair and friendly'. There are 'war stories' at Hanover of the nine widows contacted on the same day as their husbands died in an air crash. It is no fun to be there with your hand extended within hours of a customer suffering grievous loss, but it could be, after all, the best way of not having their anger, resentment and revenge inflicted on your company. Deep empathy in the immediate aftermath of loss is Hanover's rule. Such tenderness is also good business. A week later and the mood could be very different. What sustains a company of Hanover's quality is that fair, fast and friendly dealings are incredibly cheaper than the court system of the most litigious nation on earth. Not only are lawyers paid several times more per day than adjusters, but litigation seems unending, with huge yet arbitrary bonanzas, keeping nearly everyone yearning yet frustrated, expectant yet enraged by delays and disappointments.

With the help of Peter Senge's Systems Dynamics Group at MIT, Hanover has developed a Claims Game, in which Hanover's own mental model of its Claims Departments are simulated on software.[7] Here it was discovered that the claims operation had a self-perpetuating bias. Any sudden influx in the volume of claims pushed up the pending ratio (a measure of the claims waiting to be processed). This put pressure on adjusters to work faster, which led to resignations, which led to more pressure on those remaining, a serious lag in hiring and a famine of those experienced enough to handle complex claims.

All these pressures led to increases in 'quick and dirty' settlements, after insufficient investigation. The penalty for this comes later in escalating costs for litigation or money paid to keep a weak case out of court. Now the Claims Department could quickly recognize *intellectually* what was happening and could see that it would pay the company handsomely to increase the numbers, the pay and the training of adjusters to well above the industry average, since they would be amply repaid by lower settlement payments and by less litigation. I say 'intellectually' because senior claim managers openly advocated this policy, yet *when they played the Claims Game they repeated the original bias*. This fact reinforces Bill's belief that what blocks learning is less intellectual insight than ingrained emotional habits of mind. Under the stress of even simulated events these habits reassert themselves. Changing emotionally significant actions takes advanced maturity.

Advanced Maturity

The pursuit of merit by a lean organization using local initiatives which discusses the consequences of the initiatives openly results in *advanced maturity*. This includes the development of Hanover's people as individuals and as an organization. American culture puts great emphasis on physical and intellectual maturity. O'Brien stresses the emotional 'muscles' necessary to working and communicating in new ways. This begins with strong beliefs and values, invested with an emotional charge. It involves commitment to these values and a realization that they are larger than we are, that we must serve them and share their fortune. Such levels of commitment allied with a willingness to test the values in practice requires moral courage and an openness to feedback which could confound what we care about. Reality must be faced without delusion or false comfort. Free will can be exercised and experienced only by those with the courage to accept responsibility for the values they chose and how these were implemented. Finally, for gratification one must persist and wait. Mature employees will advance the purposes of Hanover, provided that Hanover teaches maturity.

Identifying Hanover's Dilemmas

After Bill O'Brien had read the author's work he immediately identified two dilemmas crucial to Hanover's future success.

The first dilemma asked: 'Can we continue to invest in and stress the quality of our staff, spending wisely to upgrade their skills and performance, while at the same time lowering our expense ratios' (the costs involved in underwriting and selling policies and administering the settlement of claims, relative to premiums sold). This was a dilemma because expenditure on the quality of human resources is a cost that raises expense ratios, while the successful training of staff in the philosophy of leanness should push the ratio down again. Could Hanover raise expenses in such a manner as to lower them, or is this all some self-contradictory nonsense?

The author pointed out that Bill's Dilemma 4.1 was, in fact, a restatement of his philosophy of leanness in a dilemma format. Investing in quality of staff could constitute the 'soft' horizontal (or whirlpool) axis while reducing the expense ratio could constitute the 'hard' vertical (or rock) axis – Dilemma 4.1.

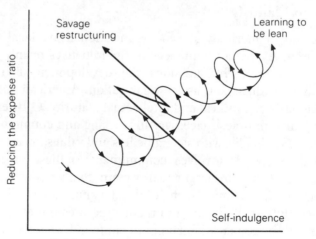

Dilemma 4.1

Bill's insight was that the objectives of increasing quality and reducing costs would need to be implemented in sequence. This is because spending money on better salaries for more qualified recruits, or on training existing staff in negotiating skills, must *in the short run* increase rather than reduce the expense ratio, while the results of better recruits, better training and improved technology should reduce this ratio *in the longer term*. The idealized pattern of progress should thus be *helical* with every increase in the expense ratio (short term) turning back on itself (longer term).

This would be facilitated if, following each increase in investment in quality, a new effort was made to reduce costs. This would, in the short run, *decrease* investment in quality but, in the longer run, ensure that all the fat had been trimmed and that investment was paying off and could therefore be *increased* further. This path steers between the 'rock' of savage restructuring and the 'whirlpool' of self-indulgence. Where the organization has indulged itself too long, there will be a sudden lunge from self-indulgence to restructing as the crisis hits. This is symbolized by the lightning bolt moving suddenly top left.

There is a second reason for tackling the two 'horns' of the dilemma sequentially. It is hard to disentangle their joint effects unless the one is held constant while the second is changed, and the second held constant while the first is changed. Hence you first try to increase quality and observe carefully what happens to costs. You then try to prune back all cost increases not essential to the quality you have attained, and you look carefully at quality indicators. Have they suffered? To return to the helmsman introduced in chapter 2, you steer for quality, then correct for costs, steer for costs, then correct for quality, and your destination is to be lean and to learn.

The second dilemma for Bill O'Brien was how to make local branch staff stronger and more self-reliant while also making the staff at National Office strong, capable and responsive. There were two perils to be avoided: a strong central staff that suppressed local initiatives and made branches dependent, and a strong local staff that resented any interference from national headquarters as an infringement of their autonomy. Once again the author argued that Bill was, in fact, restating his localism philosophy in dilemma form. Localism involved steering between the rock of isolationism and the whirlpool of dependence: Dilemma 4.2.

Now headquarters' verdict on branch initiatives will not always be positive. The purpose of negative feedback is to correct, and so there has to be a series of *temporary recursions* or reverses in which the branches try again and try to develop greater strength than before.

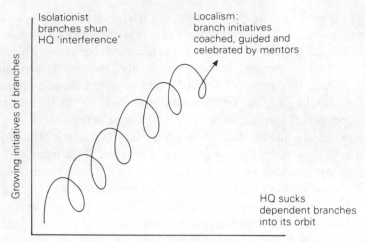

Isolationist
branches shun
HQ 'interference'

Localism:
branch initiatives
coached, guided and
celebrated by mentors

Growing initiatives of branches

HQ sucks
dependent branches
into its orbit

Strength and development of National Office

Dilemma 4.2

Nor does the growth of branch initiative in any respect reduce the long-term strength of National Office. Teaching others to develop has its own sense of fulfilment and power. There are, however, short-term reverses for the mentor as for the branch; when the first evaluates the second there can be disappointment for coaches as for performers and a temporary diminution in their sense of growth and influence.

It is also possible to express Bill O'Brien's philosophy of openness in a merit environment in terms of the dilemma between advocating and inquiring in Dilemma 4.3. On the vertical rock-like axis the individual uses model I behaviour to push his/her initial position through to victory, blocking off all qualifying messages. On the horizontal whirlpool axis the manager is so open to the currents of opinion that action and direction are lost. It is also possible to create a horrid hybrid of mixed messages as when the manager invites participation but remains fiercely committed, persuading all participants to reach the conclusions he/she began with. Only in model II behaviour, at top right, are advocacy and inquiry reconciled in a shared search for merit.

'Double-loop learning' is illustrated in Dilemma 4.4. Here the vertical axis teaches the 'hard' lesson of bringing employee performance up to the standards and values of Hanover, while the 'soft' horizontal axis peers into the depth of employees' potentials to ask whether

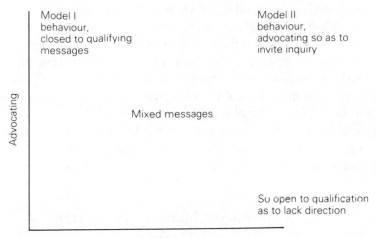

Model I
behaviour,
closed to qualifying
messages

Model II
behaviour,
advocating so as to
invite inquiry

Advocating

Mixed messages

So open to qualification
as to lack direction

Inquiring

Dilemma 4.3

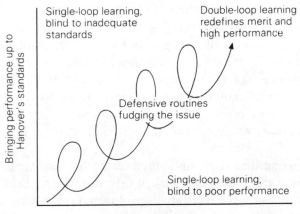

Single-loop learning,
blind to inadequate
standards

Double-loop learning
redefines merit and
high performance

Bringing performance up to
Hanover's standards

Defensive routines
fudging the issue

Single-loop learning,
blind to poor performance

Bringing standards up to the
potentials/aspirations of employees

Dilemma 4.4

standards reflect these adequately and evoke the best from people. If employees are merely reproached for failing to live up to the organization's standards, then only single-loop learning can occur, which is blind to inadequate standards. If standards are perpetually rearranged to fit what employees have accomplished, the consequences could be poor performance. Defensive routines occur when supervisors evade comparing the performance of employees with the standards or vice versa, preferring to fudge the whole issue and avoid embarrassment. Only *double-loop learning* in which the employees are judged against standards and then standards are judged against the visions and aspirations of employees can lead to steady improvement, while constantly redefining this to meet new challenges in new ways.

The process of periodically revising standards will set back in some degree the ability of employees to attain them. This 'moving of the goal posts' creates temporary reverses but longer-term gains, because the renewed standards are more motivating and more relevant to employees' aspirations and the challenges of the environment.

The Poisoned Chalice of Perfection

So Hanover must be excellent, right? It should join the Halls of Fame, for ever being described by the self-appointed arbiters of excellence.[8] The cruel truth is that such companies are no sooner extolled in print and film than cracks begin to appear in the edifice, and yesterday's idols bite the dust. There is a very good reason for this. The vast majority of managers in the West think in straight lines, what Thomas Carlyle once called '*steam-engine intellects*'.[9] It follows that if someone has dubbed you 'excellent' and many seem to agree then, clearly, you should do what you are doing now, only more so, more profit, more competition, more closeness to the customer, more 'hands on', more walking about, more sticking to more knitting and so on.

Alas, it is hard to think of a surer recipe for disaster or a quicker way to strike the rock or be sucked into the whirpool. More of any value may be too much. Declare as profit what might have been spent on upgrading the quality of your service and you may be sorry. Hanover cannot afford to believe that it has arrived, or that the perfect combination has been achieved.

Indeed, it is not too difficult to predict where Hanover is likely, even now, to be making its mistakes. The place to look is where the Greek tragedians looked. *All heroes are liable to overlearn their winning combinations*. Yesterday's triumph becomes tomorrow's excess. So when I was invited to visit some of Hanover's branches, I already had a rough idea of what I was looking for. I was looking for a tendency to take O'Brien's philosophy too literally, to turn into some straight-line 'thing' to be maximized and then run this into the ground.

Eight months later I had a second chance to collect impressions. This time at second hand. John Kittel, Hanover's new man on strategy, had convened a meeting of general managers, some of whom had recent experience in managing branches. I recorded their wider ranging discussion of current problems.

In the rest of this chapter I shall explore a few of these issues. If I seem to be critical please remember that *the helmsman steers by course corrections*. Virtue is always elusive and indefinite, a reconciliation of many values. Only rocks, whirlpools and similar forms of excess are sufficiently stereotyped to provide the recognition that allows us to steer between them. It follows that a company needs to be at least as dissatisfied as it is satisfied, and that the meaning of 'good' is that you can do even better. Only through negative feedback can a corporation learn consistently and without end. The notion of perfection is a poisoned chalice, never more lethal than when you hold it to your lips.

The Problems of Success

Nothing could be more unfair to Bill O'Brien than to call his philosophy one dimensional. Indeed, he goes to great pains to say what localism, leanness and openness are not – not putting branches on their own, not cutting into the muscle of the organization, not a vaguely benign atmosphere in which everything is accepted – and yet there is *no philosophy that cannot be transformed into mental spaghetti by being processed through a linear mind-set*. Localism, leanness etc. are reduced to slogans. The slogans are 'good', so let us all have more and more of a good thing.

There are two views of the human condition that seem to me to form a perpetual paradox. The first says that people want to grow and to learn and that this motive like an underground stream is of immense power and significance in human affairs. We cannot create wealth or anything else without it. The second view says that if people can counterfeit the process of growth they will, if they can find a way of avoiding the anxiety, danger, difficulty and effort inherent in growth they will, and that the counterfeits outnumber the genuine achievements. I believe both statements are true – of Hanover as well as other organizations. Hanover's success would suggest that the counterfeits of growth are fewer here than elsewhere, but they are still present and they consist of *pieces* of Bill's philosophy carefully contrived to build for the individual a shelter against growth.

We shall discuss four ways in which Hanover's philosophy can be falsified and turned into 'easy pieces' that can make managers look good. I do not suggest that this is rife or that the organization is riddled with evasions. I suggest rather that an organization as formidable and dynamic as Hanover is big enough to examine its own possible excesses and to steer even more intelligently. Each *excess*, as we shall see, counterfeits a *success*, the former settling like an incubus upon aspiring dreams.

Philosophy for Everyone

Bill is an outstanding corporate philosopher, and for that reason the philosophy fills and sometimes clouds hundreds of discussions. I wrote of my visit to the branches:

I was amazed and delighted to discover the extent to which the Hanover philosophy had been incorporated into the way I was personally treated and the general orientation of the managers. Yours is a living philosophy acted out in the way customers and consultants are approached and not a PR document or a Sunday sermon used to bless business-as-usual, which is what I feared I might find.

And yet there is a slight blandness and belief that an all-pervading sense of good will and basic decency will solve all our problems. The philosophy tends to be used as a catch-all and as an explanatory principle of success which gives the same answer to a large number of my questions.

What is your distinctive competence? Why is Syracuse better than most other branches? How could relationships with agents be improved? To all such questions the answer comes back 'The philosophy', 'living the philosophy', 'more philosophy'. Interviewing at least some of the managers at the more successful branches is like trying to penetrate a soft donut and being lightly dusted by confectionery sugar at every attempt.

The same issue arose at the meeting of general managers. 'Aren't we confusing strategy with getting our philosophical foundations in place?' one manager asked. 'Philosophy is our strategy,' said another. 'When I try to talk strategy to the branches', a third manager complained, 'they say "That's not the way Bill puts it. . . ." It's almost as if they want to keep it vague. They *resist* strategy in the name of philosophy.'

So I created Dilemma 4.5 from what the managers were telling me. On the 'rock-like' vertical axis are the sharp specific strategies that some speakers wanted the branches to create. On the 'whirlpool' horizontal axis is Bill's general philosophy encompassing all the branches and so expressed at high levels of abstraction.

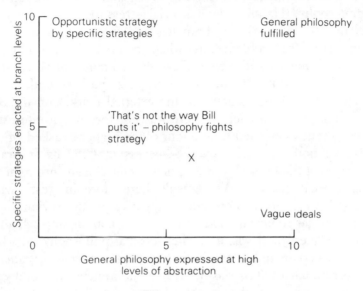

Dilemma 4.5

'What you need', I said, 'is for specific branch strategies to *fulfil* Bill's philosophy. He does not need to have his philosophy *repeated* as if you were all his clones. He's abstract because he has to be, because his ideas have to cover multiple conditions at different branches. If you reproduce that vagueness at the branch level, you create something too imprecise for commitment and too loose for useful feedback to result.'

It was the rough consensus of those at the meeting that Hanover was too close to 'vague ideals' in whose name specific strategies with achievable targets were too often being avoided. Accordingly I placed the × in the vincinity of 4/6 on the chart.

I argued that to express Bill's philosophy in the form of dilemma charts made it much harder to evade the message of that philosophy since the 'two avenues of escape' into extreme vagueness and into opportunistic precision were both flagged. If the branches were willing to be assessed on how the philosophy had been translated into strategy in their specific markets, then they could not use philosophy as a smoke machine.

Excuses of Inner Direction

A philosophical organization is usually inner directed by the values of that philosophy. Hanover puts special stress on discovering the mental models in use by its branches and functions. There is no problem here. The problem starts when you are so busy dwelling on your own interstices and having these dwelt upon that you start to neglect what is outside you, i.e. changing markets and trends. Although I invited assessments of the external market on my brief tour of some of the branches, there was not very much interest. A manager recently returned from a tour of the branches asked why no branch had bothered to study the success of Citizens Insurance Company, an affiliate of Hanover. Their senior citizens program was proving a great success. Why wasn't there more interest? 'Many branches don't perform thorough competitive pricing reviews . . .', another manager reported, 'and we review our commission schedules to agents belatedly.' It was as if the personal philosophy on which Hanover placed so much emphasis had begun to *erode attention to external events*. Clearly this was not true of all branches nor of a great many employees. Yet the group of managers I conferred with regarded it as sufficiently serious for me to draw Dilemma 4.6.

It was felt that the respect being given to mental models was being misinterpreted by at least some managers. They seemed to feel that their own thoughts and actions were of primary importance and that external events had a lower priority. This was an evasion. O'Brien's philosophy urged Hanover to take external events extremely seriously but to see these *through* the mental models of those who had brought them about. Important events were intentional. Again my group of informants placed Hanover dangerously close to the 'whirlpool' of inner-directed thoughts and too far from the 'rocks' of hard events in the external world.

The Flight to Uniqueness

This evasion takes O'Brien's ideas of localism and exaggerates it to the point where every branch is unique in all respects. It follows that no one can really understand the branch, much less evaluate it, except

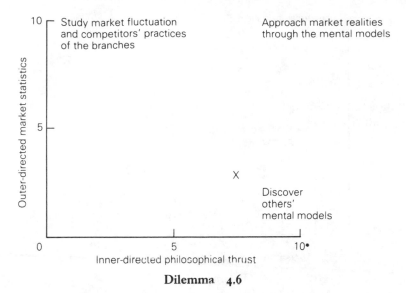

Dilemma 4.6

that branch itself. If it is unprofitable as was one branch I visited, this is because it faces a particular combination of circumstances that headquarters has never understood and never will, because their understanding is exclusive to New England.

Some branches were 'too small to be profitable', and it was not fair to expect this of them. Some, especially in the south and the west, had to compete using agents against companies using 'direct writers', i.e. in-house agents selling only their company's policies. Other branches were having central office functions devolved upon them when it was uneconomic, given their size, to do this. All in all, the local differences of the branches can be used, and in some cases *were* used, to reject 'interference' by headquarters and to claim that there was no comparability in the relative performances of different branches owing to particular handicaps. I drew Dilemma 4.7. In the case of the unprofitable branch I visited, it had just refused to sanction headquarters' request to pay a visit, citing as a reason the expense and the exceptional nature of that branch's problems, so far from the heaps of impersonal statistics compiled in Worcester.

This clearly exemplifies how a narrow stereotype of localism can be used to defeat the wider integrated concept of localism which argues that branches are *both* comparable in some respects *and* different in others. Every branch can negotiate its own criteria for assessment which takes account of those special features.

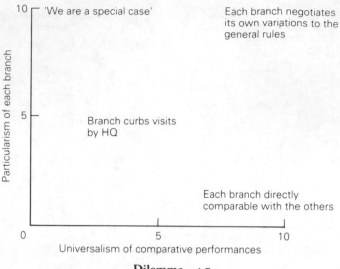

Dilemma 4.7

Ever-enlarging Wholes

It is as rare as it is wonderful to find a company that thinks holistically. The near universal bias among English-speaking economies is to analyse everything to the consistency of builder's rubble. Because Hanover is such an exciting exception I feel ungracious in pointing out that, while you can easily hide beneath great piles of meaningless data, you can equally well shelter within the mystery of wholes and those systems-within-systems-within-systems.

According to some of my informants there was a bias against detail, against statistics, against reductionism in any form. According to one company-sponsored seminar, holism was a virtue and analysis a malignant trait! 'We think connections and that's good,' one manager told me, 'but we're loosey-goosey in our response to numbers and seem to prefer general impressions.'

On my visit to the branches I took the managers through the monthly print-out of statistics asking what these meant and why they had been collected. While the successful branches were strong on company philosophy, they were not able to tell me what aspects of the philosophy the figures either supported or denied. Indeed, the usual explanation of why certain figures were collected was that it had always been so, it was required by regulators and/or that the insurance industry needed it. The figures were precise but their meanings were quite vague. It was as if the statistics and the philosophy existed in separate realms, with the first not really appropriate to the second.

This did not prevent at least two of the branches being highly successful, and I puzzled how the philosophy was being transmitted and acted upon in the absence of figures which registered its attainment.

I concluded that in the best branches the managers *modelled the philosophy in their own behaviours* and this was the form of transmission, not the information flows. Nevertheless, my informants detected a bias towards holistic thinking of a loose rather than a detailed kind. I accordingly drew Dilemma 4.8.

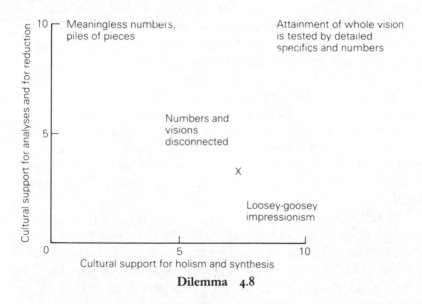

Dilemma 4.8

We finally placed the x between the looseness complained of at the meeting and the gap between visions and numbers which I had encountered in the branches I'd visited. The attainable ideal is to create whole visions and strategies for success and then to ask what data are needed to prove or to falsify their achievement. The successful organization thinks in wholes *constituted by detailed parts*, and there is no advantage in sacrificing analysis to synthesis or vice versa.

What is to be Done?

Important as it is for Hanover to steer between the misinterpretations of its own philosophy there was a more immediate issue facing John Kittel, who was charged with turning general philosophy into particular branch strategies (see Dilemma 4.5).

Given the philosophy of localism, how could branches be persuaded to create a coherent strategy in the first place, and if each branch was so different from any other, could anything as comparable as a scoreboard be devised? At this time branches were required to make annual presentations about their intended plans for the year to an 'internal board of directors', wise persons drawn from Hanover at large. While such plans were strategies of a kind, they took very different forms. Some were spoken, some written down, some were kept to guide the branch and to compare the performance with the promise, others were consigned to the waste-bin with past speeches. Some were one dimensional, 'move from urban areas to the suburbs and rural areas', others merely tactical, 'reduce our exposure in this line'. If National tried to force some general format on branches with common standards to ensure comparability, might this not offend against the principle of localism? Yet if all 'strategies' were accepted in all their variations, then very little information of use to all or most of the organization would flow through its channels. What could be done?

The author pointed out that there were two ways of understanding strategy, *prospectively* and *retrospectively*. In the *prospective* way, the branch presents its strategy to its internal board of directors to get its approval and any resources held by National Office which are necessary to the plan. Strategy is understood by comparing its prospects to its consequences. In the *retrospective* way of understanding, National approaches a branch that has been unusually and unexpectedly successful and tries to reconstruct and retrace the process by which this was achieved. The advantage of the latter approach is that you only make a study if there is something exciting to discover, and the branch is extremely likely to cooperate to the full with research aimed at showing its performance in a favourable light. Another advantage of the retrospective approach is that it can help formalize, and make reasonable, what was originally achieved by informal and intuitive judgements. Hence embryo strategies written on the back of envelopes or orally transmitted can be *written down in a format that makes them comparable.*

What we have is a helical curve moving between prospective and introspective axes in Dilemma 4.9. We start with largely retrospective strategies created with the help of National and we end with mostly prospective strategies created by the branches themselves as commitments on which they are prepared to be evaluated and scored, and, of course, *last year's* retrospectively created map can become *next year's* prospectively created map as the branch continues to chart its progress on the same coordinates.

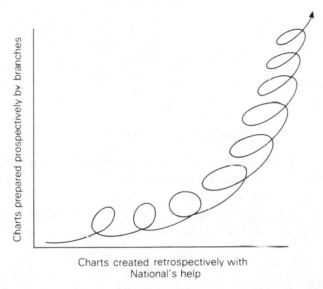

Charts created retrospectively with
National's help

Dilemma 4.9

The helix is there because strategies are improved *both* by advance preparation (prospective) and by reflection after the fact (retrospective). Indeed, there is a continuous learning cycle – figure 4.3.

The method used to map strategy retrospectively is the one introduced in chapter 3 and elaborated in this chapter. You interview the branches, create maps from their dilemmas and invite them to own these records of achievement.

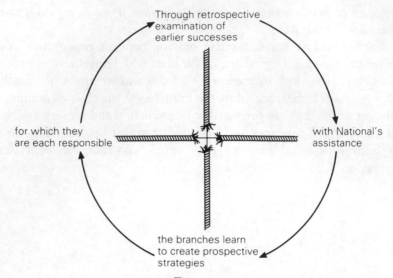

Figure 4.3

Combining the Dilemmas

Let us recall that, although dilemmas are separately presented, they are multiple dimensions of a larger reality. Let us interweave localism with openness in a merit environment. This is done by superimposing Dilemmas 4.2, 4.3 and 4.4 (figure 4.4). The learning cycle or developmental helix would read something like figure 4.5.

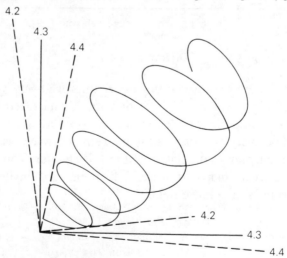

Figure 4.4   Dilemmas 4.2, 4.3 and 4.4 superimposed.

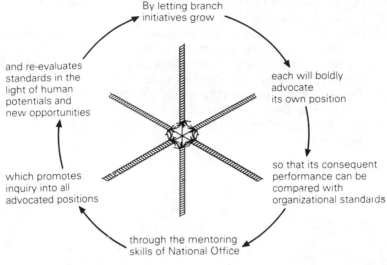

By letting branch
initiatives grow

and re-evaluates
standards in the
light of human
potentials and
new opportunities

each will boldly
advocate
its own position

which promotes
inquiry into all
advocated positions

so that its consequent
performance can be
compared with
organizational standards

through the mentoring
skills of National Office

Figure 4.5

Bill O'Brien came up to me after I had presented this cross-ropes
chart to a meeting, called by the Systems Dynamics Group of MIT in
Gstaad.[10] 'What holds the ropes together and stops them from snapping?' 'Integrity,' I replied, 'yours and that of other managers.' 'You
give me too much credit,' he replied. 'Isn't it really love, the feeling
within the community?'

I hesitated, my English reserve and pretensions to social science
giving me pause. 'May I quote you?' I asked.

Notes

1 A. P. de Geus, 'Planning as Learning', *Harvard Business Review*, March/April
   1988.
2 These pamphlets are available from the Hanover Insurance Co., 100 North
   Parkway, Worcester, Mass. See also various editions of *The Hanover News*.
3 Chris Argyris, *Strategy, Change and Defensive Routines*. Boston, Mass.:
   Pitman, 1983.
4 Lee G. Bolman and Terrence E. Deal, *Modern Approaches to Understanding
   and Managing Organizations*. San Francisco, Calif.: Jossey-Bass, 1984.
5 Donald A. Schon, *The Reflective Practitioner*. New York: Basic Books, 1982.
6 Chris Argyris and Donald A. Schon, *Organizational Learning: A Theory of
   Action Perspective*. Reading, Mass.: Addison Wesley, 1978.
7 Senge's claim game is described in 'Catalyzing Systems Thinking within

Organizations', in F. Massarik (ed.), *Advances in Organization Development*. Cambridge, Mass.: MIT Press, 1987.

8 For a good discussion of this problem see the paperback edition of Jim O'Toole's *Vanguard Management*. New York: Doubleday, 1985.

9 Thomas Carlyle, 'Signs of the Times 1829', in *Thomas Carlyle Selected Writings*. Harmondsworth: Penguin, 1971.

10 This is known as the Program in Systems Thinking and the New Management Style, coordinated at the Sloan School by Peter Senge. Members include Polaroid, Herman-Miller, Analog Devices, Ford, Hanover, Apple and others.

5

Odysseus in Silicon Valley

So far we have not examined companies in the forefront of the information revolution. Domestic appliances and insurance are not the much-touted 'industries of the future', out there on the frontiers of knowledge. They are relatively 'low tech' and humdrum. Can our dilemma methodology take the measure of the vanguard technologies, the high value-added products and the interstices of the knowledge society? It is axiomatic that we must all now deal with escalating levels of complexity in decision-making. Is dilemma analysis a self-starter in this weird world or a buggy whip?

To try and answer this question I have examined the writings of one of the major visionaries of the electronics industry, John Sculley, Chief Executive Officer of Apple Computers. This company is not simply a technological innovator but claims the status of a cultural and organizational prototype for the twenty-first century renaissance, the Florence of the electronic age. Heady stuff – but Sculley is building on the foundations laid by Apple's 'charismatic young founder', Steve Jobs, who stole fire from the corporate gods and brought it back to the people. Today the personal computer packs more power to the person than that wielded by giant computers less than a decade earlier. Sculley has incorporated the 'GAIA hypothesis' into his corporate philosophy.[1] The world is a single, unified, living system, self-organizing, self-controlling and integrated by an ecological intelligence. The world began with an apple bitten into, with fateful consequences and now used by Apple as its logo. Can Apple help to recreate an Electronic Eden, which monitors the harmonies of mankind?

Sculley and Jobs both personify 'the heroic style' of business leadership with all its powers to catalyse vast enthusiasms and all the perils of vainglory. It is said of this distinctively Californian brand of humanism that it seeks the triumphs of great drama without its tragedies, but is this possible? Will Sculley follow Jobs into *peripeteia*, the moment in Greek tragedy when vaunted values turn into their opposites?[22] If it's dangerous for man alone to aspire to greatness, is it not folly for an entire organization publicly to signal its directions and set off in headlong pursuit? Or does this give Apple a sense of mission and excitement so lacking among its competitors?

There is a final reason that an information company is crucial to my hypothesis that managers steer between dilemmas. *Information is binary, while objects are unitary*. The computer itself is based on the 'bit' or binary digits 0 or 1. Newton beheld a world of objects and celestial bodies. Information theory looks at *differences* or *contrasts*. It follows that an avant-garde information company like Apple should be up to its stalk in dilemmas and the need to reconcile these. Let us see if this is true.

As fortune would have it, in the summer of 1988 Apple University invited the author to design a systems logic based on dilemmas methodology, which might enable their university to codify, map, explain, teach, monitor, research, and even contribute to the ongoing visions and strategies of Apple Computer Inc. It might also be possible to uncover systems of values and processes of interaction which functioned in the manner of a genetic code, patterning Apple's transformation from one state to another.

The notion of an in-house corporate university has always intrigued action-researchers because any knowledge which guides action and is tested through action in the real world, as opposed to the laboratory, needs to be close to that action. Hence corporate universities, of which there are now several, could be the first institutions with a genuine mandate to change their immediate environments and study the consequences. Ironically, the corporate university could become what universities tried to become in the 1960s but were thwarted: a community of scholars with the convictions to act on their beliefs.[3]

Usually the author interviews the principals of an organization to elicit their dilemmas, but in this case, as befits the Californian culture, it was 'all hanging out'. John Sculley, Apple's CEO, had written a book, *Odyssey: From Pepsi to Apple*,[4] which was by turns ecstatic, despairing, confessional, tutorial, visionary, inspiring and humorous. Above all, he described in great detail the sensation of being pulled asunder by a myriad of new forces. The narrative was very rich for a connoisseur of inner conflict and dilemma. It consciously likened the author to a Greek hero. I therefore used this as my source material.

Sculley begins with the need to get beyond linear thinking and the rational mind-set. We have been 'falsely chasing the god of science' which stops us seeing familiar objects in a radically new light. He quotes Marvin Minsky: 'You don't really understand something until you understand it in more than one way.' It is essential, he argues, to *encourage contrarian thinking*. 'There should be a level of tension between discipline and anarchy.' '. . . [it] is like arsenic, a little is medicinal, but a lot can kill you.' The leader is an impresario whose 'artists need freedom and discipline'.

The traditional corporation has been left-brained, systematized, quantified. The entrepreneurial model often errs on the other side. It is too loose and iconoclastic . . . yet to nurture the creative impulse of any organization there needs to be some reconciliation of the two states.[5]

Sculley says of his best moments with Steve Jobs, Apple's co-founder:

Even when we disagreed it was as if were a single debater working through thesis and antithesis to reach the best conclusion . . . always examining both sides of an issue.[6]

Sculley's ideal is Sceptical Man, the successor of Rational Man who can think only in logical linear sequences, and Empirical Man who gets increasingly bogged down in a thousand pieces of data. The sceptical leader is dissatisfied with seeing only one side of an issue. He sees all views as partial, yet potentially confluent and reconcilable. Yet the dominant culture of Western business focuses on objectives and seeks ever more of the same.

Now our culture is based on amplitude. Whenever we want someone to listen to us we talk louder, we mount bigger special effects on television, use more garish colors, engage in more gyrating and twisting. We surround ourselves with what Asians call 'a very obvious culture. . . .' By contrast, Skeptical Man will communicate by details, which information offers in plenitude. *The computer will turn off amplitude and turn up contrast.* (Emphasis in original)[7]

Sculley dislikes the words 'objective' or 'end' because there are no ultimate ends or objectives. He prefers 'direction' and quotes the dictum, 'the journey is the reward'. The winding odyssey towards the resolution of increasingly vivid contraries or contrasts is its own reward. The Odyssey was, after all, a sea journey in which the wily Odysseus sailed between the rock and the whirlpool and defied the Siren songs which tried to lure him to destruction. Sculley shows great insight in charting his way between false blandishments and the media's constant attempt to hype particular achievements, but he also seems to enjoy, as Jobs did before him, the land of the Lotus-eaters which makes men forget. It is typical of the kind of heroic leadership which Sculley personifies that each triumph sets you up for a disaster. So we shall be looking admiringly at how Apple thinks and also critically at what it seems not to have grasped, for at least some of Sculley's thinking is dangerously incomplete.

We shall look at three sets of dilemmas:

1 the *transition dilemmas* resulting from Sculley's move from PepsiCo to Apple;
2 the *crisis dilemmas* of Sculley's quarrel with Jobs and the company's subsequent turnaround;
3 the *future dilemmas* which Sculley foresees.

Finally, we shall consider whether the heroic style is sustainable, or whether the 'business dramatists' do not have a kind of courtship with catastrophe that comes from thinking in such exalted terms.

The Transition Dilemmas

One 'Siren song' which could lure Apple onto the rocks is that sung by Alvin Toffler, the author of *Future Shock* and *The Third Wave*[8] or, as Daniel Bell has unkindly called it, 'Future Schlock'. Interpreting Toffler, Sculley sees Apple moving from the second wave, typified by his experience of PepsiCo, to the third wave, typified by companies undergoing continuous change and who are in the process of transforming reality (table 5.1).

For example, Sculley notes that at Pepsi the company was obsessed with *market share* – a ½ per cent gain at the expense of CocaCola was an occasion for celebration – yet at Apple it is far more important to *create the market*. Computers are 'the wings of the mind', as Jean-Louis Gassé, head of Apple's R&D, has put it. The opportunity to educate the public in the expansion of minds is infinite. In that sense *goals* and *plans* are at best way-stations on paths running in particular *directions* and pointing towards values.

Table 5.1 Contrasting paradigms

Characteristic	Second wave	Third wave
Organization	Hierarchy	Net work
Output	Market share	Market creation
Focus	Institution	Individual
Style	Structured	Flexible
Source of strength	Stability	Change
Structure	Self-sufficiency	Interdependence
Culture	Tradition	Genetic code
Mission	Goals/strategic plans	Identity/direction/values
Leadership	Dogmatic	Inspirational
Quality	Affordable best	No compromise
Expectations	Security	Personal growth
Status	Title and rank	Making a difference
Resources	Cash	Information
Advantage	Better saneness	Meaningful differences
Motivation	To complete	To build

Similarly, the old-fashioned *hierarchy* based on the fact that the boss dispensed the *cash* and could tell subordinates what to do because he knew better has given way to *networks* where authority shifts to whosoever has the relevant *information*. Where Pepsi had a highly *structured* style with a culture based on *tradition* and *stability*, Apple had a *flexible* style with a culture unfolding according to a *genetic code*, based on a blueprint for *change*.

All this is very plausible and it certainly contains a measure of truth. My difficulty is that it contradicts in several respects Sculley's statements about the contrarian nature of Sceptical Man, his strictures on the 'obvious culture' of linear thinking, his pleas to see things in more than one way and to reconcile contrasting views. Quite suddenly, Sculley claims to know that we are on a one-way trip from dogmatism to inspiration, security to personal growth and soda pop to ultimate significance. If we *really* left hierarchy behind and shoved our status in the closet, then one wonders what hit Steve Jobs and removed him from running the Macintosh Division.

My own interpretation of the third wave as the reconciliation of an earlier dilemma at least has the virtue of being consistent with the rest of Sculley's thinking. This interpretation is set out in Objectives 5.1 to 5.4 and in Dilemmas 5.1 to 5.4 on the left and right respectively of the page. All the figures have to do with John Sculley's transition from PepsiCo to Apple and all are from table 5.1 which compares Toffler's second wave with his third wave.

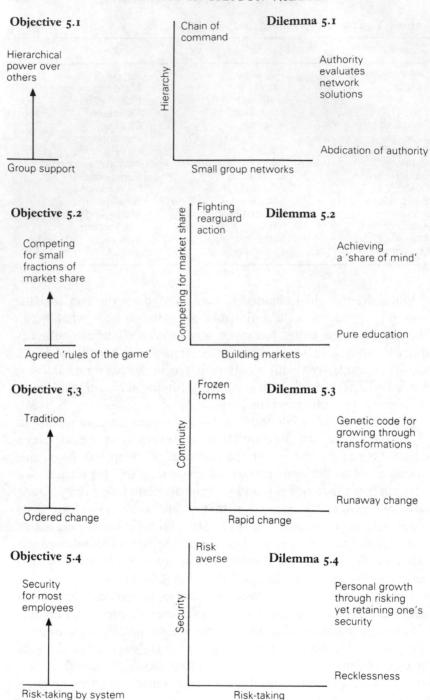

Objective 5.1

Hierarchical power over others

Group support

Dilemma 5.1

Chain of command

Hierarchy

Authority evaluates network solutions

Abdication of authority

Small group networks

Objective 5.2

Competing for small fractions of market share

Agreed 'rules of the game'

Dilemma 5.2

Fighting rearguard action

Competing for market share

Achieving a 'share of mind'

Pure education

Building markets

Objective 5.3

Tradition

Ordered change

Dilemma 5.3

Frozen forms

Continuity

Genetic code for growing through transformations

Runaway change

Rapid change

Objective 5.4

Security for most employees

Risk-taking by system designers

Dilemma 5.4

Risk averse

Security

Personal growth through risking yet retaining one's security

Recklessness

Risk-taking

On the left there is *one predominant objective*, while on the right there are two directions, constituting a dilemma, between whose values steers Sceptical Man using two 'contrarian' ways of thinking. For example, in Objective 5.1 the predominant reality is the hierarchy. You can sense it when people come into the conference room: the most junior first, distributing themselves in seats peripheral to the circle; last into the room came PepsiCo's then President, Donald M. Kendall, whereupon a Pepsi in a Tiffany tumbler was brought to him on a silver tray. Yet the staging of such displays of deference requires a network of managers who all know their place and who all play their parts. The network is there *in embryo*, shoring up the hierarchy.

In Dilemma 5.1 the small group networks have grown in power and influence until they strongly qualify the hierarchy, but it would be a serious mistake to believe that an accountability hierarchy can be transcended. It is a legal and operational constant. What is left behind to a large extent is the 'chain of command' in which the leader gives a direct order to a subordinate, who does not argue because the leader 'knows best'. In more and more situations leaders do not know how to do what they are responsible for getting done. The requisite knowledge is broadly dispersed through the network.

However, the leader remains responsible for issuing the challenge to the network and for *evaluating the quality of its creative solutions*. The hierarchy has changed in important ways but has *not* been abolished. Where it once gave specific and direct orders *before* the fact, it now mostly evaluates performances *after* the fact. In the top right-hand corner of Dilemma 5.1, hierarchy and networking are reconciled.

We see the same kind of change as Objective 5.2 moves to Dilemma 5.2. When Sculley worked for PepsiCo the predominant objective was competing against the CocaCola company for small increments of market share, worth millions. At regular intervals Nielsen, who kept the scores, presented the gains and losses, with each company in a win–lose contest for a finite amount of consumer patronage. The atmosphere of a Marine Boot-camp which Sculley reports comes from this sense of total conflict with an opponent of closely matched strength. Yet, even here there was a tacit agreement to enlarge the market where possible. Moreover, like all good competitors, they had agreed on the game to be played.

Yet Dilemma 5.2 changes this reality significantly. Here the market is not simply in a state of great expansion overall, but all consumer and software companies are teaching consumers to enlarge their capacities for thought. Ideas introduced by one company rapidly become features of a 'mindscape' shared by all. More important than market share is 'share of mind'. And consider that appetites for knowledge and mental processing skills are not quickly satiated as is a thirst for PepsiCola. Indeed, the more one *already* knows, the greater the thirst for knowledge and the more easily one learns. A knowledge-intense economy is qualitatively different from the exchange of soda pop for cash, as Steve Jobs frequently reminded John Sculley when trying to recruit him to Apple.

Yet market creation should not obscure a continuous contest for market share. After all, the creation of a contiguous market niche like Hypertext software is an effective way of gaining market share. It is no more true that one leaves market share considerations behind one than that one abandons hierarchical responsibilities. If, in time, the market for computers becomes mature, the importance of relative shares of the market will reassert itself. Apple's recent legal suit against Microsoft should remind us, if this were needed, that competition for finite resources is always a part of reality. Even where knowledge is self-generating and abundant scarcities of time and attention may remain. Once again, then, we face a dilemma. As Sculley reminded us, quoting Jerome Bruner, 'contrasting viewpoints are better than absolute judgements'.

A further simplification is Sculley's notion that tradition is giving way to a genetic code, an information 'template' for orderly transformation similar to the DNA molecule (see table 5.1). But this is to sell short the importance of tradition or, as I prefer to name it, continuity. It also ignores the fact that genetic codes encompass *both* change and continuity. The organism grows while maintaining its identity. Sculley knows this but the Sirens have been singing to him of transformation. After all, it was the Guy from Corporate America, the Boot-camp Marine, the four-miles-before-breakfast runner who is reported to have saved Apple from its counter-cultural excesses. How, then, can tradition be denied? Nor, as we have seen in earlier chapters, are traditional businesses exempt from exchanging information and reconciling dilemmas.

Objective 5.3 shows that for companies like PepsiCo tradition is stronger than change. The manicured formal gardens, the fountains turned on by the President, the 'crown princes' like Sculley groomed for an orderly succession – yet even here tradition is based on ordered changes. What has happened in Dilemma 5.3 is that change is now as strong as continuity and something akin to a genetic code must steer between frozen forms and runaway change. A company may go through a veritable transformation, but this is still encoded in its values and, as in all acts of creation, we get a 'shock of recognition'. It is still Apple after all.

Finally, like Bill O'Brien in the previous chapter, Sculley sees corporations moving from offering security to the expectations of employees to offering the opportunity for personal growth. Clearly, the excitement and enthusiasm of Apple teams, the badges inscribed 'working 90 hours a week and loving it', are not motivated by the needs of employees to feel more secure, but the notion that a secure basis has ceased to be necessary as employees ascend to 'higher realms' is surely fanciful. Were Apple a uniquely wonderful place to work, the fear of being cast out could be all the stronger.

Objective 5.4 shows that security was indeed a major motivator of employees at PepsiCo, although this was firmly based on risk-taking and personal growth of the few who built the system. What has happened at Apple is that the security provided by affluence, education and enlightened corporate practices has been qualified by the voluntary acceptance of risk by employees, which gives life more zest and excitement. This results in personal growth at the top right-hand corner of Dilemma 5.4, in which risk earns greater financial and emotional security, which in turn is invested in greater risks.

The Crisis Dilemmas

As in the last chapter I shall argue that what went wrong with Apple was an excess mounted on its own previous success. The very values that had triumphed in the past threatened catastrophe through being exaggerated, intensified and extolled. It is crucial to grasp that dilemmas are not reconciled once and for all. They have to be resolved, literally solved repeatedly. Moreover, yesterday's glorious synthesis becomes tomorrow's thesis, liable, if pushed too far, to swing suddenly over to its opposite, a process C.G. Jung called *emantiodromia* – 'the return swing of the pendulum'.[9]

How this occurs may be illustrated by comparing the Historic Dilemmas 5.5 to 5.7 with the Crisis Dilemmas 5.5 to 5.7. In each example, the historic reconciliation has become an overemphasized

Historic Dilemma 5.5

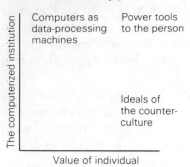

The computerized institution

Computers as data-processing machines

Power tools to the person

Ideals of the counter-culture

Value of individual

Crisis Dilemma 5.5

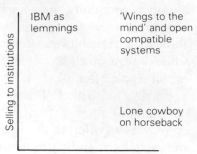

Selling to institutions

IBM as lemmings

'Wings to the mind' and open compatible systems

Lone cowboy on horseback

The empowered person

Historic Dilemma 5.6

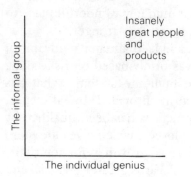

The informal group

Insanely great people and products

The individual genius

Crisis Dilemma 5.6

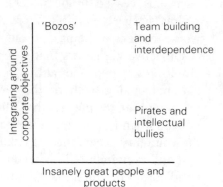

Integrating around corporate objectives

'Bozos'

Team building and interdependence

Pirates and intellectual bullies

Insanely great people and products

Historic Dilemma 5.7

The garage tradition

The hackers' revolution

'I love this product'

Crisis Dilemma 5.7

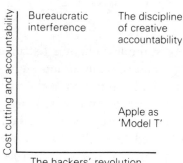

Cost cutting and accountability

Bureaucratic interference

The discipline of creative accountability

Apple as 'Model T'

The hackers' revolution

value which threatened Apple with catastrophe. Let us begin with three of Apple's historic triumphs, solutions that made the company justly famous. Apple's first triumph was to design a computer, up till then the preserve of the large corporation, and create a *power tool for the person*. The ideology was 'Aquarian' and counter-cultural, but the technology was 'user-friendly' to an unprecedented extent. 'Human being. Do not spindle, fold or mutilate.' So the placards of protesting students had once read. But Steve Jobs had changed all that by arming the radical individualist with his or her own mental power-house. A genius empowering would-be geniuses. It was quintessentially American, a voluntary association of unholy hackers, a triumph of youth over alienating institutions. Small was again beautiful.

Yet the empowered person now became a cult. It does not take long in California where roots are shallow. 'Alone Again', proclaimed Apple's TV commercials. Sculley saw it and disapproved. 'The heroic style,' he dubbed it, 'the lone cowboy on horseback.' It was the 'obvious culture' he hated, amplification instead of contrast. But worse was to come. Led by their advertising agents and the media hype about the 'Dynamic Duo' of Jobs and Sculley, Apple okayed its famous Big Brother commercial in which Orwell's 1984 was fused with the Olympics in Los Angeles. A female hammer thrower ran into a room of faceless skin-heads being harangued from a screen by Big Brother and, throwing her hammer, shattered the screen.

If the reference to IBM was still vague (some thought the target was Synanon), Apple's 'Lemming' commercial now made this explicit. Executives in business suits were shown marching in lock-step to the edge of a precipice and falling over it in turn. Sculley writes that he was appalled. Dealers were on the telephone complaining that Apple was insulting potential customers. Moreover, individuality as well as allegiance to institutions was being caricatured. And, as it turned out, the company approaching the precipice was not IBM but Apple itself. Satire is glass in which we behold all faces but our own.

Late in 1984 over-capacity and recession in the computer industry began to bite. The 'Dynamic Duo' had agreed to 'go for growth', Jobs spending on R&D, Sculley on marketing. Apple with its preponderance of non-institutional customers was worse hit than several of its competitors. The hacker market was close to saturation. The 'Mighty Mac' was late and not as cheap as Apple I and II. The institutional customers had been insulted at the very moment they were most needed. The 'Mac Office' was hastily launched as an attempt to get beyond the lone hackers who were not buying, but it was more of an idea than a reality. Apple machines were largely incompatible – even with each other. 'Pure hype', Sculley recalled.

If the marketing was badly skewed towards an ersatz individualism, so were the organizational dynamics within Apple. Once again it was a case of over-learning a once-winning combination. Apple's spectacular take-off had fused the individual geniuses of Steve Jobs, Steve Wozniak and Doug Engelbert with the fierce loyalties and authentic criticism of a small, informal group of fellow enthusiasts. It is how intense periods of creative ferment have been generated historically. It generated, as we see in Historical Dilemma 5.6, 'insanely great people and products' of which the IWM (Incredible Woz Machine) chip was typical.

But it is a short step from these triumphs to the excesses of mutual admiration and the insanity of the great and would-be great. Sculley was concerned by the way meetings were conducted. It was a rap session in which individuals got to express themselves at indefinite length, while decisions died among the duelling. 'Come on,' I shouted, 'we've got to cut this out. Let's focus on the issues and not on personalities.'

'We were intellectual bullies,' said Debi Coleman looking back on those days. Today 'there is more willingness to listen to the other side, to not win the battle for the sake of winning a battle [but] waiting, measuring and making tradeoffs.'

A disturbing sign that 'genius' had run amok were the competing fiefdoms. Those not working in the elite MAC group with Jobs were called 'Bozos'. The MAC group even sported a button which barred a clown: 'No Bozos Here'. Hardly had a product been completed when the creators grew bored – nay contemptuous – of it. LISA had a 'Cro-magnon Look'. Steve's elite called themselves 'The Pirates', but the pillage was of the rest of Apple. The worst aspects of the 1960s radical style was emerging – the curious tendency of radical individualism to sap institutions, even their own. 'They were ill disciplined, unbridled, fiercely independent . . .', Sculley recalled, and too emancipated to answer the telephone. Sculley got furious complaints from those working on Apple II that the Mighty Mac was getting all the limelight.

Our third historic Dilemma 5.7 shows how Apple was created in typical entrepreneurial fashion by the 'frugality of the garage tradition' combined with the 'love for the product being made'. Entrepreneurs make do with what they have, which is usually very little, and need intense devotion to their product to see it through. It is this crucible of parsimony reconciled with devotion that helped

Apple to arise – and much American entrepreneurialism in general.

'This product means more to me than anything I've ever done in my life,' Steve said to John. 'I love this product, and I want to share it with you. I want you to be the first person outside Apple to see it.'[10]

At this stage in the take-off of a new company, the entrepreneur's vision and the market revolution are one. There has been an intuition – a direct perception – of what enthusiasts want from one of their own. But this early symbiosis rarely lasts, and 'the hackers' revolution' passed quickly from being right to being rigid, as with the recession Apple's cheering section faded. Sculley noted:

No one could give me a satisfactory answer to the benefits to the end user. . . . I would get strange looks. 'There's a revolution out there,' I was told. 'People are lined up trying to buy them. The Macintosh is even better and easier to use, so more people will try to buy it.'[11]

So we have three examples of excess on the horizontal axes of Dilemmas 5.5, 5.6 and 5.7. In each case the historical solution became the over-vaunted value in the crises to come.

For by June 1985 Apple was in deep trouble. Its market value had dropped to less than $900 million. It was awash in unsold stock and surplus inventory. 1,500 temporary workers had to be laid off and two of six factories closed. The 'Macintosh Office' had failed. LISA had to be abandoned.

Tragically, Steve Jobs and John Sculley had come to personify the opposed values in Dilemmas 5.5 to 5.7. Steve still extolled the empowered person, the insanely great products and their people, and the hackers' revolution somewhere 'out there'. Sculley, trained in PepsiCo and still believing in institutions, urged Apple's individualists to integrate themselves around corporate objectives and saw a desperate need to start controlling its runaway costs. In a sense, each responded to the crisis by reverting to form. Steve retreated to his small band of MAC enthusiasts, recreating the garage of folklore and hoping to invent his way out of trouble. John looked to the market and to his past triumphs as PepsiCo's cost cutter.

As the dispute between Sculley and Jobs intensified, there was a pattern of oscillation between the horns of the three dilemmas, with increased plans for selling to institutions and cutting costs met by more determined praise for one man – one computer and more faith in the Apple as the 'Model T' of its own industry, a miracle complete unto itself, far beyond the conceptions of mere cost accountants.

What developed in effect was a *vicious circle* of the kind explored in chapter 2, where the ropes holding the system together have snapped, leading to 'runaway' or positive feedback, so that the system is self-exciting. Employing the six axes from dilemmas 5.5 to 5.7, it would read as figure 5.1.

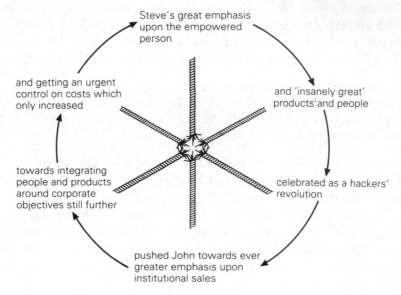

Steve's great emphasis upon the empowered person

and getting an urgent control on costs which only increased

and 'insanely great' products and people

towards integrating people and products around corporate objectives still further

celebrated as a hackers' revolution

pushed John towards ever greater emphasis upon institutional sales

Figure 5.1

Here, then, was a fierce ideological clash between the heir of 'Woodstock and Haight-Ashbury', as John saw it, who had 'absorbed the decade's ideals without being scarred by its tragedies', and the Wharton MBA, winner of the Sugared Water Olympiad, as Steve liked to call it. The outcome was not in doubt because John had the power as CEO to remove Steve from leadership of the Macintosh Division, which he did, with the backing of the Board of which Steve was still chairman. The confrontation left both men devastated. John recalls that his eyes were red with weeping. He had ousted Apple's 'charismatic, young founder' from the company he'd built and from the product he loved.

Yet, if Steve and John were irreconcilable, then *the values for which each had fought were reconcilable* and it is to Sculley's credit that, instead of smashing Steve's contrarian ideas, he built these into the syntheses described in the top right-hand corners of Dilemmas 5.5, 5.6 and 5.7.

The future of Apple was neither to stick with the isolated hackers and their closed boxes, nor sell out to soulless institutions, but to give wings to the mind through open systems and high compatibility. Hostility to IBM was counter-productive because IBM was a large part of the industry and market environment.

In a major change to Apple's philosophy I had publicly announced that we would begin to introduce devices that would allow Apple users to plug into IBM and Digital Equipment Corp communications networks.[12]

From now on Apple was selling solutions, even if these solutions used products of another company. 'For Apple to succeed, IBM does not have to fail,' Sculley insisted. Rather Apple must build the market with IBM. If possible faster and with superior solutions to users' problems. 'We were . . . trying to build a foundation for interpersonal computing by moving from stand-alone to connectivity, using a range of systems products.'

Within Apple the extraordinary individualists were to be organized into teams, in which Sculley was the chief listener and the ideal was interdependence and the fusing of contrasting ideas. The team Sculley chose to turn Apple around was in itself a resolution of opposites, a combination of remarkable individuals.

What a group to lead Apple out of its quagmire: a soda-pop executive from the East; a solid, though untested, Apple II manager; an Ivy League football coach; a French intellectual; a German conceptual thinker; an English literature major; a seasoned attorney; a Baptist philosopher; and a laid-back surfer![13]

For Debi Coleman it was a total transformation from caterpillar to butterfly. The wholes created were more than the sum of their parts. It required Taoism, biology or architecture to capture what had happened. What harmonizes teams is their learning together and innovating together, two skills crucial to creating value.

The third dilemma Sculley reconciled is set out in Dilemma 5.7. Here he insisted that creative people could and must be able to control costs. He called this creative accountability and discipline.

We had to make it acceptable to talk about accountability with the same reverence as we talk about creativity. Something as creative as architecture requires discipline. . . . For a creative-driven organization, control has negative connotations, while discipline is an underlying process integral to innovation.[14]

The discipline once imposed by the austerity of the garage in which Woz and Steve began it all had to be rediscovered.

As the dilemmas were reconciled – and the three covered here were but a part – the organization began first to heal and then to rebound. By April 1987 the company's market value had climbed from its 1985 low of $900 million to $5.5 billion. Its stock price rose from $15 to $70 in the same interval. Moreover, the Mighty Mac was selling at more than 50,000 units a month and more than 50 per cent gross margin. These targets set in the depth of the crisis two years earlier had been exceeded.

Apple's Contemporary Dilemmas

What challenges does Sculley see immediately ahead for Apple Inc? On at least three more issues his thinking is strikingly original. He takes well-worn dichotomies and designs creative syntheses. These are set out in Dilemmas 5.8, 5.9 and 5.10.

Sculley first challenges the notion of either being a domestic company or a multinational. Is Silicon Valley to be a technological equivalent of Renaissance Florence, blooming miraculously in one extraordinary town in one short epoch, or is this the beginning of another US multinational making 'what works in America' into *a world standard* and teaching 'the American way' to a less enlightened world? Neither, argues Sculley. Apple is to be *multi-local*. Just as Apple, France, once run by Jean-Louis Gassé has contributed unique ideas to the whole Apple network, so will each Apple company contribute viewpoints based in its culture to the whole system. A potentially important development is Apple in Japan and its work with *kanji*, letters borrowed from the Chinese and used to symbolize combinations of ideas and words.

Kanji are important because they stand between the world of letters and the world of pictures. They have the literary precision of the rock and the visuo-spatial configuration of the whirlpool. They join the analysing reductive left hemisphere of the brain to the synthesizing elaborating right hemisphere of the brain. *Kanji*, in short, is a language able to express the resolution of contrarian ideas.

Dilemma 5.8

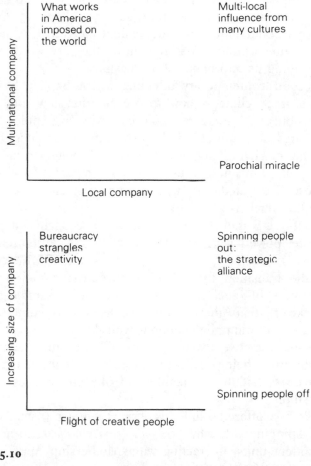

What works
in America
imposed on
the world

Multi-local
influence from
many cultures

Multinational company

Parochial miracle

Local company

Increasing size of company

Bureaucracy
strangles
creativity

Spinning people
out:
the strategic
alliance

Spinning people off

Flight of creative people

Dilemma 5.10

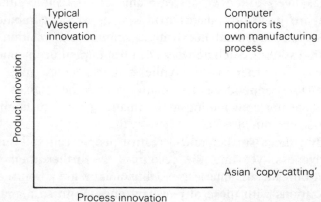

Typical
Western
innovation

Computer
monitors its
own manufacturing
process

Product innovation

Asian 'copy-catting'

Process innovation

Might not Apple, led by its Japanese unit, create a language of picturegrams and composite ideas to give the West an equivalent of *kanji*? Even two to three hundred equivalents of 'multi-local', 'creative accountability', 'interdependent individualists' could enrich business immeasurably. Without these, the very words we use will keep dividing us into opposite persuasions.

A second contemporary dilemma which Sculley has ingenious ideas for reconciling is how to prevent the slow, but inexorable, stranglehold of bureaucracy on creativity as Apple gets larger. Traditionally, the only alternative to becoming bureaucratized is flight from the petrifying organization to start again from scratch, or spinning off. Thus numerous computer companies have been started by those frustrated in larger companies and prevented from proceeding further.

Arguably US industry has never really reconciled the bigness of corporate power with the ingenuity of its entrepreneurs. The literature of organizational development is full of those who failed to make the transition from brilliant inventiveness to organizational effectiveness, of which Steve Jobs is one more example. It is shortly after 'take off' that American business seems most vulnerable. Silicon Valley as a cultural phenomenon is typical in this respect. Brilliant in its trail-blazing inventiveness, it stumbled at the stage when new inventions were being challenged by lower-cost alternatives and when inventiveness had to be qualified by the effectiveness of a larger organization.

Sculley's proffered solution is of great interest. Instead of your best people spinning off, why not *spin them out deliberately* into semi-independent units, interacting with 'Mothership Apple'. Elsewhere this has been called a 'strategic alliance' or 'value-added chain'. There are great advantages to a system which combines a large measure of independence with a continuing relationship in a federated system. Such networks can be coupled or uncoupled at the initiative of either party. While a bureaucracy may retain an unprofitable appendage for many years, the signals from any appendage not contributing to an alliance or not sustaining its own existence are much faster.

Within these smaller units creative people can still sustain their inventiveness, yet find the resources to further their inventions without bureaucratic interference, thus uniting the advantages of small organizations with those of powerful ones. With so many spin-offs,

Apple itself remains small, able to change the patterns formed by its units quickly, so that each new situation can be met with new configurations of the strategic alliance.

Apple's third reconciliation of its contemporary dilemmas is the one between product innovation and process innovation. Of the two, process innovation has long been the weaker. For years we accused the Japanese of copying our products in a sterile and unimaginative way when, in fact, their manufacturing processes were remarkably novel, often eliminating several manufacturing steps and creating 'the same' product at a fraction of the cost. Process innovation can be hidden for months or years, while a novel product immediately draws attention to itself and invites imitators.

The peculiar advantage of manufacturing a computer is its ability to *participate in the process of its own creation*. You do not simply design the machine for fewer manufacturing steps and easier assembly, you get the computer to 'talk' to its makers about how well it is being made.

After the assembled MAC gets a brain – its screen lights up and it tells the line's human operator how it's doing: 'I'm okay,' or, 'Fix me, I've got a problem with a drive.'[15]

After that the MACs go for a stress test monitored by another MAC, while a third MAC keeps count of the number of times the inventory turns over a year. Under Debi Coleman's supervision, this rose from three to thirty-six, while computerized reordering brought the parts in just in time. Essentially, *the product is conversing with the process* and each feeds back vital corrective information about the other as they achieve synergy in the top right-hand corner of Dilemma 5.10.

The Leader as Visionary

In one sense John Sculley had no choice but to hit the headlines and put Apple on a roller-coaster ride from boom to bust to boom to where? He had replaced a legendary leader and had to keep up the dramatic momentum of the world's most romantic company. He could not afford to be the anticlimax following Steve's departure and so he wove his own mythology around shared exploits. He could not be as inventive as Steve around the basic technology, and so he became a business philosopher and an avatar of new paradigms and third waves.

For Sculley the personal computer will be to the twenty-first century what the printing press was to the sixteenth. We are on the threshold of a renaissance for which the PC is the breakthrough tool. He foresees a Knowledge Navigator sailing through vast data bases and comparing culture to culture, discipline to discipline. For the huge advantage of this new technology is its mediation between contrarian ways of thinking, its visual capacities interacting with text and the thousands of cross-disciplinary, cross-hemispherical connections of which it is capable. The MAC, using hyper text, is nothing less than a creativity machine, making possible a massive shift to a holistic viewpoint and an ecological sense of the interdependence of all living things.

With such machines, tailored to whatever learning bias the individual may have, the United States may be enabled to create value and turn around its sliding economic fortunes. It has the specialists, the Nobel prizes and the 'firsts' in many fields. What it lacks are the myriad cross-connections between fields of knowledge which create valuable products. Here, again, Apple has the answers. For the edge America has over the Japanese is its stress upon the individual. Because the cells in a single brain are the first to grasp a creative connection, the culture that connects individuals *without* any diminution of the uniqueness of their characters must innovate more successfully. With Apple's products, the age-old quest to communicate without coalescing, to be an individual and yet sustain and be sustained by others, is now within reach.

This same technology can bring immense enjoyment to learning and richness to the intellectual environment. By thinking analogically, the MAC is a tool for culture and the humanities. By simulating tasks in which error would normally be dangerous, challenges like flying a jet or operating machinery can be cut to a fraction of what was formerly necessary.

Is the Heroic Style Sustainable?

Clearly, this author finds all this captivating, a cerebral 'garden of delights'. But is it sustainable? Can the Real Apple ever come close to the Ideal Apple and is there not a risk of burning out the fevered imaginations of the faithful? Can a CEO announce before the world what he wants without precipitating a rush within the organization towards one end or the other of a delicate balance?

It is now some time since Sculley wrote his epistle to the expectant, and Apple is again pregnant with products or hysteria. It is hard to know which. Much as I would like to believe in this new marriage of business and intellectual excitement, parts of me remain sceptical. It can't be *that* much fun! When will the next catastrophe strike? Press reports are worrying and rumour is rife. There has been a considerable amount of exiting from the organization, a fact which suggests frustration with the ratio between promise and fulfilment. A *New York Times* report speaks of a fascination with the future but a neglect of the present. It asks what will succeed the MAC now that Jobs has gone and where are the geniuses?[16]

Friends speak of turmoil caused by reorganization after reorganization. The Mothership Apple appears to suffer from 'information overload', with its spin-outs all trying to speak at once and very few messages getting through. Another candidate for Apple's Achilles' heel is the repeated attempt to flatten the organization and say farewell to the old 'hierarchical paradigm'. But hierarchies help to control anxiety and they are something to fall back on when exchanging information fails us. The reported quarrelling among would-be successors to the Philosopher King could be one consequence of this too assiduous pursuit of formal equality.

The company is also on a collision course with Sun Microsystems as PCs and work stations converge upon each other. Yet, if, as Sculley insists, 'the journey is the reward', then Apple has already had more fun than most other companies, and the outcome may be less important than the triumphs of the process thus far. For those who compare themselves with Greek heroes, the important outcomes are *the lessons to be learned.* Even if dramatic behaviour can be perilous, it teaches the rest of us.

This was what I told Apple University: 'You have in your midst a living lesson in action science. Be the groaning Greek chorus on the edges of the stage, warning the actors and advising them. It is a wonderful chance to learn some classic truths, and to try and forestall *hubris* and promote *harmonia.*

Notes

1 Norman Myers (ed.), *GAIA: An Atlas of Planet Management*. New York: Anchor Press, Doubleday, 1984.

2 For the categories in Greek drama corresponding to various crises in organization see maps 1, 2, 57 and 58 in Charles Hampden-Turner, *Maps of the Mind*. New York: Macmillan, 1981.

3 For this author's earlier interest in the community of scholars see *Radical Man: Towards a Theory of Psycho-social Development*. New York: Anchor, 1971; London: Duckworth, 1973; especially chs 11 and 12.

4 John Sculley, *Odyssey: From Pepsi to Apple*. New York: Harper and Row, 1987.

5 Ibid. p. 184.

6 Ibid. p. 169.

7 Ibid. p. 152.

8 Alvin Toffler, *Future Shock*. New York: Bantam, 1970; *The Third Wave*. New York: Bantam, 1980.

9 Joseph Campbell (ed.), *The Portable Jung*. New York: Viking, 1971.

10 Sculley, *Odyssey: From Pepsi to Apple*, p. 301.

11 Ibid. p. 274.

12 Ibid. p. 329.

13 Ibid. p. 283.

14 Ibid. p. 320.

15 Ibid. p. 290.

16 'John Sculley's Biggest Test', *New York Times*, Business Section, 26 February 1989.

6

Seven Steps to Reconciling
Dilemmas Strategically

Thus far we examined the dynamics of creating value (chapter 1) and
of steering an organization (chapter 2). We have seen how dilemmas
are charted (chapter 3) and how an entire organization sets itself up to
learn how to steer between contrasting 'horns' (chapter 4). We noted
that such an 'odyssey' lends itself to visionary leadership and self-
dramatization, with all the advantages and pitfalls of such heroic styles
(chapter 5). We have yet to consider in detail *how dilemmas are
resolved*. It is all very fine to say that you will 'steer between' values
which are in tension or will 'combine' these. In practice this is quite
difficult and needs particular ways of thinking and acting which are
not the usual ways.

Moreover, most organizations will actively *resist* seeing more
problems than they can solve, or surfacing more dilemmas than can
be reconciled. Where time for making decisions is limited and the
energy needed is near exhaustion, managers will quite rightly refuse
to take on more than they can handle or admit to disputes which make
it difficult to live with colleagues. It may therefore be crucial to
demonstrate that 'opposed' values *can* be resolved. Unless there is
sufficient faith in the dilemma-reconciling concepts, the dilemmas
may not be volunteered in the first place.

The organization which assisted me more than any other in the
early formulation of my dilemmas' reconciliation was the Shell
International Petroleum Company, now the world's largest corporation.
I owe to its Group Planning Department, located on London's South
Bank, and its Coordinator, Arie de Geus, a considerable debt of
gratitude for hosting my early efforts and for recognizing before any
other corporation whatever merits these had. I worked for two years

in Group Planning, after which they generously supported me at the Centre for Business Strategy at London Business School, where I was Shell Senior Research Fellow for three years.

It is extraordinary, when I think back on it, that the first 'guinea pigs' of as yet untested methods were the fifty-four most senior members of this formidable multinational. They were first interviewed in depth by two senior managers in the Group Planning Department, Kees van der Heijden and Gareth Price. It was only after a great number of quite discrepant viewpoints had been collected that this author was asked to comb the transcripts for reconcilable dilemmas. It is important to grasp that the process of gathering issues through interviews and then feeding these back to those interviewed is itself dilemma prone. If this 'reflection' shows more problems than can possibly be dealt with, the consultants are likely to be seen as non-constructive, as indeed they are.

If, on the other hand, the organization's main dilemmas are unveiled with methods of reconciling these, then the sheer extent of opposed opinion is far less threatening. *E pluribus unum* becomes more than just a motto but a tenable prospect. A wide range of diverse opinions is exciting, *provided* there are ways of rendering these compatible, and so it proved in this case. 'Beyond the Looking Glass' and its later version 'Approaching Dilemmas' were immediately restricted to those senior enough to be informed, but they quickly gained the underground notoriety of a *samizdat*, being featured in three Dutch newspapers who obtained copies illegally.[1]

I cannot, unfortunately, reveal even today the statements made by interviewees or show how I 'mapped' these. Shell, unlike Apple, does not believe in 'letting it all hang out', and that is its right. I can reveal in outline the 'seven steps for reconciling dilemmas', since these are now part of my general practice. I will apply these seven steps, not to what Shell told me, but to an imagined composite chemical company called Multichem. In fact, I have presented my dilemmas methodology to Dow Chemical (Eastern Division, USA), DSM (Dutch State Mines), AKZO and ICI (Australia), in each case asking those I addressed to volunteer their dilemmas from the floor or from small groups convened to discuss and implement these methods. Multichem is a hybrid of their responses, with preference given to the most frequently recurring dilemmas.

Clearly, dilemmas surfaced in this way may be relatively superficial. There is no reason to suppose the companies concerned would trust an itinerant foreigner with the anguish of their private deliberations. Nonetheless, the dilemmas are good enough to demonstrate the methods of resolution. It is also of interest how very similar such dilemmas are, even across three continents! Companies often believe that they are alone in the uniqueness of their perplexities. This is very rarely the case.

In the descriptions that follow, all statements have been paraphrased. All dilemmas were raised by *at least* two companies, some by three, and one by all four. Nothing unique to any one company has been revealed or described. No statements made in confidence have been repeated.

The steps take the form of sequential processes, each building upon and extending the previous step. They are as follows:

1 Eliciting through humour
2 Mapping
3 Processing
4 Framing/contextualizing
5 Sequencing
6 Waving/cycling
7 Synergizing

Eliciting Dilemmas through Humour

Humour is necessary in my experience because the rational model which still dominates business thinking is a curiously solemn affair and takes itself very seriously. The admission that dilemmas even exist tends to be difficult for some companies, and discussions may show strain or embarrassment. After all, one is suggesting the absence of a perfect consensus on the goals to be achieved and on the means of realizing these most efficiently. The more pristine rationalists may resent this. 'Is this worth more than a bowl of warm spit?' one such sceptic asked of my approach.

An effective way of freeing up the channels of communication is to make use of the corporation's own in-jokes and to present in a humorous way the mutual impedance among key ideas in that environment. In this way people laugh at what might otherwise provoke anxiety or shame. Laughter is like 'first aid'. The Greek dramatists believed that if you could not laugh at their comedies, you would end up weeping at their tragedies. In the annual Dionysian festivals the comedies came first, in December, with the tragedies in April and May.

It is best when poking fun to start with yourself and your own ideas. Cartoon 1 introduces *Dilemma* as a cross-eyed beast with horns.[2] Cartoon 2 makes light of the serious point that a dilemma not reconciled in its early stages may become an *Impasse*, a much more formidable beast. There are serious dilemmas inherent in my own role as a consultant or researcher. How come, if I'm so smart, that I'm not sitting at the top of giant corporations like several of my clients? Is 'strategic thinking' really a generalizable subject, and do those specializing in it have anything to teach those who have already won their way to the top of organizations? Cartoon 3 makes mock of the pretensions in the field of strategy and allows managers to find me every bit as ridiculous as they wish.

It is also vital, if this dilemma approach is to win any credence within the organization, to deflate the notion that there has to be a consensus on which values are most important. This is done in cartoon 4. So long as managers believe they ought to feel the same, talk the same and want the same objectives, the very existence of dilemmas is a reproach to them. What, in fact, is needed for learning to occur is *not* that everyone seeks the same ends, but that they grasp the interdependence of the ends they are pursuing and that they learn how to reconcile their preferences. A, an idealist, needs to learn that only with the help of B, a realist, can his/her ideals be realized. C, a research and development specialist, needs to learn that only with the help of D, a marketing expert, can his/her precious product attract sufficient customers.

There has to be a consensus on how values are tested and how best to reconcile values so that A gets what he/she wants as a consequence or as a precursor of B, C and D getting what they want. But this is a consensus about procedure, about methods, about how to treat people so that the exchange of ideas and information is enriched. It is not a consensus about who or what is most important or 'ultimately valuable'. Another way of calming the corporate nervous system is to say, in effect, that 'it's okay to be anxious'. Anxieties shared through laughter are diminished and the arrival of a consultant on strategy is usually enough to raise the *Qualm Quotient* (cartoon 5).

A fairly safe joke in most multinational chemical companies who have gathered together in conference is that senior managers rarely

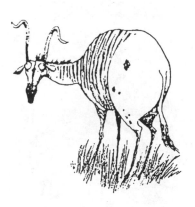

1   The Dilemma. A mottled quadruped with a pronounced squint, one eye being focused upon each of its two horns. Contrary to popular superstition, the Dilemma is not usually dangerous and can easily be domesticated.

2   The Impasse. A much more formidable beast than its cousin, The Dilemma. Those unwilling or unable to domesticate Dilemmas may have no choice but to confront the Impasse.

3   The Strategic Thinker. A reptile of amazing craft and subtlety who calculates on the run.

4   The Consensus. A sloth-like beast of mythical properties, long thought to be of great value to hunters. In fact, a Consensus of any size is very hard to find, and tends to vanish as mysteriously as it first appeared. Much time and effort can be saved by not seeking it.

QUALMS

5 Qualms. Small timid creatures, which emit a cheeping sound. Qualms, typically, gather at meetings discussing chemical toxicity and ecological crises.

6 The Gathering Momentum. All multinational corporations have a large Momentum which, once it gathers, is difficult to stop. Unwary directors who speak in very loud voices may cause a great Gathering of Momenta to rush too far in one direction.

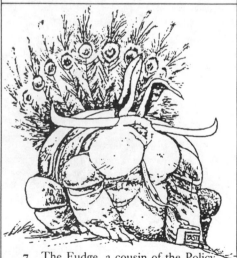

7 The Fudge, a cousin of the Policy Statement, resembles a paste-up of many different species: its peacock's tail attracts attention, while a hard shell protects it. Popular as a house pet, it has an awkward habit of climbing to the top of abstraction ladders and refusing to come down.

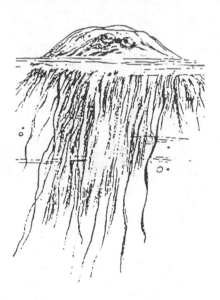

8 The Random Grope or *conglomeratus major* feeds on targets of opportunity using its multiple tentacles. It is thought to suffer from an identity crisis.

say anything which is particular new, interesting or memorable. This is not because they lack competence, far from it, but because anything definite like 'steer left' or 'steer right' is likely to be emphasized by the first echelon, re-emphasized by the second, further exaggerated by the third . . . until you have hit the rock or been pulled into the whirlpool. Any competent leader or helmsman is rightly concerned with the *Gathering Momentum* (cartoon 6) around any statement he/she might make.

What they do instead is to make balanced statements at such high levels of abstraction and with such obvious nobility of intention that no one could possibly disagree. At such a height above the concrete level of day-to-day events, any cracks in the edifice are invisible. Top managers agree with all factions but especially that these should reach better agreements among themselves. Cartoon 7 laughs at the *Fudge* (or Policy Statement) with its pseudo-consensus and mere juxtaposition of incompatible views.

Because of their sheer size most multinationals are extremely difficult to steer from any point at the centre. While those at HQ vaguely felt they should have 'a strategy', they tended to be perplexed about how to do this. Most Multichem respondents felt that HQ had little influence on them or, if at HQ, that national companies should have considerable discretion to get on with it. Many felt that their company was expanding in a haphazard way, 'feeding off targets of opportunity'. We named this creature the *Random Grope* (cartoon 8), with tentacles extending in all directions.

It is rare for Multichem cultures to tolerate 'bold' or 'charismatic' leaders. Much fun is poked at those who might even try to give orders. Where an organization is widely dispersed across the globe, central leadership only knows what it is told or what is statistically reported. The danger of pretending one knows about remote operations because they are formally accountable is that others may support the leader out of deference or out of ambition to succeed him.

For this reason there are strong norms against any 'strong' leadership style. Widely dispersed operations have serious misgiving about central leadership.

Mapping the Dilemmas

Having used humour to help surface dilemmas in their least offensive forms we are now in a position to take a second step towards reconciling them. This consists of mapping or charting our dilemmas as was done in chapters 3, 4 and 5. In fact, we can create a map from several of the cartoons just introduced. For example, three of the creatures from our bestiary, the Fudge or the Consensus and the Random Grope, constitute two ways of not reconciling the dilemma of decisive leadership versus the pluralism of local initiatives. This tension is set out in Dilemma 6.1, in which the Fudge or Policy Statement, which papers over the necessary diversity of viewpoints by talking in extreme generalities, represents a pseudo-consensus between the two extremes, an unsatisfactory compromise which gets little genuine decisiveness or diversity into the way the corporation forms its strategies. The reconciliation of this dilemma is through the Strategic Thinker (cartoon 3) who must continue to be a figure of fun until his reptilian wiles have been justified.

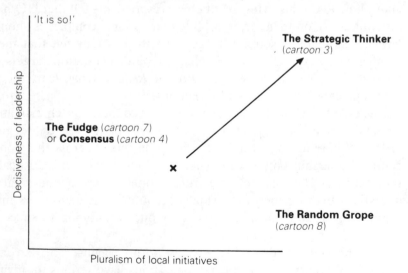

Dilemma 6.1

Having used humour and company 'in-jokes' along with interviews with those convening the conference, I am now in a position to map and to summarize four of the most frequently recurring dilemmas. These may be stated as follows.

1 Given the wide pluralism of local initiatives, is it possible to exercise any decisive or strategic leadership which is applicable to all the units concerned?

2 Given the necessity to compete strongly so that the best organization, people and products arise to prominence in world markets, what is the role of cooperation in this process. Can it strengthen competition or does it weaken it?

3 Given the obvious desirability of paying employees according to the value of their performance to the company, is it possible to achieve this while maintaining authentic communications and mutually sustaining relationships?

4 Given life-long commitments to the professions and disciplines such as chemistry and engineering, is it really possible for employees to develop an equivalent concern for the diverse and special needs of customers and the fleeting potentials of the market?

Dilemma 6.1 has already been mapped. Note that most Multichem respondents located themselves in the vicinity of the Fudge and the Random Grope, and nearly all wished to find a way of steering their larger organizations strategically.

Dilemma 6.2 is mapped between the vertical axis of competition and the horizontal axis of cooperation. The 'rock' of too much competing leads to factionalism and arch-rivalry. The 'whirlpool' of too much cooperating leads to collusion and mutual protectionism.

Dilemma 6.2

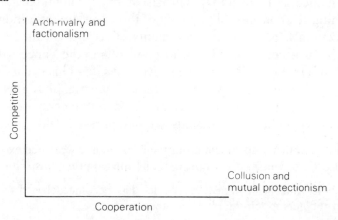

Respondents drew attention to this dilemma in words paraphrased below.

Our products are supposed to compete even with each other . . . but in reality the development of one is key to the development of several more. I wish we could help each other more in this respect.

If senior managers are known to have 'pet projects', this saps the morale of everyone concerned. We should compete fairly among ourselves.

We frequently put two or three teams on the urgent solution to a problem. The idea is that when the best answer has been found, all teams will unite around it. I'm afraid that doesn't happen. . . .

You can't innovate unless the people you are working with are genuinely constructive in their criticism. Unfortunately, there are factions who take great pleasure in shooting down any ideas created by rivals.

Why do we get angry when customers complain? They aren't our adversaries. They are our teachers.

You can't give a customer proper service unless products supplied by different units are coordinated.

Our delivery dates are being set back by the slowest units in our organization. We seem afraid to complain or to pressure them.

Most of these remarks complain of excessive rivalry and the inability to harmonize the efforts of different units. But at least two complain of relationships which are too cosy or collusive. The *Arch-rival* (cartoon 9) belongs at the top left of Dilemma 6.2, while the *Collusion* (cartoon 10) belongs at the bottom right.

Dilemma 6.3 is mapped between the vertical axis of pay for performance and the horizontal axis of open communications and sustaining relationships. The 'rock' of too eager an imposition of the organization's standards via increments of reward is called the *Cold Appraisal* (cartoon 11). The 'whirlpool' of infinite concern for the feeling of employees is called sensitive and safe. This occurs when a supervisor, anxious at all costs to remain on friendly terms with a poorly performing employee, is tactful about incompetence. The words of Multichem respondents are paraphrased below.

Did you know that 75 per cent of our total work-force was rated excellent in the last review? And it costs us the earth in inflated premiums and bonuses!

The whole concept of high performance has become debased by people without the guts to tell the truth to subordinates.

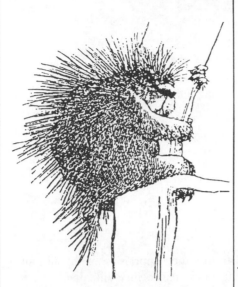

9 The Arch-rival occupies a high position above its enemies and succeeds in barring their ascent.

10 The Collusion. An inhabitant of smoke-filled rooms and back alleyways. It avoids open conflict if it can.

11 The Cold Appraisal. This famously fussy eater examines its prey at great length to ensure it conforms to required standards.

Dilemma   6.3

This year we forced managers to distribute their appraisals among all four categories of performance: excellent, good, satisfactory and poor, but it seems they are now bad-mouthing the system itself.

I am being asked to pass judgements on employees who can judge themselves far better than I can and have much more information.

In these cosy evaluation sessions the buck gets passed to those not in the room.

If a supervisor–subordinate relationship is not resilient enough to stand some honest evaluation, then there are bound to be evasions.

The 'standards' by which we expected to evaluate our people are a joke as far as I'm concerned. You could say 'I go through the motions' but what else can I do? My people deserve better methods of evaluation and they know it!

Supervisor speak with false tongue.

In fact, the most usual condition of 'pay for performance' schemes is what Chris Argyris and Donald Schon have called *defensive routines* in which both the performance and the relationship are compromised by the *skilled incompetence* of those involved.[3] Fearing the attenuation of the relationship and that the subordinate may go out of control – emotionally and behaviourally – the supervisor glosses over *both* the mediocre performance and possible errors in the method of evaluation. This situation is captured in cartoon 12, the *Mixed Message*.

Dilemma 6.4 is mapped between the vertical axis 'Commitment to profession' and the horizontal axis 'Identification with customers'

14 The Disciplinarian. Its narrow vision tends to focus on what its tools can best accomplish.

12 The Mixed Message is easily made nervous and adopts a curious stumbling gait or defensive routine.

15 The Customers' Creature, tongue protruding, runs to meet its master, a common inhabitant of advertising agencies.

13 The Compromising Position, a relative of The Mounting Crisis.

Dilemma   6.4

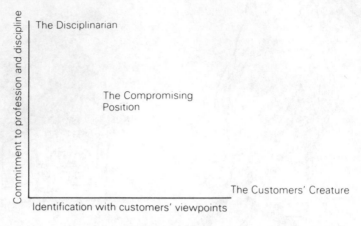

viewpoint'. The rock of narrow discipline is counter-pointed by the customer's creature, who, tongue already out, rushes to meet its master. In fact the latter is very rare, especially in Multichem where the organization tends to be larger and more powerful than customers and where prime allegiance is often to one's scientific profession. What is more usual is that 'attention to customers' is seen as a *Compromising Position* (cartoon 13) for professionals to adopt. Nearly all Multichem respondents placed themselves at the top left of this dilemma. Statements were paraphrased as follows:

I can't get my people to care about what the product will do for people's lives. They're interested in its development but not the result.

I say 'Damn it! This fibre's so tough you can build a *bridge* from it. It's six times stronger than steel. Let's use our imagination about what customers might do with it. How can we convince them? How can we get the insurers on board? And I'm met with blank indifference.

The important issue is how to help people live longer and healthier lives. Now part of this problem is pharmaceutical, but another part has to do with diagnostics and instruments in the home, and another part with good diet, good exercise, good habits and good information. I say we have to have it *all*, but if it isn't pharmaceutical, my people tune out.

What customers need is organized around the customers' priorities. They want to be in the driver's seat. But for us, the customer is the last link in a chain stretching from the research lab to the environment. We have to reverse the direction of our thinking. We have to enter a world that is not our own.

I heard this story in which a group of salesmen stopped competing on the sales they closed and started competing who had learned most from customers that month. The irony was that they closed more sales as a result of concentrating on others. We should try that.[4]

All these statements tend to criticize the 'professional' horn of the dilemma or the vertical axis. Accordingly I found the *Disciplinarian* (cartoon 14) to personify this bias and balanced it with the *Customers' Creature* (cartoon 15). At this point all four dilemmas have been mapped and all respondents have located their positions. Now the process of reconciliation begins.

Processing Dilemmas

The third step is to rid ourselves of nouns. They sound harder and more like solid things. Decisiveness of leaders, for example, sounds impervious to the pluralism of local initiatives. Competition versus cooperation are sacred ideals around which a cold war was recently fought. Discipline clashes with customers' needs and each polarized term sounds as if it were a commandment chiselled in stone. By adding *ing* to these words we convert the noun form to the present participle: not decisiveness but deciding, not competition but competing, not discipline but disciplining.

Once expressed in this way, they are process words which are free to mingle and qualify each other like ripples on the surface of a pond, so that disciplining is qualified by customizing, competing with cooperating, deciding with pluralizing, evaluating subordinates with relating to them. Quite suddenly the oppositions are softened and the *adversary structure* disappears.

Processes form intricate patterns and are mutually modifying. They take us out of Newton's world of solid objects and into the *frequency realm* of waves and currents in which the whole patterns the parts rather than the parts constituting the whole.

Framing and Contextualizing Dilemmas

Another useful step in reconciling dilemmas is to make *each side in turn the frame or the context for the other*. Let us go through some of our dilemmas to see how this works.

Our top management strategist must excel at deciding, yet these decisions must have relevance to the pluralizing of a number of business units. We can express this idea by making each process a picture surrounded by a frame and then making the frame change places with the picture (figure 6.1).

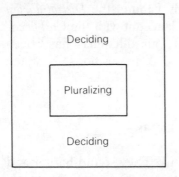 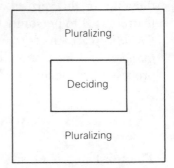

Figure 6.1

Context is from *contextere*, to weave together. Indeed, frame and picture are now inseparable. There are a pluralizing number of initiatives to be encompassed by deciding, and deciding must take place within a plural context. Each stands out in turn from the background constituted by the other. 'Text' and 'context' are reversible.

It is important to grasp that each value is *contained within* and *constrained by* its opposite. For example, nothing about the process of deciding should diminish the plurality of contexts to which it can be applied. Nothing about the plurality of contexts can be allowed to affect the importance of deciding. What this means, in effect, is that deciding has to operate at a level of abstraction above pluralizing, and that pluralizing has to operate at a level of abstraction above deciding. If the line below represents the different levels of abstraction, then the reconciliation reads like this:

HQ creates the plural context . . .

. . . in which each business unit decides

and

HQ decides key features . . .

. . . which recur in plural contexts.

How might this work specifically? Well, HQ could decide that the whole company should aim for higher value-added products, yet leave to business units the choice of which of these products to make. Increasing the level of knowledge intensity along with the training of employees and the recruitment of top talent could thereby become the *context* in which each business unit decides its own future. Harold Mintzberg has called this an 'umbrella strategy'.[5]

In addition, HQ might decide to move out of bulk chemicals into speciality chemicals or pharmaceuticals because of the higher margins to be found there. This policy was so common among my Multichem respondents that we created cartoon 16 which contrasted the ubiquitous *Bulk Chemical* with the rarer elusive niche-dwelling *Speciality Chemical*, much sought after but difficult to capture. Difficulty in moving from the first to the second is so routinely blamed on the *Corporate Culture* that we included this as well (cartoon 17).

The framing and contextualizing step can be used on several of our other dilemmas. For example, competing and cooperating (figure 6.2). To argue that competing is framed by cooperating or vice versa is to insist that how well a supplier competes with other suppliers is a measure of how well he has cooperated with his customers. You could say that the internal cooperating or harmony within a unit was a function of how strongly it competed externally and vice versa.

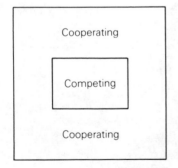
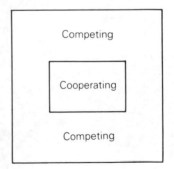

Figure 6.2

This is an important principle because the kind of competing which weakens the capacity for cooperating with customers is the *Arch-rival* depicted in cartoon 9 and the factionalism at top left in Dilemma 6.2. The kind of cooperating internally that weakens external competition is the collusion and protectionism at bottom right in Dilemma 6.2. Only if competing contains and constrains the excesses of cooperating and only if cooperating contains and

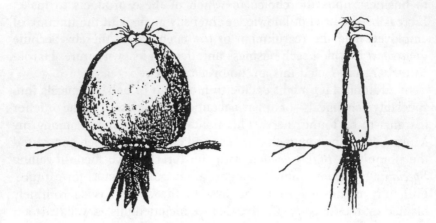

16   The Bulk Product (left) and The Speciality Product (right). There is great concern to find and capture the much rarer niche-dwelling Speciality Products, but these have proved elusive and scrawnier than expected. Hunting them takes expertise which is often lacking among bulk finders.

17   The Corporate Culture. A chameleon-like lizard of such variegated hues that, while everyone acknowledges its splendour, few can agree on a description.

constrains the excesses of competing will the two processes keep each other honest and integral, woven together as text and context.

The same figure and ground relationship applies to the pay for performance problem. Evaluating the performance of employees is contained within and constrained by the need for continued relating between manager and managed. This evaluating must not damage the relationship in which it occurs. Similarly, the relating of manager and subordinate is contained within and constrained by the need for honest and authentic evaluating. That is what the relationship is for.

Where the evaluating damages the relating we know that the latter is too weak. And where the relating obscures the evaluating we know that the latter is evasive and false. Only where picture and frame, text and context retain their integrity and their strength will paying-for-performance work.

Sequencing Dilemmas

What makes contrasting values *seem* so oppositional is that each is presented to us at one moment in time. It is hard to see how, in evaluating a subordinate critically, you can relate warmly to that person *at the same time*. Can you simultaneously compete with someone and be seen as cooperating? Surely not. The very use of contrasting terms denotes a difference, not an identity.

But in reality time is used to mediate these contrasts. Indeed, timing is a large part of strategy.[6] You do something first to create the context or background for what you do second and there is meaning to such sequences. If, for example, each business unit of Multichem *first* prepares a strategy *and then* brings it to HQ for approval and funding, then a *pluralizing* of local initiatives has been combined with a later deciding by HQ as to whether the project should go forward or not. Two researchers, Michael Goold and Andrew Campbell, have called this process *strategic control*.[7] There are plural strategies, but central controls.

If a supervisor has related closely to a subordinate for six months to a year *prior to* evaluating him or her, then evaluating can take place within the context of relating. If no such relationship has been established over time, then any authentic evaluating of performance is unlikely to occur. Indeed, elapsed time can be a good measure of how seriously values are taken in an organization. If a supervisor has spent ten minutes in a year relating to a subordinate and now expects to evaluate him or her in another ten minutes, then the relationship is unlikely to survive the evaluation.

If close cooperating has taken place for several months within a new product group, then we should see fierce competing in the market-place, achieved through that earlier cooperating. Or we may set several problem-solving groups competing with each other so that later all can start cooperating around the best solution which emerged. The fact that during their college days and their early employment with Multichem, managers were committing themselves to professional disciplines does not mean that they cannot now develop in identifying with the customers' viewpoints. All such 'contrary' goals can become *sequential processes*.

The ancient Greeks had two gods representing time: Chronos and Kairos.[8] Chronos was 'the march of time' – to use a recent metaphor – time seen in successive increments as on the teeth of a clock wheel. Kairos was the god of opportunity, time used in strategic ways, as in 'seize the time!' It is time to tell a subordinate that his/her performance is lacklustre when the relationship is strong enough. It is time to start cooperating when several alternative proposals are on the table and the best needs to be implemented. It is time to commend the best strategies from a host of plural policies after these have been presented by the business units concerned. Timing is crucial to the reconciliation of values.

Waving/Cycling Dilemmas

To say that the two sides of a dilemma can be emphasized in sequences suggests that they constitute a *wave-form* moving between the axes of a dilemma. If, for example, we *first* allow environmental inputs to pluralize and *then* decide at HQ which of these inputs to incorporate into our global strategy, we have a *wave-form or cycle* encompassing both pluralism and decision. Henry Mintzberg has called this *emergent strategy*.[9] The plural business units initiate many experiments, some surprisingly successful, and top management decides to designate which of these are 'flowers' and which 'weeds', which are local aberrations or adaptations unique to a particular culture and which hold lessons from which the whole of Multichem would be wise to learn.

Now a wave-form is really part of a cycle operating over time. Suppose that all the plurality of initiatives were carefully evaluated over a six-month period. Suppose that over a second six months a strategy were prepared incorporating the best of these initiatives, and this global strategy was returned to the business units for their edification and criticism. We would then have established an *annual cycle in which the headquarters learned from and in turn educated* their own plurality of business units. Such a cycle is illustrated in Dilemma 6.5. The *Strategic Thinker* (cartoon 3) both learns and decides, is changed by what he/she discovers in the environment and changes that environment.

Dilemma   6.5

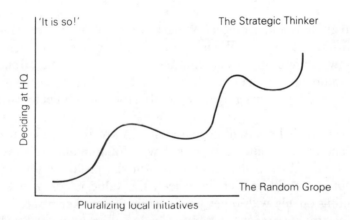

The same general rule can be applied to Dilemma 6.6. How well a group has cooperated internally can be discovered by how well it now competes externally which, in turn, is the feedback for more internal cooperating. How well the employees of a company have competed with each other (which directs the most competent to the key roles and shifts employees towards those tasks they can best perform) can be discovered by the quality of their cooperating with customers. Cooperating feeds back on competing which feeds back on cooperating. During the early stages of a meeting it may help to get many competing ideas on the table, yet in the later stages it helps if those ideas can cooperate in achieving a solution. Yet in time that solution must again be subjected to competing approaches. The cycle never ends but spirals in the direction of collaborative competing.

In reality, competing and cooperating are two ways of knowing,

Dilemma   6.6

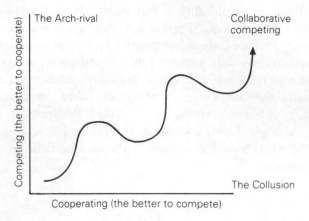

akin to analysis and synthesis. We ask 'which of these ideas show the most promise and why?' We must then ask 'if we combine these ideas into new configurations and mutualities would they be stronger in some combinations than in others?' This question, in turn, can only be answered by allowing the new combinations to compete with each other.

It's especially important in a company like Multichem to introduce both 'cooperating' and 'competing' ways of thinking into everyday calculations: 'What is the value of a particular product?' for example. Most of us would answer 'its price', the value it commands when competing openly with other products in the market-place. But this overlooks the *integral* or 'cooperative' value of inventing or developing a particular product. It may contribute a vital competitive edge to fifty *additional* products, as would a better solvent to a line of paint products. Most economists will remind you with an indulgent smile that the solvent, too, has a price on the open market. If you cannot make it cheaper than others, buy it.

But this misses the whole strategic calculus that it can pay you to control the development of a particular product in house if that product has multiple uses to other products, *even if* that ingredient itself has a price that fails to recoup costs. This is so because the competitors of Multichem, especially the Japanese and other Asians, have a grasp of integral value, which has the effect of *depressing the unit value of many strategic products*. It follows that, if you back out of every product that does not pay for itself, you will leave in the hands of the Japanese the chemical equivalents of the microchip, a low margin or no margin product that gives a 'brain' to thousands of other products who then succeed with this cooperation.

Dilemma 6.7 can, similarly, be encompassed by a cycle of supervisors *relating* to their subordinates and then *evaluating* them, so that pay commensurate with performance is achieved over time. But this may not be enough. Let us recall from our study of Hanover Insurance in chapter 4 that the standards used for judging 'high performance' are not immune from criticism or guaranteed against obsolescence. What constitutes 'excellence' in rapidly changing circumstances is continually open to question. Accordingly the learning organization must not only evaluate the employee against standards but evaluate the standards against the aspirations of employees. This was considered so important that we made the *Double-loop Learners*[10] into another item in our bestiary (cartoon 18).

Dilemma 6.7

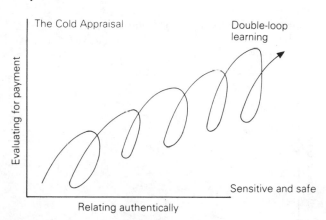

Dilemma 6.8 uses a similar wave-form or cycle to spiral upwards between the axes of committing to a profession or discipline and identifying with the customers' viewpoints. Once again these are two interdependent aspects of learning to create value. You need a disciplined grasp of what constitutes a safe, stable and high quality chemical product, and you need to be able to enter the inner world of the customers and grasp that these 'impresarios' organize a *scenario of satisfactions* around their own purposes.[11] Chemistry may, *or may not*, be the theme that organizes this scenario. The theme may be 'waste management', 'a reasonable quality of life in old age' or 'pest control'. In this event, biology, medical diagnostics or entomology may be

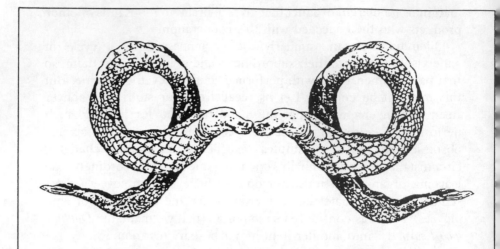

18   The Double-loop Learners engage in an amazing mirror-image dance that puts them in unusually close communication. They adapt themselves to their habitat and their habitat to themselves.

Dilemma   6.8

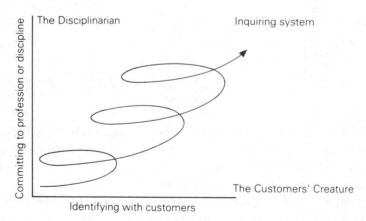

more important to the customers than chemistry and, in order to serve them well, we must be in all those fields and not just one.

Here we encounter *two* logics which we shall examine more closely in chapter 7, an inner-directed logic of the 'one best way', which starts from an exact science, and an other-directed logic which begins with what the customer wants and upon which one must 'home in' as upon a beacon, by a process of error correction. The two mentalities are far apart, yet a learning cycle joins the two, as when developing technology is pulled towards those who need it most. What we are really doing is moving from the *Bloated Bureaucracy* (cartoon 19), long considered a necessary evil, to the design of an *Inquiring System* (cartoon 20), which not only has its own scientific disciplines but inquires into how these might best be matched to the demands of customers.

Synergizing Dilemmas

Our last step in the process of reconciling dilemmas is really a criterion for judging how well this job of reconciling has been done. The test is synergy – from the Greek *syn-ergo* or 'work together'.[12] Has the total system been so designed that deciding works with pluralizing, competing with cooperating, evaluating with relating, and committing oneself to a discipline with identifying with customers?

Synergy may be mathematically demonstrable as when customer satisfaction rises along with the number of professional credentials achieved. Social surveys can show that both the managers of business units and those at HQ feel they have 'more influence on strategy'. You could ask employees being evaluated by supervisors: 'Do you feel that even criticisms contribute to an improvement in relationships with your supervisor?' 'Do you feel that you have some control over the criteria used to evaluate you?' 'Yes' answers to both of these suggest synergy. 'No' suggests its lack.

It is important to grasp that synergy is often *more* than a mere combination of the processes represented by the two axes. It can represent the creation of something new. 'Double-loop learning', for example, is more than just evaluating and relating, more than just evaluating performance by standards and then evaluating standards by feedback from performers. It is also a dialogue between different sources of knowledge and, of course, a spiral that accumulates knowledge of many kinds.

Similarly, the Strategic Thinker does more than take inputs from the plural environment and work these into a global strategy. There are scores of economies, trade-offs, technology transfers and useful exchanges in this process. Much duplication can be avoided and

19   The Bloated Bureaucracy swims in a pool of talent which it depletes.

20   The Inquiring System. Is this an important alternative to the Bloated Bureaucracy?

considerable experience codified into expert systems. With proper exchange of information every company embarking on a similar policy should benefit from the condensation of earlier experience. HQ is really a central nervous system, the brain of the firm.[13]

Collaborative competing is also much more than either process alone, or even the two 'added together' were this possible. Collaborative competing learns which of several options works better, combines the better elements of these better competitors in novel cooperative forms and then runs these forms against each other competitively once more. *The whole system has an intelligence which its parts lack.*

But perhaps the best definition of synergy is the 'virtuous circles' we encountered in chapters 2, 3, 4 and 5. We can make a strategic policy circle out of Dilemmas 6.5, 6.6 and 6.8, which constitutes a synergy of synergies, a 'brain' with greater learning capacity. The virtuous circle could read as in figure 6.3. Dilemma 6.7 has been omitted only because longer loops become more cumbersome and less useful. It is not possible to write a grammatical policy statement using only present participles, and so this rule has been modified. The notion that the sentence 'starts' at 12 o'clock is artificial. A learning loop can start with any of its elements. Only a grammatical sentence has to start somewhere.

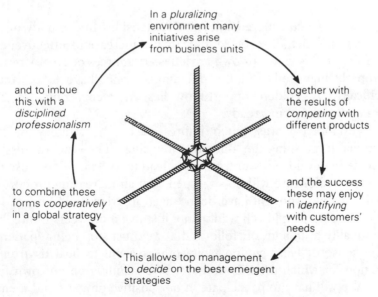

In a *pluralizing* environment many initiatives arise from business units

together with the results of *competing* with different products

and the success these may enjoy in *identifying* with customers' needs

This allows top management to *decide* on the best emergent strategies

to combine these forms *cooperatively* in a global strategy

and to imbue this with a *disciplined professionalism*

Figure 6.3

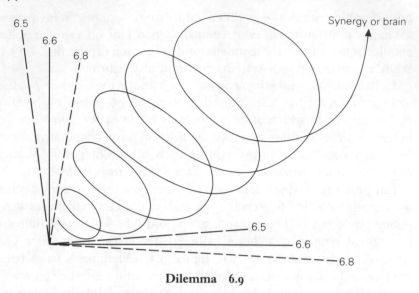

Dilemma 6.9

Dilemma 6.9 shows the virtuous synergistic circle encompassing Dilemmas 6.5, 6.6 and 6.8 in a developing helix.

Environmental Dilemmas as Market Opportunities

So far we have considered dilemmas as tensions in the body of the organization which, if resolved, quickly will increase its effectiveness. According to this view our own anxieties are sources of great strength if properly managed. But the dilemmas do not have to be 'ours' specifically. A golden opportunity lies in recognizing 'societal dilemmas' and making ready.

For example, I was much impressed by the strategy of ICI (Australia) in grasping the 'dilemma of ageing'. The very 'success' of medicine in developed countries could lead to its 'failure' because the system of health care will be swamped with an increasing proportion of older people who will have been 'saved to grow frail'.

What ageing people will want is not just five more years of life, but some quality to this life. It follows that we must stop being 'patients' in the sense of lying supine while others claim to heal us from a condition for which there is no cure, save standing on our own feet again. We will have to participate in our positive physical and mental health and that means monitoring our own health in our own homes and avoiding 'germ city', otherwise known as hospital. What people will need is a seemless web of good eating, good exercise, good diagnosis, good monitoring and good information, whether or not these derive from chemistry. If ICI can accomplish this, it deserves its success.

Avoiding the Monstrous Dilemmas

I was a shade disappointed that my Multichem informants shied away from the really 'monstrous' dilemmas. Perhaps they did not care to discuss these before me. For example, our environment is becoming 'addicted' in the sense of a cumulative pesticide habit. When the genes of the pests mutate to develop immunities and when insect predators are poisoned, it takes *more* and newer poisons to save the same amount of crops.[14]

This is no one's fault and nothing is achieved by name-calling. The farmers may be desperate for the pesticide and the other 'horn' of this dilemma is often starvation itself. But the dilemma is lethal unless solved soon. The whole system of capitalism is based on the principle that satisfying customers at a profit will benefit everyone concerned. But this does not hold true where environmental damage is involved.

The flip side is that solving such dilemmas is as beneficent and as praiseworthy as the original predicament was monstrous. We need to create wealth more effectively but, more than that, we need leaders who can stare into the face of the absurd and find in it meanings that could save us all.

Notes

1 Charles M. Hampden-Turner, 'Approaching Dilemmas', *Shell Guides to Planning*, No. 3, 1985. The paper is still confidential.
2 These and all subsequent cartoons have been borrowed from *A Political Bestiary*, by Eugene N. McCarthy and James K. Kilpatrick, illustrated by Jeff MacNelly (New York: McGraw-Hill, 1978). Some but not all the captions have been changed in order to convert US politics to corporate politics.
3 This situation has been extensively discussed by Chris Argyris and Donald Schon; see especially 'Rigor or Relevance? Normal Science and Action Science Compared', Harvard University and MIT, September 1988 (mimeo).

4 This story told to the author independently by Tim Gallwey, author of *The Inner Game of Tennis*. New York: Doubleday, 1974.

5 Henry Mintzberg, 'Opening up the Definition of Strategy', in J. M. Quinn, H. Mintzberg and R. M. James (eds), *The Strategy Process*. Englewood Cliffs, N.J.: Prentice-Hall, 1987.

6 I am much indebted to Elliot Jaques, *The Form of Time*. New York: Crane Russak, 1982.

7 Michael Goold and Andrew Campbell, *Strategies and Styles*. Oxford: Basil Blackwell, 1987.

8 Jaques, *The Form of Time*.

9 Henry Mintzberg, 'Crafting Strategy', *Harvard Business Review*, March/April 1987, pp. 66–75.

10 Chris Argyris and Donald A. Schon, *Organizational Learning: A Theory of Action Perspective*. Reading, Mass.: Addison Wesley, 1978.

11 Charles M. Hampden-Turner, *Lifestyle Marketing*. Menlo Park, Calif.: SRI International, Leading Edge Publications, 1986.

12 The concept is ably described in Abraham Maslow, *Motivation and Personality*. New York: Harper and Row, 1954. See also Peter A. Corning and Susan Corning, *Winning with Synergy*. New York: Harper and Row, 1986.

13 See Stafford Beer, *The Brain of the Firm*. New York: Wiley, 1981.

14 Norman Myers (ed.), *GAIA: An Atlas of Planet Management*. New York: Anchor Press, Doubleday, 1984.

7

Efficiency and Effectiveness:
Two Logics of Learning

Several years ago Peter Drucker contrasted efficiency with effectiveness.[1] This author discovered the difference when invited by the Canadian National Oil Company, located in Western Ontario, to examine growing levels of tension between the Manufacturing Function (MF) in charge of the building, design, engineering, maintenance and safety of oil refineries (a technology of daunting complexity) and the local refineries themselves organized into regions of North America and the world for marketing purposes.

Until quite recently oil prices had been high, and Canadian Oil's world-wide strategy of 'upgrading the oil barrel' to sell more refined products of higher value-added quality had paid off handsomely. The company's 'technology-push' style of operating had elevated the MF to a point where it personified many of the company's principal virtues. It was staffed very largely by Canadian engineers, many educated at the University of Waterloo, arguably Canada's finest school for process and chemical engineering. Its manufacturers are widely respected both as the 'Presbyterian conscience' of the oil industry and as an example of its most expert and sophisticated practices.

Extensive interviews conducted with senior managers in Manufacturing and with those in charge of refineries and coordinating refineries in the regions revealed a clear bifurcation in the thinking of the two major groupings. Both were articulate, both confident, and both were committed to those values central to their tasks. Both were flawlessly logical, proceeding from premise via tested means to their conclusion without detectable error. One left the presence of either group perplexed as to how such eminently reasonable and obviously decent people could be giving each other such a hard time. To listen to either side was to be carried along by the force of their argument. How right, how cogent! Would there were more people of such calibre.

And yet, they were utterly at odds. The numbers of upwardly directed complaints from both sides about the unresponsiveness of the other were now so numerous that something had to be done to discover how, with the best will in the world, two groups could talk so completely past each other. Manufacturing's nickname was significant: they were called the 'Teccies'. Looking at the transcripts of the interviews it was not difficult to detect two compelling, yet opposing, points of view.

The procedure now followed was the one described in chapter 3. The interviews were combed for the expression of dilemmas and conflicts, after which the procedures described in chapter 6 were used to reconcile the dilemmas which had emerged. Humour was not needed because the interviews had been frank and revelatory. This was a conflict among friends and both sides were eager to reconcile it, as was senior management who had been hearing the complaints. Another advantage was that both sides saw the other's logic and even granted it some legitimacy. Their problem was to reconcile it with their own logic, which seemed more trenchant and persuasive.

In the account which follows, the dilemma is expressed first and is then bifurcated into two 'horns'. Statements in support of Manufacturing's traditional function are made at the head of the left column. Statements made by regional companies (Regcos) questioning this function are in the right column. Both these columns are pro the horn above them. The bottom of each column contains statements rebutting the horn above.

Dilemma 7.1

Given CANO's tradition of technology-based long-term innovation and continuity and its history of world leadership in petroleum engineering, is it reasonable to ask this successful organization to adopt a market-based, shorter-term flexible and commercial orientation?

TECHNOLOGY-BASED LONG-TERM INNOVATION AND CONTINUITY	VS	MARKET-BASED, SHORTER-TERM, FLEXIBLE AND COMMERCIAL INNOVATION
Better tech. means better business		Teccies should study our most successfully competing refineries
We have the brains, the concepts		
We must push beyond the routine		More emphasis on licensing would test our market sense
Good people are attracted and held by an in-depth approach		
We are 'rigid yet reliable'		Teccies should concern themselves with Regcos' commercial strategies
		Only we persist in shale processes. Are others all wrong?
Where are we going to learn about world technological thrusts?		*Commercialized research people won't even do good research*
Teccies have two ears and one mouth . . . there's a moral there		*It takes many years and a long-term orientation to develop something really good*
How do Teccies know that their services to us are genuinely what we need?		*To justify technological development of a short-term commercial type is just not possible. It's all too complex and interrelated*
How much can you learn from a captive?		

Discussion

There are substantial reasons for CANO to maintain its pursuit of technological excellence. An earlier decision to 'upgrade the oil barrel' by moving into more refined products with higher margins paid off handsomely when oil prices rose in the 1970s. With under-capacity in the industry, CANO's reserves of technological sophistication and its habit of pushing ahead of market demand was also vindicated.

Although the Manufacturing Function is not concerned with the exploration for oil and gas and pumping it from the wellhead, the reputation of Drilling and Production (D and P) within CANO greatly enhances the value of technology push in general. When there is the prospect of vast oil reserves beneath a difficult terrain, the owners' first concern is not how cheaply the drilling can be done but whether the oil can be found and recovered at all. Preference is likely to be given to the world's most sophisticated drillers, since the costs of recovery are small compared with the bonanza of finding the oil in the first place and getting most of it out of the ground by the latest techniques of enhanced recovery. CANO engineers therefore value technological excellence very highly and believe in pushing their discipline beyond its present boundaries to new frontiers.

In thus raising up their eyes to the hills, the short-term needs to get competitively priced products to the right customers at the right time tended to get less relative attention, and the refineries who felt the full heat of market forces were asking for more help. Even if a product was the latest thing, and a new refining process was 'state of the art', the customers had to be found to cover these costs and it was getting very difficult. Not everything which MF wanted to make was saleable in the present state of chronic over-capacity, which was very different from just a few years ago. CANO must respond more quickly to market demands which were, after all, decentralized the world over, which brings us to the next dilemma.

Dilemma 7.2

Given the vital role played by Manufacturing's centralized intelligence and its capacity to universalize the principles it had developed and discovered to refineries in every part of the world, could it also give greater influence to the decentralized operations of all refineries which are the keys to success in particular instances?

CENTRALIZED INTELLIGENCE IS universalized	VS	DECENTRALIZED AND PARTICULAR OPERATIONS ARE THE KEY
We are an invaluable centre of excellence and the leading edge of technology		CANO's local coloration is the key to her success
The one HQ with access to many refineries is a potentially brilliant structure for learning and operating successfully		We need to *do things better* in concrete instances
		Our needs are quite special
		We need to see an identifiable Teccie team at work on our project
		Stiffen the backs of MF people working for Regcos
We often feel patronized		*Many off-beat requests plunge us into chaos*
The unanticipated request does not get very good service and is most likely to suffer cost overruns		*It doesn't help when contractors fail to check with us, or don't keep project heads advised*
If you're in Plastics a wisdom based on oil or gas is not invariably relevant		

Discussion

The second dilemma pits the advantages of centralization techniques that can be developed by scientists and then universalized against a stress on the unique, local, decentralized and particular operations performed by Regcos taking on the coloration of their particular country.

A 'scientific centre' conducting an ongoing multiplicity of experiments world-wide is a powerful model of rapid learning, for deductive as well as inductive thinking and for the economy and parsimony of performing one set of calculations which can apply to innumerable instances all over the world, *e pluribus unum* as Americans say.

But the ideal has its critics too. Many particular instances are not examples of a universal rule but are unique problems requiring specific and not general answers. Chemicals, especially, felt that MF's generalities were often irrelevant, and that oil-based axioms were not applicable to their situations. Requests for specialized services not only resulted in a poorer level of services but in serious cost overruns. It was sometimes possible to identify a distinctive team at MF willing to work on a specific project, see it through to the end and take responsibility for its value to the Regcos which had requested it, but only for mega-projects.

Those at the refinery end were also critical of the notion that all virtue somehow resided with MF's 'conscience' and that this constituted the organization's 'integrity', a concern that introduces the next dilemma.

Dilemma 7.3

Given that much of the system's knowledge-based integrity and its collective conscience was in Manufacturing, was there not another ethic, every bit as important, which was the responsibility of the refineries to discharge, namely responsibility to customers and the user?

KNOWLEDGE-BASED INTEGRITY AND CONSCIENCE	VS	CUSTOMER ORIENTED, RESPONSIBLE TO USER
Canadians are solid engineers Presbyterian about excellence		We need to inject our own specifications. It's hard and expensive

KNOWLEDGE-BASED INTEGRITY AND CONSCIENCE	VS CUSTOMER ORIENTED, RESPONSIBLE TO USER
Our access to company technology is the cement of our business	When dealing with customers, there is more uncertainty and equality and less hierarchy than in MF
The MF engineer is more sophisticated than the D and P counterpart	Joint venture partners are refusing to pay Teccies bills
Large-scale investing is our competitive edge	Business context needed
We often feel that MF does not respect us	*Complaining Regcos can shop around if they want to, but they won't find similar value*
MF is expensive, perfectionist and too formal	*We have to avoid being turned into a cafeteria*
Something that is state of the art and represents excellence in engineering may be simply too costly and unprofitable to operate	

Discussion

The third major dilemma revolved around this issue of whether the company's conscience, integrity and world-class standards could legitimately be said to reside at least partly, if not wholly, within Manufacturing. The solidity of Canadian process engineering, the Scots' Presbyterianism of its search for excellence, the sophistication of its expertise, and the sheer extent of investments, which consisted of projects Manufacturing performed and/or promised could be done, all these capacities constituted a weighty moral commitment for the company as a whole. With the possible exception of D and P, it was hard to find any function on whose judgement so much of the company's money and reputation was pledged.

This attempt to assume the moral high ground attracted more derogatory comments than any other single claim. MF was 'arrogant', 'hierarchical and expensive'. It was every bit as 'moral' to serve customers at a competitive rate as to aspire to quality engineering, and the Regcos were MF's customers who could only give good value if they received it.

The great concern in MF was that it would be expected to run like a cafeteria, serving side dishes to all comers and fragmented by multiple requests. But this was seen by the refineries as typical of

MF's concern with process and its relative disinterest in results, which constitutes our next dilemma.

Dilemma 7.4

Given Manufacturing's legitimate concern with the processes and the procedures by which refineries were best operated, could it also concern itself with the comparative results in terms of costs, prices, margins and sales?

PROCESS AND PROCEDURE ORIENTATION	vs	COMPARATIVE RESULTS ORIENTATION
MF's role is to think constantly in terms of process tech.		Decision-making must be joined to accountability
MF's requirement that others fit into its perspectives is not unreasonable		MF needs to operate like a Regco with a bottom line
On the feasibility of major projects MF is *the* authority		How can Teccies test the external consequences of their activities?

Simply 'following the book' does not help us to develop as people

Advice tends to be anonymous but we who implement it in circumstances not always envisaged by MF put ourselves on the line

Risks should be shared, uncertainties acknowledged

The multiple signatures on telex syndrome

Cheap contractors don't have our overheads and expertise

We shouldn't be asked to do minor jobs. Only in certain areas are we the best

Discussion

The fourth dilemma concerned the procedural structure of MF. It 'laid down the law' in the sense of specifying procedures which others had to follow. This gave it a 'natural right' to set the agenda and have its own logic followed by everyone else. Indeed, the feasibility of major projects depended on this logic, its reliability and the extent to which it was followed by Regcos.

Yet critics pointed out that simply following other peoples' procedures stultifies the mind. Moreover, the specification books avoided all risks attendant upon abstract rules encountering concrete situations. No matter what problems you had encountered at the refinery end, you were advised in a telex with multiple signatures to follow the procedures the signatories had laid down before you raised that problem. The advice was elegant, authorless and passed the buck to the refinery for any problem not foreseen from afar.

MF did not seem to grasp that what ultimately mattered were better *results* compared with those of competitors. Their decisions were at least partly buffered from accountability, since they could 'sell' their processes to Regcos regardless of whether the Regcos could sell the resulting products to customers. The danger was that MF could believe it was 'succeeding' even after the Regcos had started to fail through an excess of gold plating and over-engineered plants. This tendency was intensified by MF's habit of seeing everything in terms of machinery *analysable* into discrete parts, which constituted our fifth dilemma.

Dilemma 7.5

Given that MF was full of specialists with highly differentiated and analytical points of view which dissolved every problem into pieces, was it not equally important to integrate these pieces and employ generalists with holistic orientations able to see the big picture and markets in their entirety?

SPECIALISTS WITH HIGHLY DIFFERENTIATED ANALYTICAL ORIENTATIONS	VS	GENERALISTS WITH HIGHLY INTEGRATIVE HOLISTIC ORIENTATIONS
We must not lose key capacities as Plastics have		MF needs vision
If skills are not used they die		Can Teccies *stay* with a project from start to finish?
Knowledge never stops being differentiated		Project managers need to know more of what's going on, and must prevail over junior specialists
Appraisals fight shy of business issues and tend to be relentlessly technical		*Ex-specialists do not want to return. You may lose the only people you can really rely on*
No one seems to have settled on a context or a direction for the company as a whole		*Specialized expertise is our sheet-anchor, our reality principle. Don't let it go*
Coherence falls between the stools of specialists		
Who answers for MF as a whole?		

Discussion

The fifth dilemma has to do with the disputed strength of specialists' analytical culture within MF. Its supporters argue that a large number of key capacities are indispensable, that unused skills will die and so specialists must keep busy, and that an ever-differentiating process characterizes the development of new knowledge. Because one division of labour depends upon another, you cannot simply abandon special skills which are currently in low demand. A skill pool consists of a total array of specialists, and to do things narrowly is a crucial part of doing them reliably and well. If you move specialists to broader responsibilities, they rarely wish to return.

The critics do not dispute the need for specialization as much as they bewail the lack of concern for wider issues. The appraisals carried out at refineries rarely touch on broader business issues. There is no indication of where the larger company is going and the instant specialists prove to be reluctant generalists. MF does not seem to have a vision that could give it coherence. Even MF interviewees complained that project managers with seniority over specialists in their teams were obliged to defer to juniors 'armed' as it were by their specializations. It was part of the culture. You lost influence if you tried to think holistically. The main emphasis was on avoiding mistakes, or even approximations. Herein lay the last dilemma.

Dilemma 7.6

Given that building, operating and maintaining a refinery requires of MF a 'mistake-free' orientation to perfect prediction and control, is it also possible to learn quickly by making rough approximations and then correcting the resulting errors?

RATIONAL 'MISTAKE-FREE' ORIENTATION TO PERFECT PREDICTION AND CONTROL	VS	QUICK LEARNING, ERROR-CORRECTING ORIENTATION TO UNCERTAINTY AND APPROXIMATION
Catcracker went into smooth operation the very first time		We need to scan the environment
'No mistakes' expertise is the key		Task forces are needed to gather external intelligence
		We must alter the culture for faster adaptation

RATIONAL 'MISTAKE-FREE' ORIENTATION TO PERFECT PREDICTION AND CONTROL	VS	QUICK LEARNING, ERROR-CORRECTING ORIENTATION TO UNCERTAINTY AND APPROXIMATION
We need only be approximately right if we are quicker than our competitors		*The traditional Teccie culture is not going to be changed. They'll return to their old ways at the first opportunity*
Refineries are 'foolproof'. And the 'fools' are not too pleased		
We could go broke and still be right on every detail and every signature		

Discussion

The sixth dilemma is a conflict of 'rationalities' between two contrasting ways of learning. Manufacturing's concept of rationality is of the traditional kind described by Hobbes, i.e. the capacity to 'reckon the consequences' by predicting and controlling the precise operations of its technologies. Of this, there were several impressive examples. Complicated plant went into smooth operations the very first time. MF specializes in techniques so dependent upon each other that expertise must be 'mistake free' if the final assembly is to work. MF's culture is shaped by this requirement.

Yet critics asked for 85 per cent rather than 100 per cent solutions. There are, after all, competent engineers with the Regcos, yet MF works towards a state where no one at the refinery level needs to think any more, because everything has been laid down in advance.

There are other ways of thinking which, while they don't amount to formal rationality, are not irrational either, but vital to certain situations. The company needs to learn quickly from its environment and the best way to do this is to act, however haphazardly, and then swiftly correct the error. The motto at Cadbury-Schweppes was 'ready–fire–aim'. Not *until* one has fired can the aim be corrected. The initial thrust is uncertain, approximate and heuristic, for the purpose is rapid adaptation to a changing environment. Supporters of this type of thinking wanted groups to monitor the environment and task forces to test reality and gather feedback. There was danger in MF being so absorbed within itself that crucial changes in the environment would evoke a tardy response.

A Dilemma of Dilemmas

It is possible to summarize dilemmas or to collapse them into a common theme. Do our six dilemmas share such a theme? I believe so.

1 Technology-based long-term innovation
2 The universalization of centralized intelligence
3 A knowledge-based integrity and conscience ... are all *inner-directed* motives, which derive from within MF.
4 An orientation to process and procedure
5 A specialized, differentiated and analytical orientation
6 A rational atttempt to predict and control

1 Market-based, short-term, flexible innovation
2 Decentralized and particular operations
3 Customer-oriented response to users ... are all *outer-directed* motives, which derive from influences bearing on MF.
4 An orientation to comparative results
5 Integrative and holistic orientations
6 Quick learning, error-correcting orientation

Hence the Dilemma of Dilemmas is as follows.

Should MF be steered by or **Should MF respond to**
inner-directed *concerns for* **outer-directed, market-**
technology-based and **pulled, decentralized and**
universalized codes of good **customer-oriented**
practice, achieved by a **commercial results, using a**
process-oriented **holistic approach to**
predictable rationality? **accelerated learning?**

Since we are not usng the humour described in the last chapter to loosen up the organization, there remain only six steps to resolving the dilemma. These are

1 Mapping
2 Processing
3 Framing/contextualizing
4 Sequencing
5 Waving/Cycling
6 Synergizing

Step 1   Mapping

To save space and time let us map the Dilemma of Dilemmas as in figure 7.1. Let value A represent MF's inner-directedness. Let value B represent MF's outer-directedness. In this event five conditions are possible.

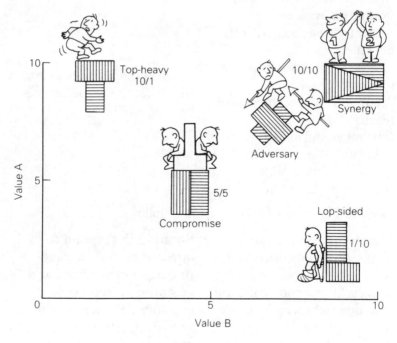

Figure 7.1

1   MF could be top-heavy with a far greater inner-directed, innovative thrust than its willingness or capacity to learn from market forces (10/1 on the diagram).
2   MF could be lop-sided towards the outer-directed demands of the market and so lose its own innovative thrust (1/10 on the diagram).
3   Persistent demands by Regcos and other functions could create an adversary relationship between MF and its clients, with the dangers of *oscillation* between 10/1 and 1/10 and persistent tensions.
4   To avoid these strains a lacklustre compromise could emerge (5/5 on the diagram).
5   Yet to the extent that the dilemmas are reconciled *both* a higher degree of inner-directed thrust and a ready capacity to respond to the environment can be achieved through synergy (10/10 on the diagram).

We may conclude from what we have already heard that something approaching an *adversary* situation existed between MF and the refineries, although this was conducted in a civilized and respectful dispute among friends.

Having located MF and the Regcos between the axes or 'horns', we are now in a position to try reconciliatory procedures.

Step 2   Processing

Processing turns nouns, like universalism, into present participles, i.e. universalizing, which end in 'ing'. This converts solid-sounding 'things' into liquid-like processes. It is no coincidence that the word 'solution' means both reconciling and a liquid.

When we turn our six dilemmas into present participles, their 'hard edges' and mutual oppositions have already started to melt, so:

1   Technically innovating   vs   Flexibly marketing
2   Universalizing principles   vs   Particularizing operations
3   Integrating knowledge   vs   Responding to users
4   Creating processes   vs   Comparing results
5   Differentiating specialists   vs   Integrating wholes
6   Predicting and controlling   vs   Correcting and learning quickly
    rationally

Step 3   Framing/Contextualizing

This simplest context is an abstraction ladder. You weave processes together by 'dovetailing' them at different levels of abstraction (figure 7.2). The higher level of abstraction represents the purpose for which principles are universalized or processes are created. Neither universalizing nor creating processes/procedures are ends in themselves, but are done for the purpose higher on the ladder. We could argue equally well that 'we particularize the better to universalize such attributes as are in common' and 'we compare results so as to discover which processes are more effective'.

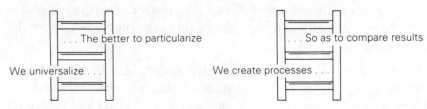

Figure 7.2

An alternative way of contextualizing 'opposed' values is by putting them in figure/ground relationships or on a 'picture within a frame'. This is done in figure 7.3. Hence the process of specialist differentiation takes place within the frame of integrating the whole of the resulting skills.

The processes of predicting and controlling rationally are contained

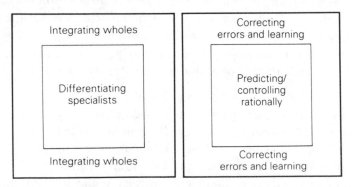

Figure 7.3   Every 'picture' must be contained and constrained by its frame.

within and constrained by a process of testing the market environment, rapidly correcting for errors and learning.

Note that text–context, picture–frame, and figure–ground are all *reversible* so that the differentiated specialities also frame the processes of integration. The integration must be of the fine details and must not lose them in the process of combination. Correcting errors and homing in on market needs must be framed by rationally conceived techniques that are as error-free as possible to satisfy these needs.

Step 4   Sequencing

One of the chief reasons we feel trapped within dilemmas is because we ignore the variable of *time*. Two sides or 'horns' of a dilemma can be processed *sequentially*, although one sequence may in all or some circumstances be better than another. For example, innovating technically can be followed by marketing flexibly or vice versa. Universalizing scientific and technical discoveries can be followed by discovering how useful they are in which particular instances. Predicting and controlling the rational operations of refineries can be followed by learning which products are most in demand and correcting for customer trends.

Such sequences can be reversed if it is believed that values in the right-hand column are being subordinated. It is best to *start* a sequence with whichever of two values is neglected in the present arrangement. Since in this case the inner-directed, rational, left-hand column, or vertical axis, was dominant over the outer-directed, error-correcting right-hand column, or horizontal axis, it may help to start with the latter. In that case the refineries and those closest to customers may wish to

- explain that their flexible marketing strategies can use only some of the current technical innovations;
- show which particular instances are covered by MF's universal rules and which are not;
- show how responding to users needs some but not all of MF's integrity and other resources beside;
- show how comparing the results of marketing strategies makes some processes more valuable than others;

- explain that the whole policies and entire scenarios are more than the specialist functions that go into them;
- show that correcting quickly for changes in market demand makes some of MF's predicting and controlling more relevant and some less relevant.

By treating the refineries as the initiators for once, it becomes possible for MF to respond in some measure to their agendas.

Step 5   Waving/Cycling

But, of course, a sequence charted between two axes becomes a wave-form, and these wave-forms have strategic significance by which one value is consummated first in order to better consummate the second value, to create an organization which is most 'values intense'.

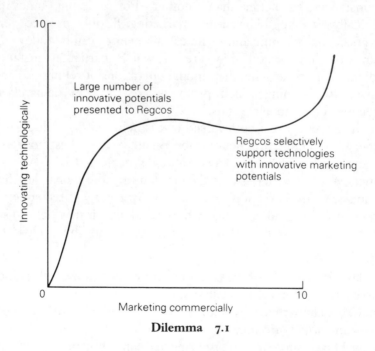

Dilemma   7.1

Consider Dilemma 7.1 in which on the vertical axis MF innovates technologically and on the horizontal axis the refineries market commercially. Since major innovations designed to keep CANO ahead of competitors emanate from MF, I have drawn the wave in such a way that MF *first* presents the innovative potentials on improving technology to the refineries. The refineries within the Regcos then choose which of these improvements are of the greatest interest to them in marketing competitively, and which merely threaten to increase costs. The initiative thus moves *from MF to* the Regcos and back *over time*.

Of course, this alone may not solve all the issues. Suppose MF wants a new process installed, not because it will lower costs in the short term but because it is a vital first step to upgrading refinery operations generally. There are various ways of handling this: if the refineries still object to the costs of this improvement, then a special joint task force could be set up to monitor its longer-term pay-off. In the meantime its costs will be assigned to MF, as will the profits if MF's judgement is vindicated, or the improved technology could be installed only at consenting refineries with agreement to compare their performance with those withholding their consent. The question is not who is right *but how can we best learn together about effective strategy?* The parties should be free to disagree, but are never free from the *consequences* of that choice, which will be evaluated. If one party or the other is discovered to have sounder judgement, then their opinions will gain the weight they deserve. In the meantime, the technologies with positive effects on commercial strategy are obviously to be preferred. The wave-form is designed to give heightened influence to *both* areas of the dilemma.

Or consider the question of whether MF has access to the universal principles of refinery operation the world over, or whether each particular case is different enough to deserve special attention. It is possible to entertain these hypotheses by turns and let each correct the other in a sequential wave, as illustrated in Dilemma 7.2. Here we have begun by having the refineries and Regcos enumerate all particular cases in which they wanted help from MF, and no particular rule or principle covered that particular instance, so that assistance was either not forthcoming or slow. MF's response to these cases is to show either that rules *did* cover these, or to create new rules that now cover them, or to admit that this or that particular problem really is unique or unusual but that the cost of solving it, from afar, at a single refinery is uneconomical.

By turns, the refineries are presenting particular cases, while MF is trying to incorporate these, where justified, under an improved rule.

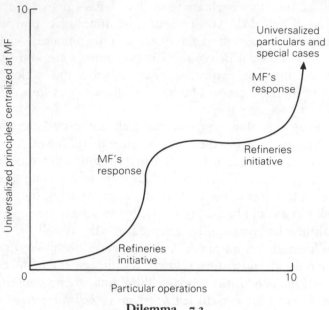

Dilemma 7.2

Where this is done effectively, *more particular operations will be covered by better formulated principles*, or universalized particulars and special cases (see Dilemma 7.2). But what about the residue of special cases?

One possibility would be to rewrite the rules for when local contractors could be employed. If the problem encountered was exceptional, MF would have less to learn by solving it than if that problem were applicable to many refineries. Jobs performed by external contractors could be examined once a year to make sure the MF was not missing out on any development for which a universal solution was needed. MF's costs might be kept in line by requiring it not to charge more than, say, 20 per cent above the bids of local contractors. Such a margin might be needed because MF has higher overheads and wage rates than many local contractors, but also a capacity to learn from its world-wide projects, which is worth sustaining.

In any event, agreement must be reached not only to universalize more particulars, but also to apply *ad hoc* solutions to particular problems not likely to be covered by more general rules.

Waves as Cycles

But, of course, a wave is part of a cycle with a particular amplitude and frequency. The knowledge-based integrity of MF must be allowed to modify what the customer is asking for, *and* customers, by way of marketing, must be allowed to modify what MF deems to be important. 'Responsiveness to the user' in CANO's far-flung empire is *no less* important and *no more* important than MF's integrity about what its technology can and should achieve. Each of these values-in-tension must be allowed to feed back upon the other to correct it in a cycle of eternal return, as shown in Dilemma 7.3; otherwise, uncorrected technological 'conscience' will become opinionated and stiff, and uncorrected responsiveness will become random reactions disintegrating any coherent policy.

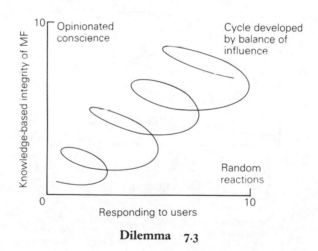

Dilemma 7.3

But there were forces militating against the helix in Dilemma 7.3. One practice which gave MF far too much power *vis-à-vis* the refineries, as the Regcos saw it, was the convention that MF was the 'substitute shareholder' with the role of inspecting and appraising refineries for their safety and conformity to best practice. This had the effect of making MF not simply the supplier of technology, procedures and consulting, but the judge and jury of those they supplied. In practice, 'company standards' were maintained by following MF's original instructions! Some redress in the balance of influence was badly needed, the Regcos argued, and why serving customers as well as possible took less 'integrity' or was of less concern to shareholders was a mystery.

This issue was important because unless changes were made MF could modify the refineries' attempts to serve customers, while the refineries *lacked* the influence to modify MF's insistence that customers should pay for all recent developments. A virtuous cycle could develop only if both parties could correct each other's potential excesses. For the cycle to balance, powers of influence and feedback must be approximately equal. This exercise can be repeated for Dilemmas 7.4, 7.5 and 7.6. In all cases virtuous cycles encompass both axes.

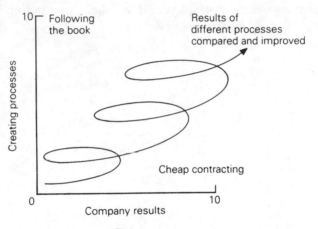

Dilemma 7.4

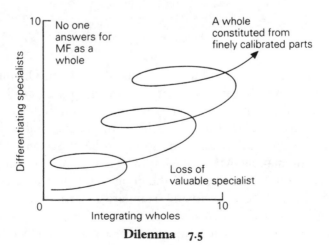

Dilemma 7.5

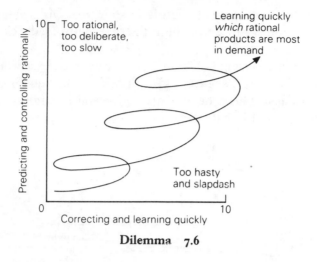

Dilemma 7.6

Step 6 Synergizing

We saw in chapter 6 that synergy, or working together optimally, could be represented by a virtuous cycle. The advantage of cycles is that they can include elements from two or more dilemmas. For example, the cycle in figure 7.4 takes the Dilemmas 7.2 and 7.4 and combines them. The reason for having much heavier arrows on the

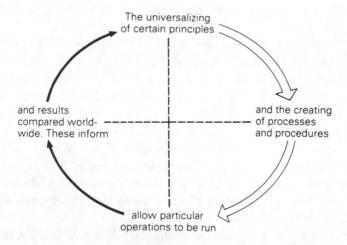

Figure 7.4

right of the cycle than on the left is to show that MF's values were tending to dominate those of the refineries whose feedback on MF was weaker.

The same relationship holds for Dilemmas 7.5 and 7.1 which have been placed in a circle (figure 7.5) with MF's values dominating the refineries values. These helices are only semi-synergistic because their values are not in balance.

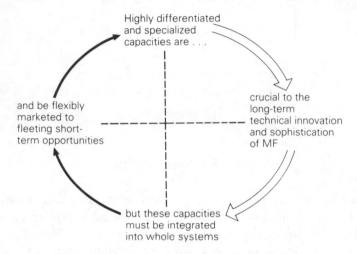

Figure 7.5

In order for MF and the refineries to have *mutually developing values*, their weights have to be rebalanced and fine-tuned. Such a virtuous cycle, consisting of Dilemmas 7.4, 7.5 and 7.6, is shown in figure 7.6.

In contrast with the two previous cycles, the cycle in figure 7.6 is balanced and fine-tuned, and if MF could build such a relationship with its refineries it would learn in *two ways*, from technical reason (or scientific calculation) *before* the fact, and from error correction (or reflection) *after* the fact. These 'opposed' ways of learning are represented by the right-hand side and left-hand side of the circle.

Arguably, the right- and left-hand sides of the human body have these biases too. Both types of rationality are perfectly legitimate, but were at loggerheads in this case, with 'right-hand reason' the stronger of the two. Figure 7.7 shows all these dilemmas encompassed by an ascending helix.

We are now in a position to reconsider Peter Drucker's original distinction between efficiency and effectiveness. An operation is said

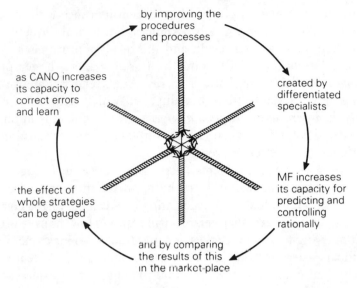

by improving the
procedures
and processes

created by
differentiated
specialists

as CANO increases
its capacity to
correct errors
and learn

MF increases
its capacity for
predicting and
controlling
rationally

the effect of
whole strategies
can be gauged

and by comparing
the results of this
in the market-place

Figure 7.6

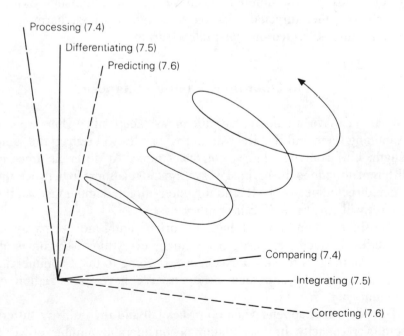

Processing (7.4)

Differentiating (7.5)

Predicting (7.6)

Comparing (7.4)

Integrating (7.5)

Correcting (7.6)

Figure 7.7 Dilemmas 7.4, 7.5 and 7.6 superimposed.

to be efficient when an effect follows upon its cause with minimum waste of energy, when there is a smooth and logical sequence from conception, to action, to result, and the result approximates to what was initially conceived. But effectiveness is a much larger process *encompassing the entire learning circle*. As Gregory Bateson once observed, cause-and-effect thinking, of which efficiency is one variety, is *an arc abstracted from a larger circle*.[2] Think only in terms of this arc and you miss crucial variables in the process of learning from experience how better to create wealth.

There are many problems, especially those involving human relations, where we mainly learn by approximation and correction. There are no reliable ways of calculating, in advance, what a customer will want, or how particular persons will respond to your overtures. So far from trying to avoid mistakes, it could be wise to make many small and inexpensive mistakes as soon as possible so as to learn more quickly than competitors. This is *not* to suggest that catcrackers be thrown together so that they take months to debug. What is needed is a logic suitable to the machine *joined to* a logic suitable to social relationships with the simultaneous development of both logics within a cycle of inner-directed technology-driven learning, harmonized with an outer-directed market-pulled learning.

Do Dilemmas Change Shape?

So far we have assumed that dilemmas 'keep still' while we are examining them and that the two 'horns' or axes will remain the same length. Unfortunately, life is not that simple. At different times in different situations the optimal or synergistic relationship between the inner-directed needs of MF and the outer-directed imperatives of the market will *vary in their relative salience*.

Consider a condition of high oil prices and under-capacity in refineries. In such circumstances, virtually everything MF comes up with, assuming its technical excellence, is going to be of commercial value to refineries and their products. We have the situation of Dilemma 7.7.

But see what happens when oil prices fall and the industry suffers from over-capacity. In this situation, a considerable number of MF's excellent engineering processes either lie idle or are not fully utilized. Anything which adds further to refineries' fixed costs may be

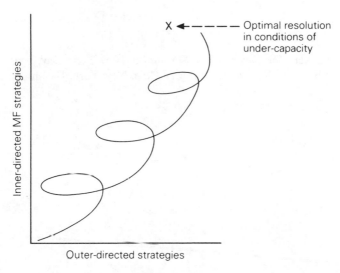

Dilemma 7.7

burdensome. Technological excellence is needed as always, but *within the anticipated patterns of demand* and not outside them. Moreover, the aims of process engineering may need to alter, with more emphasis on economy and maintenance and a demonstrated capacity to meet special requests from customers. As before, we are aiming at *synergy*, *but the relative proportions of inner and outer-directed values have shifted*, as shown in Dilemma 7.8. The marketing end and signals from the refineries have become more important in conditions of over-capacity. The refineries need all the orders they can get to defray their high overheads and the speed of MF's response may be crucial.

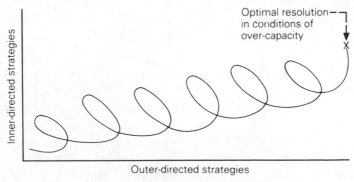

Dilemma   7.8

Notes

1 Peter Drucker, *The Concept of the Corporation*. New York: Day, 1946.
2 Gregory Bateson, *Steps to an Ecology of Mind*. New York: Ballantine, 1974.

8

Strategically Outclassed: Culture and Strategy in the Pacific Rim

So far we have not examined the challenge posed to Europe and North America by Japan and the nations of the Pacific Rim. Do our most successful Asian competitors, Japan, South Korea, Taiwan, Singapore and Hong Kong, think in the terms described in this book, i.e. dilemmas, circles and synergies? Are there reasons to believe that their habitual ways of thinking give them crucial advantages over Western corporations? Are there aspects of corporate strategy to which we are culturally blind, or slow to see, but which they grasp more readily? Above all, can we see emerging a distinctive type of Asian capitalism, sometimes called 'cheating' by the rules which the West has invented and now enforces,[1] but actually more effective competitively? Might we be wise to adapt to these strategies so that capitalism as a system evolves to even greater capacities to create wealth? My answer to all these questions is at least a qualified 'yes'.

The qualification is necessary because dilemmas methodology is designed to loosen knots in an Occidental mind-set. This book has argued in effect that separate elements which appear to be antagonistic and opposed can often be reconciled. Generally speaking, Asians see neither separate atoms as we do, nor stubborn antagonisms among these, but are sensitized to complementarities. The famous *T'ai Chi* or 'Diagram of the Supreme Ultimate' is composed of *yin* and *yang*, literally 'the dark and the sunny side of the hill'. These are complementary principles which constitute the *Tao* or 'The way of the universe'. They constitute one primordial breath, *chi*, which divided into the lighter mountain mist and the darker earth vapour but are alternating, cyclical, harmonious and rhythmic.[2]

Hence the ways of reconciling dilemmas discussed in chapter 6, processing, contextualizing, sequencing, waving/cycling and synergizing, are cultural 'givens' for our Asian competitors. They would not have to learn them. *Yin* and *yang* are processes, for ever ebbing and flowing. They are interwoven contextually. They are both sequential and cyclical as is dawn and dusk, light and dark, while the central Japanese cultural axiom is *wā*, or harmony, roughly what we have been calling synergy.

As for the vortices and helices I have drawn to represent the development and learning of organizations, these, too, lie deep in Asian thought.

One day Confucius and his pupils were walking by a turbulent river. They saw an old man playing in the raging waters around the rocks. Suddenly, he disappeared from view and Confucius sent his pupils racing to the rescue, but the old man as suddenly emerged by the bank. Confucius asked him how he could survive the torrents. He answered, 'Oh, I know how to go in with the descending vortex, and come out by the ascending one'. He knew the Tao.[3]

Shinto, the official Japanese religion, means 'the way of the gods'. The gods (or *kami*) are all imports from Japan's neighbours, many from Buddhism, in a way reminiscent of the borrowing of Western technology. But Shinto is not an alien religion. Its own distinctive contribution is to render all its gods harmonious with each other. *Kami* live within the forces of nature in mountains, rivers, rocks and trees and in the processes of creativity, growth and healing. In contrast with Christianity there is no 'after life'. Death is neither fought nor triumphed over, but is reconciled with life and seen as emphasis necessary to its enhancement. Life at its best involves harnessing oneself to the *kami* of natural forces, so as to flow with them and be carried in favourable directions.[4]

Man alone is weak, but harnessed to nature he becomes strong through his understanding of these forces. This contrasts strongly with Western traditions of man-as-stronger-than-nature, as embodied in Hercules, Gargantua and Superman.

The major symbols of Shinto religion include the *torii* or wooden gate which stands at the entry to shrines. It is a symbol of unity and reconciliation. Two pillars represent posts which support the sky, while the cross-bars symbolize the earth. The *torii* unifies earth and sky. Shinto morality is closely allied to a sense of aestheticism. Honesty, kindness, respect, care and love make relationships more beautiful and whole and release more natural energy for shared advantage. Creativity is a new and potent combination of natural forces to which one is drawn by aesthetic sensitivities.

Troubled or tense relationships are ugly and disjointed. Thus sexual promiscuity would be wrong, not because it indulged an appetite sinful in its origins, but because physical intimacy was out of balance with psychological and spiritual intimacies.

Asian Martial Arts

Asians have the same paradoxical attitudes to competition. Their major contributions to the martial arts are *ju-jitsu* (or judo), literally 'the gentle way', and *karate*, 'the empty hand'. These are both excellent examples of force by indirection. Both may be influenced in part by the fact that many Asians are lightly framed compared with Africans or Occidentals and must harness themselves to the might and the momentum generated by opponents. The key to both forms of combat are balance and lightning changes of direction in response to a move by the other. Strength may be offset by speed, force countered by altering its direction, weight may be countered by flexibility. No single value confers a decisive advantage. It is a question of coordination, or deploying the *kami* of the whole system to the best advantage.

Judo is not simply a question of winning, although its Western versions usually are. In *kata* the contest is in style, precision and elegance of specific techniques which are exhibited in sequence. In *randori* a repertory of techniques can be used in order to defeat an opponent, but points are also awarded for correct procedure. The sport owes much to Jigoro Kano who reorganized it in 1882, eliminating the more dangerous techniques. It is a form of mental discipline as well as a sport and, most importantly, *a form of instruction and learning*, which transcends winning or losing. Two of Kano's slogans were 'Maximum efficiency with minimum effort' and 'Mutual welfare and benefit'. The point was to demonstrate how well you could harness yourself to the maelstrom of natural forces in the arena. No wonder the Japanese regard Western culture with its biggest, tallest, strongest, largest, fastest, longest obsessions as an 'obvious culture', a *Guinness Book of Records* for inebriated braggarts. Neither in judo nor in business do you clash head-on if you have any sense. Rather you create *from* that struggle a more elegant and efficient combination of forces than you had before. That your opponent sails through the air is merely a demonstration of your developing skills, and that you cooperate with his powers even while competing with him is not anomalous but natural. A highly popular Japanese TV series is called 'The Way of Monkey', the hero of which ceaselessly deflects and outwits opponents of far greater might.

The Use of *Kanji*

The Japanese language may create another important advantage in reconciling dilemmas. There is no sequence in a Japanese sentence, no subject doing something transitive to an object, with the tacit implication that the first is *causing* the second to respond. The verb comes last in the sentence and the nouns are mediated or related by that verb in complex combinations. Even more important is the presence of *kanji* or picturegram words borrowed from the Chinese that often represent subtle syntheses among ideas and mental processes.

For example, it is a monotonous fact of commerce that waves of bullish optimism are followed by waves of bearish pessimism as the stock market oscillates. It's also a matter of record that Asian stock markets are less volatile. Figure 8.1 shows that while Western optimism and pessimism are topics of deserved ridicule, the Japanese *kanji* are able to express the fusion or reconciliation of the two. The three *kanji* at top right may be translated as 'easy going optimism', 'naive (literally heavenly) optimism' or 'optimism unaware of pessimistic possibilities'. The *kanji* at bottom right mean 'optimism aware of pessimistic possibilities', 'realistic optimism' or 'optimism based on careful evaluation'. The varying interpretations come from different Japanese informants and show that the fusion and subtlety of thoughts are not achieved without some loss in precision. The Japanese will sometimes trace a *kanji* on the palm of another's hand to communicate what they mean. Words are inadequate.

Are there Distinctive Asian Strategies?

Are there patterns to be found within Asian competitive strategies which are distinctive and predictable? Has the massive increase in

Optimistic Syndrome

楽天的

楽観的

Pessimistic Syndrome

Figure 8.1 Optimistic Syndrome and Pessimistic Syndrome. Westerners have no difficulty with optimism and pessimism as easily identifiable extremes. But we can express their mutual qualification only with difficulty and circumlocution. The *kanji* on the right represent naive or unqualified optimism (top) and optimism-aware-of-pessimistic-possibilities (bottom). With *kanji* subtle syntheses of mood become possible.

their world-market share been achieved by describable forms? I believe there are clear outlines to their strategies, which we shall examine under the following headlines:

1 The pursuit of knowledge intensity and integral value
2 Market share and profitability

3   Beyond generic strategies
4   Process innovation and product innovation
5   The *kaisha* with stabilizers
6   Stakeholders united
7   The revolution in flexible manufacturing

The Pursuit of Knowledge Intensity and Integral Value

One of the most consistent biases in the conventional wisdom of Western economics is that the value of a particular product is 'nothing but' the price which consumers will pay for each additional unit of that product. An impersonal market mechanism decrees where the demand curve meets the supply curve, and their conjunction decides the amount purchased and at what price.

According to this view, values are purely subjective and entirely relative to personal idiosyncrasies *until* the aggregate behaviour of consumers gives these values an objective price in the market-place.[5] There is no a priori strategy, however artful, that is not abrogated by the will of customers. 'Pushpin is as good as poetry,' Bentham said. Nay, it is better than poetry to Economic Man if it fetches a higher price.

The dismal science is a harsh antidote to the naive idealism of self-styled intellectuals. It is a bulwark of Anglo-American empiricism against the pseudo-science and false rationalism infecting parts of continental Europe and much of Asia. For isn't the belief that the whole is more than the sum of its parts a totalitarian temptation? Did not Germany, Italy, Japan and the Soviets, among others, succumb to the false god of a society which could allegedly transcend the individuality of its members?[6]

Even today, some of these governments dabble in the dubious practice of 'picking winners' and targeting certain products and key industries for special favours. What gnostic wisdom is this which settles on the minds of unelected bureaucrats? What dogma of immaculate perception informs them of what we will in future buy? And why distort market forces with predictions of doubtful validity? Ever since the post-war Labour government in Britain promoted groundnuts in East Africa and succeeded only in feeding an obvious vein of obscene humour, and promoted snoek piquante (otherwise known as canned barracuda) which finally had to be fed to cats, the notion of the state choosing for us has seemed derisory. Surely, this nonsense is implicated in the collapse of Eastern bloc economies.

It is certainly easy to stomp all over the idea of targeting, but it is difficult to see *how* the otherwise brilliantly successful economies of the Pacific Rim could be so 'foolish', or why the 'wise' advocates of total consumer sovereignty in the United States and Britain should be presiding over such calamitous deficits in their international balance of trade. Could there be elements in Asian calculations which elude us?

Nothing better illustrates our total incomprehension of Asian strategy than the imputation that they are 'picking winners'. This vision of a horse race or a demolition derby with every product racing against every other product is how we think, in bits and pieces, and in aggregations of individualists. Unlike us, *they* look out upon a world of complementarities and connections. For them the economy is a whole organism.

As we saw briefly in chapters 2 and 6, wealth creation involves a *configuration of values*. Products have at least two sources of value, their *unit value*, the price that product fetches on the market, and their *integral value*, the value of that product to *other* products, present or future, and the value inherent in teaching or developing those who invent, apply, manufacture, market, consume and use that product. It simply is not true that, say, a case of plastic cocktail swivel sticks worth $50 is as valuable to an organization or an economy as a battery-operated radio and cassette player worth $50. This is because the latter product is higher in knowledge intensity, i.e. more learning goes into every phase of its development and use. The finished product is itself a major means of disseminating information even in the absence of electricity and is crucial to communication in much of the Third World.

In other words, products have widely differing capacities to elicit greater potentials from their makers and consumers. Asians are not 'picking winners' so much as *picking teachers*, products that will supply the knowledge and skills to make other products and develop the economy's human resources at the same time. While it is perfectly true that only customers can vindicate a decision to supply particular products or services, not all vindications are of equal value, even where they fetch equal prices.

Nor is it true that there is no way of predicting, in advance of the customer's decision, which kinds of product it would be most valuable to create. The more knowledge is organized into a particular product the less likely it is that you will have many competitors, especially low-wage competition. This is because the skills and learning necessary to create products of rich complexity are scarce. Only cultures with high levels of education contain the necessary human resources, other things being equal. Therefore, products of high knowledge intensity will command higher rents and profit margins.[7] Leading in the race to learn tends to be progressive if not exponential. The more you already know, the faster you learn. The development of products A and B is not simply profitable in itself (unit value) but makes possible the creation of products C, D and E and has a value integral to the entire product family and beyond. Indeed, the sheer number of potential niches increases rapidly as you reach the information end of a resource-intense knowledge-intense continuum (figure 8.2), as do the connections between product and product represented by the white horizontal bars.

If we consider what Asians have targeted over the years, steel, machine tools, robots, microchips, metal ceramics and language translation (or 'fifth generation') computers, then the calculus becomes clearer. The cheapness and quality of steel, for example, ramifies on everything made from steel. Thousands of products start with a competitive advantage if Asian steel is cheaper and better, or with a massive disadvantage as when American speciality steel is protected by quotas and tariffs. This even spreads to services of, say, consulting engineers, whose competitive tender is bundled with the price of steel.[8]

However, advantage in steel making has moved from Japan to Korea, where wages are lower, and it is only by targeting more complex products that a developed economy can pay good wages and provide valuable education. Machine tools are an obvious target because they are *the tools that makes the tools*. Any economy with the finest machine tools will tend to have the best-tooled factories. Just as complexity in human thought goes up the abstraction ladder, so there are 'tools' and 'meta-tools' and 'meta-meta-tools', i.e. the machine tools which make the knife-grinding machines which are then sold to manufacturers of blades, saws and cutlery, which then cut their produce. It is obvious to Asians, but seemingly not to us, that, if your machine tools are the best in the world, then most of the other goods you manufacture will benefit.

The case of microchips is even more persuasive. The Japanese call

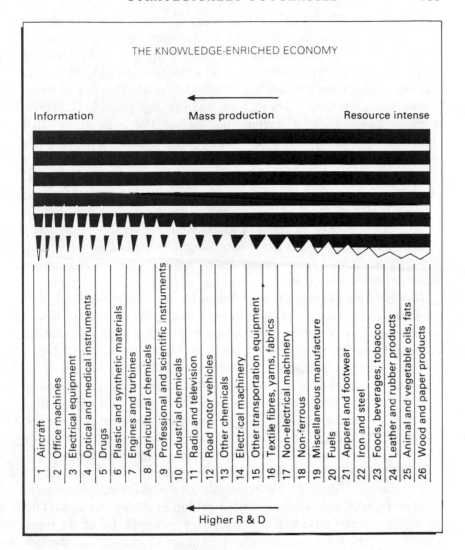

Figure 8.2 This rank ordering of industries by their degrees of knowledge intensity is taken from Bruce Scott, who showed that Japan, Singapore, Hong Kong, South Korea and Taiwan have been 'climbing' the information ladder, while the United States has been falling and Britain has been marking time: knowledge intensity is here measured by the ratio of R&D to total product costs. This deepens and multiplies niches (hence the toothcomb effect) as the economy approaches the information end of the continuum. Knowledge intensity only approximates the 'integral value' of a product to other products. Aeronautics and space, for example, and much defence expenditure may be too esoteric and too secret to benefit the industrial infrastructure.

these 'the rice of industry' and they speak of 'food chains' with certain key products nourishing the rest.[9] A microchip can put a brain into anything from a road system to a child's toy and makes tens of thousands of otherwise inanimate products intelligent and responsive. All this occurs naturally to a people who see *kami* in rocks and trees, mountains and rivers. Microchips animate the physical universe, creating a multitude of purposeful objects. The point is not that microchips, machine tools or robots are winners, although this happens to be true, but that incalculable benefits accrue to the entire economy by making these products as well and as cheaply as possible. The decision to target thém is *not*, therefore, predicated on the gamble that they will win, but on the certainty that every degree of improvement in such linchpin products would repay this effort many times over in the sheer variety of products enhanced. We are back again to the judo of Jigoro Kano where minimal effort is designed to produce maximum effect.

Just as targeted products are chosen for their catalytic properties, so important syntheses may be achieved among the targeted products themselves. Cross-fertilize microchips and electronics with machine tools and you get number-controlled machine tools in which Japan now leads the world. Robots are another targeted technology. Indeed, they can be leased from the Japanese government without a company having to invest long term in obsolescent robotics. With every new advance in technology, the older robots can be exchanged for the latest ones under the same lease agreement. The consequence is not simply another winner, but a world lead in factory automation.

An important principle of dilemma resolution or, as Asians might see it, the connecting of complementarities is that strategies always have at least two reasons and often multiples of two reasons. The reason for targeting metal ceramics, for example, is, at its most elementary, the profits to be made from the product itself and the fact that all engines made from such heat-conserving materials will be several times more efficient. But it does not end there. Ceramic engines could revolutionize Japan's already burgeoning automobile industry and, by making possible a 300-mile-per-gallon engine, they could slash Japan's oil import bills, greatly reducing its perilous reliance on Middle East politics, and combat its serious pollution problem. Fifth generation computers are similarly targeted for many reasons. Quite apart from 'slipping the field' in the race to learn, Japan's minority language, so different from most other languages, places a massive burden on translation skills which these computers could lift.

The strategy of systematically increasing the knowledge intensity of one's products has a corollary. Low-knowledge products must be phased out, preferably *before* low-wage competition from the developing world causes them to collapse, with all the accompanying dislocation and distress this causes. Indeed, buying simple manufactures from newly industrializing countries assists their economic development, while trying to go on making mass-market boots, shoes and textiles tends to impoverish whole areas of advanced economies. Japan's relationship to its co-prosperity sphere is much stronger as a result of this strategy than is the US policy of trying to keep Latin American peasants on the land producing cash crops and raw materials.[10]

What are the *yin* and the *yang* which are harmonized by the knowledge-intensive strategy? I would argue that this strategy creates the 'virtuous circle' in figure 8.3. The tensions or complementarities are between rationalism and empiricism (A–(a)), between knowledge intensity and earning a premium price (B–(b)) and between integral value and unit value (C–(c)). Note that everything typically sought by Western corporations through direct manipulation is in the arc (a)–(c), or from 6 o'clock to 10 o'clock. The Asians get these too, but *by indirection*, by 'the gentle way'.

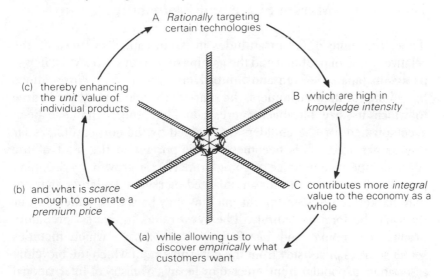

Figure 8.3

We can also draw this dynamic as a developmental helix, encompassing three complementarities A–(a), B–(b) and C–(c). This is done in Dilemma 8.1.

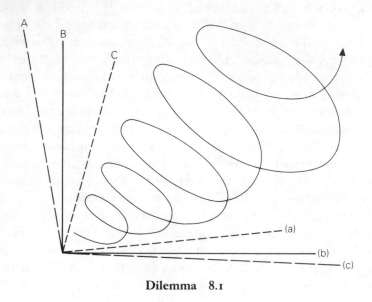

Dilemma 8.1

Market Share and Profitability

There are quite different attitudes in Asian capitalism towards the relative values of profiting and the gaining of market share. Most news-papers in Japan, Taiwan and South Korea report what corporations have done for their customers, the share of the market and the degree to which its size has been increased. The profit, what has been accomplished for shareholders or retained by the corporation, is far less emphasized. This becomes very important in the light of the Asian competitive practice of going primarily for growth, by dropping prices and going flat out for an enlarged market and a larger share of that market. To this end profit margins may be shaved wafer thin or they may be forgone entirely. The West refers to this as 'predatory pricing', 'dumping' and *The Japanese Conspiracy*,[11] which includes secret sources of subsidy from the government, of which the bicycling association, a 'popular front' erected by Japan's Ministry of International Trade and Industry (MITI), is the most notorious example. The resulting calls for 'a level playing field' assumes that the Asians are playing the same game as the one we play. But are they? It is similar in some ways to a contest between a heavyweight boxer and a judo champion. The argument on rules is illusory. Each is fighting according to the rules of his own culture.[12]

The Asians stand poised between the axes of profitability and market share (Dilemma 8.2). But they then 'move to the right', going all out for market share and forgoing profits for the short term. This has a disastrous effect on their opponents' profitability. If you are losing market share to a lower-cost competitor, your profits are likely to be squeezed severely. Hence the 'move to the right' *imposes upon your opponent a severe dilemma between falling market share and falling profits.*

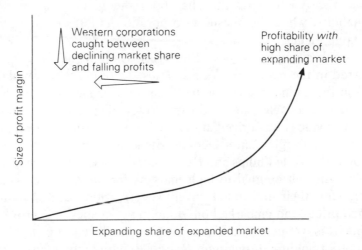

Dilemma 8.2

Now the style of Western corporations is to maintain high margins at all cost. This is partly cultural – profit is perceived as the supreme value – and partly structural – Western corporations need to pay dividends to shareholders, many of which are pension funds. In contrast Asian companies are more 'highly geared'. They have more debt compared with equity, and their shareholders are more interested in growth than in dividends.

This means that in a contest for market share by cutting prices, the Asian corporation is likely to hold out longer than the Western one. It also has the benefit of a lower cost of capital, with long-term low-interest loans from industrial banks which may themselves have invested in their client's growth. Asian industry has the kind of privileged borrowing position which in the West is reserved for the home mortgage market.

Another reason why Asian competitors may be prepared to absorb losses in the sale of a particular product is because they are focused on its integral value, while we are concerned exclusively with unit value. It may pay a corporation to take temporary losses on its metal ceramics as a product if those same ceramics are a 'strategic' ingredient in twenty *other* products still being profitably sold.

But it is crucial to grasp that *the sacrifice of profitability is only short term*. The idea is to make the competitor withdraw from the contest and this is what will typically occur. In the end, as Dilemma 8.2 shows, the Asian competitor has both the market share *and* the profitability, while the Western corporation is left defending a few profitable niches.

A good example of how the West is strategically outclassed occurred in the market for VCRs. These were developed initially by RCA in the United States and by Philips in Europe and were used in the video and television industry. A smaller tape machine for consumer videos was priced at over $1,000. The story is well told by James C. Abegglen and George Stalk in *Kaisha: The Japanese Corporation*. While Philips and RCA waited to see how demand would develop and felt entitled to high margins for modest sales as a due reward for their individual inventiveness, Sony and Matsushito slashed prices and embarked on 'doubling strategies', i.e. growing by as much as 50 per cent a year by repeatedly cutting prices as a function of volume throughput. Robert Reich commented:

In 1979, the RCA Corporation complained publicly that it lacked the $200 million that would be needed to develop a consumer video-cassette recorder, although recorders are the fastest-growing appliance of the decade. But RCA had no qualms about buying a lack-lustre finance company that same year.[13]

Presumably the profits from this acquisition were higher, but the story illustrates that the search for profits at all cost diverts the corporation from learning how to master and how to elaborate its core technologies.

It is, of course, a far more complex strategy than merely trading off short-term profits for increased market share and later recouping the profits. The 'virtuous circle' as Abegglen and Stalk call it, operates roughly as follows: the slashing of prices precipitates a greatly enlarged market and so increases volume throughput and the variety of possible models. This saves much of the income forgone by slashing prices and helps restore profits as the corporation learns faster than its competition how to produce VCRs more efficiently and more effectively.

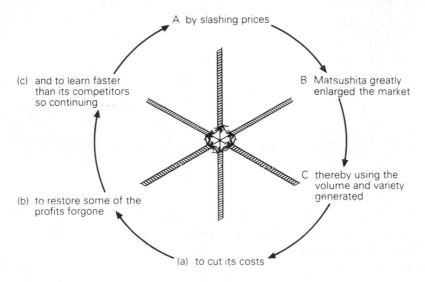

A by slashing prices

(c) and to learn faster
than its competitors
so continuing . . .

B Matsushita greatly
enlarged the market

C thereby using the
volume and variety
generated

(b) to restore some of the
profits forgone

(a) to cut its costs

Figure 8.4

The virtuous circle is shown in figure 8.4. The tension between the enlarged market and the need to restore profitability, B–(b), has already been commented on. Equally crucial is the need to compensate for slashing prices by cutting costs, A–(a), and the need to use increased volume and greater variety to gain greater experience and learn faster than competitors, C–(c). There are, in fact, three dilemmas all resolved by the 'ascending vortex' of the *Tao* (Dilemma 8.3).

Yet we should not leave this strategy without noting its devastating effect on Western industries. It has all the momentum of a scythed chariot cutting up an opposing army. Because it relies on indigenous Asian advantages in the way corporations are financed and the different position of shareholders, it may be unstoppable. What has happened – and we must not ignore this – is that the Japanese have gained every market they have targeted and held it until, starved of profits, Western corporations retreated. It is as if an invading army

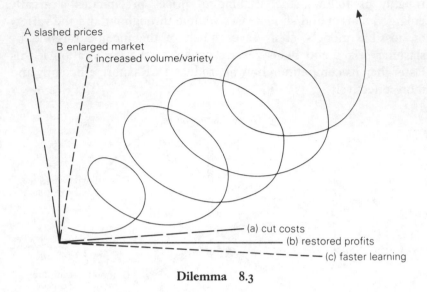

A slashed prices
B enlarged market
C increased volume/variety

(a) cut costs
(b) restored profits
(c) faster learning

Dilemma 8.3

held all the crossroads and all the strategic hilltops and passes between, so that we have had to retreat to scattered niches that could be defended more easily and at higher gain.

Beyond Generic Strategies

How long before this retreat becomes a rout? Consider the positions occupied by RCA and Philips in Dilemma 8.2, compared with Matsushita. It is essentially similar to the position of Jaguar and Rolls Royce. British automobiles retreat up-market to special luxury niches, leaving to the Japanese and now Koreans much of the lower-cost volume car market. This enables the Asians to start building high-quality cars like the Honda Legend and move inexorably up-market *using their volume car business to absorb overheads and create a competitively priced quality car.* This progress is illustrated in Dilemma 8.4 where Michael Porter's so-called generic strategies (meaning a strategy of one exclusive kind) are in the process of being reconciled over time.[14] The Asians typically go for high volume, low cost first, but then use this as a base for moving top right to combine *both* quality and value for money, the kind of frugal aesthetic embodied in the Japanese garden where everything is pruned to its essentials and

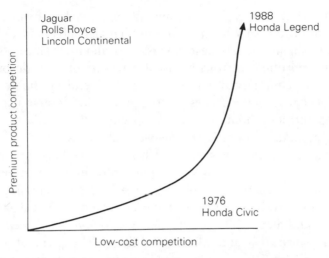

Dilemma   8.4

there is nothing spare and nothing missing.[15] That Michael Porter, perhaps the Western world's most renowned academic strategist, should think these two strategies were naturally separate, whereas for the Japanese they are naturally combined (albeit over time), says volumes about the difference between Oriental and Occidental thought patterns. Perhaps we simply cannot grasp what is happening to us.

Process Innovation and Product Innovation

Another repetitive pattern often seen is that Asians innovate in the process of production some years before they innovate in the products themselves. This leads to the famous 'copy-cat' accusation that lulled so many Western economies into believing that competition from the Far East was creatively sterile. In fact, imitation is a form of study and learning. It is also a sensible precaution when approaching an almost totally alien culture where the preferences of consumers are mysterious to you. If you know that consumers buy Ronson cigarette lighters you make something as near in appearance to them as you can.

In the meantime your innovation takes place behind factory walls, far away from the export market you are aiming for. This innovation consists in making 'the same' lighter but with half the manufacturing steps and with far easier assembly. When it reaches the market, Robin Day, the British TV host, whips out identical lighters from behind his back to shame the Japanese ambassador who loses face on screen and retires mortified. Britons as usual win wars of rhetoric only to lose those of commercial substance. The 'identical' lighter was not identical at all in the process of its composition. It wasn't so much low wages and long hours by ant-like orientals that made it inexpensive but a genuine form of *innovation* we could not see and did not grasp.

And then comes the surprise. Having tracked Western products for several years and innovated significantly in the manner of their making, the Asians suddenly leap-frog Western technology to create innovative products, while we fall over ourselves and gasp in surprise. How could they? All too easily, *since process innovation lies at the roots of product innovation* and what *looked* like a 'cheap imitation' was the result of a radically reorganized factory and redesigned production techniques.

The West, especially the English-speaking countries, are rarely strong on process innovation, although there are an increasing number of exceptions. It is too collectivized and is incompatible with troubled labour relations.[16] Process innovation is 'bottom up' rather than 'top down'. More consistent with Western individualism is the creative unit invented by the creative individual and then manufactured as cheaply as possible by the vulgar masses, if necessary in low-wage countries abroad. None of this helps process innovation or rapid learning.

Dilemma 8.5 tracks Asian strategy from its 'low-profile' process innovation, out of sight of its competitors, to its sudden leap-frog over Western products to the forefront. It is a powerful combination, using the West's own strength to propel the *kaisha* past it.

The *Kaisha* with Stabilizers

No one surveying the contemporary business scene could describe it as stable or placid. As international competition heats up corporations are subjected to ever greater turbulence and shock waves. These are not simply aspects of the business cycle or the rise and fall and rise of energy prices, but are the consequences of the 'predatory' pricing and doubling strategies discussed above. In such circumstances a major competitive advantage – almost a strategy in itself – consists of

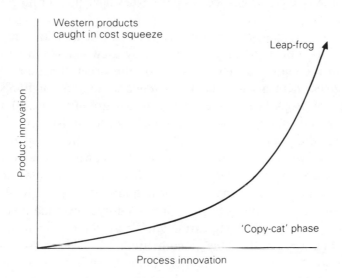

Dilemma 8.5

navigating environments of such high turbulence that competitors are severely distressed or swamped, while the victorious corporation rides the waves with comparative ease.

Severe turbulence will typically trigger disputes within Western corporations. A 20 per cent to 30 per cent down-turn in sales can lead to massive lay-offs and redundancies along with the possibility of strikes and the certainty of disaffection among its victims, usually blue-collar workers and last-hired staff. The lowest paid tend to be the victims because more senior personnel are protected by contracts and severance payments, by the scarcity of their skills and the value of their information to competitors. But, above all, they are protected by the doctrine of individual self-interest and the belief that this is somehow praiseworthy (see Peter Jay's *Management and Machiavelli*).[17] Those with the power to protect their own positions will do so, even if this involves shifting the penalties for their own misjudgement or the collective misfortune so as to inflict these exclusively on subordinates. The reliance by leading Western economies on hostile takeovers to restructure corporations is another source of periodic upheaval. It has been estimated that 1.8 million American employees were 'let go' in the 1981–3 recession.[18] Although most found new employment, the ceaseless churning of individuals like ingredients stirred in a plum pudding makes many western corporations much less resilient in the face of adverse circumstances as employees have little or no company loyalty.

Even where layed-off workers are rehired when business turns up, they will have been with the company only a few years before the next down-turn comes and they are again on the street. 'Last hired – first fired' gives them a shuttlecock existence as the corporation's most expendable people. Resentment and cynicism are inevitable. Moreover, by the most elementary canons of justice those punished in a down-turn are the least responsible for managing the company more effectively, while those protected by their own power from any penalties are the most responsible. Horrendous examples abound. The GM managers, in the midst of negotiating a large give-back of wages and fringe benefits from their work-force, awarded themselves a bonus from what they had extracted. There comes *The Reckoning* as David Halberstam has ably documented.[19] It takes myriad forms: chronic absenteeism, high sickness benefits, industrial unrest, poor quality, petty grievances and legalisms, stealing, sabotage and lethargy. Above all, workers learn only what they as individuals can sell in the open market into which they are periodically pitchforked. They do not learn how to cooperate, how to marshal several skills and accumulate information in stable networks, or how to make teams work by choosing from their skills repertory the ones most appropriate to the situation.

They do not learn how to manage themselves in a way that makes first-line and even second-line supervisors obsolete, how to solve problems on the spot and create their own solutions and how to make the highest quality a value which the entire group supports and pursues free of inspection. As the world rapidly complexifies, only subtle minds communicating subtle information to intimately experienced co-workers are able to master this burgeoning complexity of knowledge.

The Japanese *kaisha* achieves these goals by stabilizing its social system in the midst of great turbulence. It does this primarily by paying as much as 30 per cent of the staff remuneration in year-end bonuses. This not only helps maintain a high savings rate – so much money being difficult to spend immediately – but it reminds all staff that their jobs are closely tied to the success of the corporation as a whole. Everyone is in the same boat.[20]

But more important still, it means that in a down-turn or set-back *everyone's salary is reduced in proportion to their status in the company and their degree of responsibility*. Those who might have seen it coming fare commensurately worse and lose more pay than those innocent of such awareness. In the *kaisha* ill-fortune is not compounded by injustice and victimization.[21]

Indeed, the *kaisha*'s management goes further than this as a visiting delegation of Japanese trade unionists explained to me. 'They first call us in to say the situation looks bad. It is their responsibility. They will take a cut in their salary. We go away, but we know who will be next if things do not improve and, of course, we do everything we can in the next six months to improve productivity and raise quality. . . .'[22]

The philosophy is one of optimal balance and resilience. Those with most money and greatest responsibility take the first shock of recession. Those protected rush to shore up the corporation that protected them. Dilemma 8.6 illustrates the high oscillation of the typical Western corporation buffeted by economic storms, compared with the progress of self-stabilization in even the roughest seas achieved by the *kaisha*.

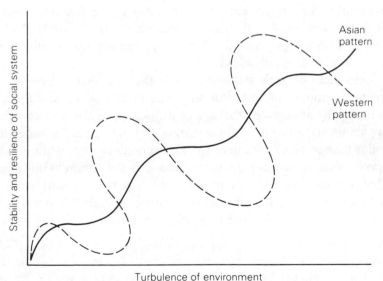

Dilemma 8.6

Stakeholders United

The Asian corporation is more often 'owned' by its employees and stakeholders than are corporations in the West, a fact that makes long-term commitment and dedication to the interests of the corporation and its employees far stronger and far more enduring. The difference is one of structure as well as style.

The legal convention in both regions is clear. The shareholders own the company but here the resemblance ends. In the West, governed as it is by the norm of self-interest, a board is appointed to make sure that top executives run the company in the interests of shareholders. These are the checks and balances familiar to American civic culture. No group's self-interest may be unlimited, and so the board yokes the managers of the company to the interests of the absentee owners. Since these shareholders are not a deliberative body but an aggregate of scattered interests, each aiming to maximize his/her investment, their rights are not really negotiable or capable of being qualified by offsetting considerations. The question of whether they might be prepared to postpone short-term profitability for longer-term gains cannot really be posed to them and much less answered. If the share price falls they may sell. If dividends are cut, who will pay the members of the pension fund, retirees who, in the longer term, are dead?

The result of such arrangements is that the share price becomes the most important indicator of a company's success, and this is substantially affected by the size of dividends, so that US companies pay about 50 per cent of their earnings in dividends. In order to tie senior managers to the interests of shareholders, they will often have a profit-sharing bonus plan, sometimes with the option to buy stock at a lower price than recently attained and so pocket the difference. All this gives Western managements a strong incentive to improve and maintain earnings. Abegglen and Stalk comment:

The Western corporate pattern might be described as an alliance of senior management and shareholders to optimize current earnings from the company to mutual benefit. The company becomes a vehicle for profit optimization or, at worst, profit maximization. . . . Not surprisingly, then, lower-ranking employees, especially as represented by their trade unions, also seek to optimize and, in fact, seek to maximize their share of current earnings. In this process the company becomes an organization external to the interests of its members, to be used to further their earnings advantage to the maximum.[23]

It is the triumph of sectional self-interests over the integrity of the organization as a whole. Senior managers and their subordinates are trapped in a perpetual internecine struggle to use the organization for the greater relative enrichment of one faction or the other. Such an organization hesitates to invest heavily in its human resources, especially if the alternative is to give more money to shareholders now and if an acquisitor is in danger of making such an offer. Money spent training workers could increase their bargaining power and their wage demands. If disaffected workers leave or are layed off in the next down-turn, the corporation could find that it has trained those now working for a competitor. For all such reasons Western corporations, compared with Asian ones, *chronically under-invest in human resources and corporate learning.*[24]

The *kaisha* has quite different priorities. It pays only about 2.0 per cent of its earnings on average in dividends, which frees up the rest for rapid reinvestment and 'doubling' strategies. It has less equity in its total financing and most of its shareholders are looking for growth rather than dividends. It is less likely to have external members on its board and treats shareholders as 'outside investors' who must be paid adequately for their funds but are not 'in control' of the company in even a theoretical sense. Board members are typically career employees representing all sections of the work-force.

Surveys which compare the attitudes of US and Japanese executives reveal that share price is *not* a major objective for the Japanese, who put it last of nine objectives, or did not endorse it at all, while American managers placed it second, just behind return on investment.

Because share price, dividend payments and short-term performance are not the preoccupations for Asian corporations that they are for Western ones, the money is freed for heavy investments in human resources, which will stay with the *kaisha* long term because all staff are identified with the growth of 'their' corporation. The dynamics which divide Western corporations into pro-shareholder and anti-shareholder factions are not salient here. The *kaisha* is a celebration of *wā* or harmony.

The difference between Western and Asian corporations, with the American and Japanese varieties used as prototypes, is captured in the

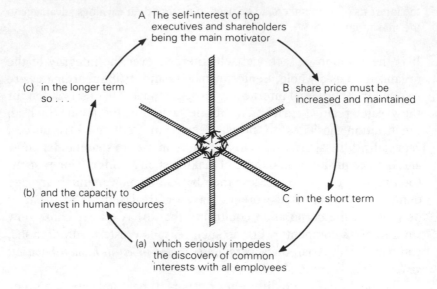

A The self-interest of top
executives and shareholders
being the main motivator

B share price must be
increased and maintained

C in the short term

(a) which seriously impedes
the discovery of common
interests with all employees

(b) and the capacity to
invest in human resources

(c) in the longer term
so . . .

Figure 8.5

following 'vicious' and 'virtuous' circles. The typical US corporation is split between factions and between processes – figure 8.5. Self-interest is split off from the common interest. The massaging upward of share price in the short term is split off from the investment in human resources in the longer term, and the corporation often fails to establish the close and productive relationships vital to the mastering of complexity.

The *kaisha*, in contrast, approaches the 'same' cycle from the notion of finding a common interest among all employees that is at point (a) or 6 o'clock. Because this is the prime emphasis, the virtuous circle may be seen as 'starting' from this point (figure 8.6).

Note that the long-term orientation *encompasses* numerous short-term exigencies as policies, laid down years earlier, bear fruit in the immediate present and the next few months. Similarly, the interests of shareholders are encompassed by the fast growth of the entire company. The ropes at the centre of the circle hold, so that the entire dynamic develops. In so far as the ropes split – as in the typical American and British corporation, dominated as they are by the demands of Wall Street and the City to make money from money – so the development of the cycle stalls and lags behind.

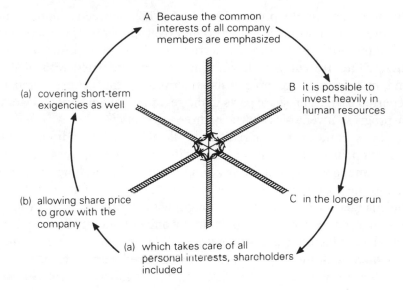

A Because the common interests of all company members are emphasized

(a) covering short-term exigencies as well

B it is possible to invest heavily in human resources

(b) allowing share price to grow with the company

C in the longer run

(a) which takes care of all personal interests, sharcholders included

Figure 8.6

The Revolution in Flexible Manufacturing

This brings us to the final Asian strategy, devastating in its impact, barely credible and reminiscent of the martial arts in its virtuoso weaving between 'opposites', which are widely regarded in the West as alternatives. The strategy consists of *both* the economies of scale with a high volume of standard components, *and* economies of scope or flexibility. We touched on it in chapter 3, Dilemma 3.3. In the market-place this involves offering greater variety at lower cost, a feat which flies in the face of traditional experience, namely that product variety sharply increases overheads. Indeed, it flies in the face of quite recent 'focus strategies' used by Taiwan, South Korea, Japan and other Pacific Rim economies. The strategies consist of producing only part of a range of Western products, the part most in demand, thereby reducing overheads and increasing turnover.[25]

How, then, can greater variety and lower costs be achieved? By several means. One ingredient is the *kanban* system, better known as Just in Time (JIT). Suppliers bring the parts needed for different products right into the plant minutes before they are needed. Typically, there is only *one* source for these parts, leading to lower costs based on the understanding that the supplier will not blackmail the producer and the producer will not switch between suppliers and 'motivate' them with sticks, carrots and rival suppliers. If the suppliers do their job right, overheads due to inventory, ordering and dispatching are cut way down. The system originated with Toyota and, in a dramatic example of its effectiveness, the Yanmar company reported savings on spare parts in the region of 50 per cent and work-in-progress inventories down by three-quarters.[26]

The second major ingredient in flexible manufacturing is the reduction in changeover costs. Traditionally, setting up a machine takes time, and resetting it for a product of different dimensions will add to the cost with two shorter runs instead of one long run. But if the changeover process is fast enough, with flexible tools that can be reset in seconds, or several tools run by one operator, then short runs can save on handling and storage costs. The economic order quantity may then be in the vicinity of fifty to a hundred with costs increasing over that number and under that number. It follows that *variety can lower costs* by making many short or medium runs more economic than few very long runs, or than a job-shop that supplies individual orders and small batches.

Western corporations, thinking in terms of units, atoms and individuals, have traditionally put one worker to one machine, and since machines could be more easily manipulated and improved than could people, it was up to the individual to *serve the machine* by maximizing throughput and utilization. The objective of multimachine manning is precisely the opposite – to have several different machines optimizing the workers' productivity, i.e. to *serve the worker* and enhance his/her skills. The machines can all be adjusted in their cycle times so as to be attended to in sequence. The worker moves from one to another *harmonizing their functions to his/her own rhythm*. Such machine combinations result in a very wide skill repertory. Each 'poly-machinist' is extraordinarily flexible in what the combination of machines can accomplish, provided the development of these skills is encouraged. Conversion to multimachine manning is credited with raising productivity between 30 and 80 per cent in such companies as Mazda, Toyota, Sanei Metal and Yanmar.

The *kaisha* typically uses a 'pull' system. The finished product is envisioned and every step towards its final synthesis and assembly is mapped so that the 'branches' converge upon the 'trunk' at just the right time. The West typically uses a 'push' system with production parts fabricated and pushed into inventories, whether or not they are needed. Once again the Asians think from the whole back to the parts from which it is derived. The West tends to start with parts and push these towards assembly.[27]

Flexible manufacturing is an excellent example of how the reconciliation of one dilemma helps to resolve other tensions. Because greater variety can be manufactured at lower relative cost, the marketing department which typically wants more variety can be reconciled with the production department which typically wants less. More important still, the ever burgeoning variety of demands in the environment can be matched by a requisite variety within the corporation. The *kaisha* has achieved a balancing act of which the practitioners of judo and karate would be proud. The answer for Western corporations is to learn by conscious deliberation and reflection – strategies which have come more easily and naturally to the Pacific Rim.

Notes

1 A good example of the 'unfair' charge and the 'wily oriental' theory may be found in Marvin J. Wolf, *The Japanese Conspiracy*. New York: Empire Books, 1983.
2 Alan Watts, *The Way of Zen*. New York: Vintage, 1959. See also *I Ching* or *Book of Changes*. Princeton, N.J.: Princeton University Press, 1967.
3 Quoted by Watts, *The Way of Zen*, p. 32.
4 My sources for insight into Japanese culture are Ezra Vogel, *Japan as No 1* (New York: Harper, 1979), and Takie Sugiyama Lebra, *Japanese Patterns of Behavior* (Honolulu, Hawaii: University Press of Hawaii, 1976).
5 The case is well argued in Walter Weisskopj, *Alienation and Economics*. New York: Dutton, 1971.
6 This is strenuously argued by Isaiah Berlin in *Two Concepts of Liberty* (Oxford: Clarendon Press 1958) and *The Hedgehog and the Fox* (New York: Mentor, 1965).
7 The point is made well by Bruce Scott in chapters 2 and 3 of Bruce Scott and George C. Lodge (eds), *American Competitiveness*. Boston, Mass.: Harvard Business School Press, 1985. See also George C. Lodge and Ezra F. Vogel (eds), *Ideology and National Competitiveness*. Boston, Mass.: Harvard Business School Press, 1987.
8 Robert Reich discusses this issue in *The Next American Frontier*, New York: Times, 1983. See also Stephen Cohen and John Zysman, *Manufacturing Matters*. New York: Basic Books, 1987.
9 Bruce Scott, personal communication.
10 George C. Lodge, personal communication.
11 Wolf, *The Japanese Conspiracy*.

12 Here, and for much of the rest of this chapter, I am indebted to Richard Abegglen and George Stalk Jr, *Kaisha: The Japanese Corporation*. New York: Basic Books, 1985.

13 Reich, *The Next American Frontier*, p. 71.

14 Michael E. Porter, *Competitive Strategy: Tehniques for Analyzing Industries and Competitors*. New York: Free Press, 1980.

15 This point is made by Iain Mittroff in *Business NOT as Usual*. San Francisco, Calif.: Jossey-Bass, 1987, last chapter.

16 Abegglen and Stalk, *Kaisha*, ch. 6.

17 Peter Jay, *Management and Machiavelli*. Harmondsworth: Penguin Books, 1967.

18 Lester C. Thurow, *The Zero Sum Solution*. New York: Simon and Schuster, 1985.

19 David Halberstam, *The Reckoning*. New York: Avon, 1986.

20 Abegglen and Stalk, *Kaisha*, ch. 7.

21 For the argument that corporate effectiveness is sustained by a sense of being treated justly, see James O'Toole, *Vanguard Management*. New York: Doubleday, 1985, ch. 12.

22 Personal communication with trade union delegation visiting the Niagra Institute, Canada, October 1987.

23 Abegglen and Stalk, *Kaisha*, p. 146. A conclusion also reached by Robert Reich; see *Tales of a New America*. New York: Times, 1987, p. 226.

24 Abegglen and Stalk, *Kaisha*, p. 141.

25 Abegglen and Stalk, *Kaisha*, pp. 131–7.

26 See also Lester C. Thurow (ed.), *The Management Challenge: Japanese Views*. Cambridge, Mass.: MIT Press, 1985, for the views of Japanese managers themselves.

27 The domination of high quality small-batch manufacturing is a major theme of Reich, *The Next American Frontier*.

9

The Shotgun Wedding: Industry and Academia

In the autumn of 1987 I was invited by the Niagara Institute to use my dilemmas methodology to 'mediate' a meeting of the deans of arts and sciences at Ontario universities. The theme was to be 'The university and its partners', including Canadian industry and state and federal governments, professional associations, students, parents and alumni. I have this irresistible urge to insinuate myself between rocks and hard places but this was stonier than usual. The experience reminded me of Dean Swift's famous adage, 'Hell hath no fury as when a friend of both parties tactfully intervenes.'

The problem of how business and government might better relate to universities and vice versa is not, of course, confined to Canada. As I write, university lecturers in Britain are refusing to mark university exams, thereby threatening the careers of tens of thousands of students. Their pay in real terms has fallen 30 per cent in the last eight years. They are refusing a pay offer 2 per cent lower than the annual rate of inflation. The Reagan years similarly witnessed a significant reduction in Federal support for US universities.

How can it be that three conservative governments and pro-business champions of free enterprise could under-fund their educational sectors in the midst of the greatest explosion of knowledge-intensive industries in the history of economic development? Who, looking back over this decade, will believe the sheer depth of this folly? Mrs Thatcher has beaten the teachers in the state system, but how well or wisely do beaten people teach?

The extraordinary spectacle of pro-business forces trashing the only institution that can save them, as low-wage countries capture the markets for simple products, cries out for explanation. There is no quicker way of discovering the answer than to place yourself in the midst of the contending political forces and to feel yourself an academic/business hybrid, if not a mongrel, pulled in several directions simultaneously. This conference was such an experience.

The speeches from the floor were mostly statesmanlike, eloquent and responsible, calls to a partnership vital to the economic future of Canada. A casual visitor might think that here was a country with a clear sense of where its future lay and with broad agreement on how to get there. The small-group meetings which convened after each plenary session to discuss the issues raised were something else. Here the real bitterness emerged, and the rage of the academicians against business and government was forcefully expressed, not least against the miserably compromised mediator who stood in their midst – the 'servant of power', the 'creature of the cooptables' were two of the more memorable phrases.

The Case for Partnership

Adam Zimmerman, President and CEO of Noranda Mines, began by asking 'who sets the agenda?' Surely, academics with their conceptual and intellectual skills, their capacity to grasp issues, their many objections to the way things were currently done, had the capacity to initiate upon the wider society their assessments of what was wrong and what could be done to improve things. Noranda desperately needed help and persistently invited academics to assist the company. He was at a loss to understand how any group of experts with valuable knowledge to contribute could lose control of the agenda. Organizations like the Fraser Institute were examples of how academic experts could participate in their own way and on their own terms, because they had a coherent body of knowledge to contribute. Fraser and similar centres were attracting money away from universities. The universities had to argue the benefits of particular projects to business and to academia jointly and *take the lead* in identifying social problems, environmental problems and potential crises in the future. No large industry was unaffected by such problems and funds would be forthcoming if the case was forcefully made.

This plea was reinforced by Dr William Sibley. Universities needed *autonomy* rather than independence. There was an important difference: independence meant that the university stood aside, an oasis of freedom, with a special variant of 'academic freedom' for those who talked but did not act politically. What was needed today was autonomy, literally self-rule, or the ability to set the rules in discussions with industry in a way that protected and advanced the integrity of the knowledge being communicated.

For Douglas Wright, President of the University of Waterloo, Canada was suffering from seriously outmoded attitudes. 'We think that abundant natural resources are guarantors of wealth.' But, in fact, most primary producers of raw materials in the world were far poorer than those who added value to those materials. Raw material prices were down and likely to stay down. It was not Riccardo's 'natural advantage' but *learned* advantage which created modern wealth.[1] Canada could not protect its manufacturing base against newly industrializing countries unless she went up the knowledge ladder fast and filled everything the economy made with all the information at its command. Those who could not read the writing on the wall would find their backs up against it. The gulf between industry and academia was a threat to all our futures. It had to be bridged.

This world shift to knowledge intensity offered universities a historic opportunity. It is one area in which Japan does not excel. Their universities are far apart from their business and, if we can build bridges faster, the trends of the last four decades can still be reversed. Thanks to the near universality of the English language, we have a massive advantage in making world information flow into wealth-creating processes. Nearly all knowledge is now of economic importance. Maths used to be largely academic but is now widely used in technology, computers and communications. You can't make language computers without help from psychologists, linguists, philosophers, educators and modern languages. The experience of putting the *New Oxford Dictionary* on software was a major task encompassing half a dozen disciplines.

Help from universities could take many forms and need not be confined to commerce. Why were social science departments not offering to assist governments in making social programmes more effective and to give the tax payer better value for money? Nor should help be confined to 'high tech'. We have to be 'more than hewers of silicon and drawers of software'. The humanities were every bit as important because they could make products or environments more aesthetic, better designed and more valuable in human terms. They could make services into a richer and more informative experience. William Sibley concurred that almost every product but those in exquisite taste and of masterful complexity could be made cheaper in the Third World.

But none of this would be possible, said Dr Alvin Lee, President and Vice Chancellor of McMaster University, unless the university could impart the process of moral evaluation, which included the discipline of detaching oneself from any one view and describing all conflicting values in a fair and balanced manner, so as to assist society in choosing wisely. Such detachment only becomes neutrality or indifference if one fails to engage the environment. Academics, fully committed to the solution of their society's problems, need to show how judgements can be weighed and views reconciled. Man was now recovering for himself the moral attributes he had earlier projected upon God, and was becoming a self-conscious self-reflecting moral agent. The values we chose to produce and to personify were moral choices with which the universities should be deeply concerned.

The Reluctant Groom

Yet, despite all these imperatives, academia was proving a reluctant groom. 'Government is standing over us with a shotgun', said one discussant, 'and saying, "you marry industry or else!" In the meantime, our pappy is cutting off our money and I'm saying, "Look, this is a hag – I don't want her. I never did. Just because she seduced a few friends of mine. . . ." But the heat is on.'

Why are the ample opportunities described by the speakers not being seized with greater alacrity? Why aren't Canadian universities celebrating the influent society in which they could become the knowledge elite, described by Daniel Bell?[2] Perhaps government is holding a 'shotgun', but the 'bride' is both wealthy and educable and the future of millions is at stake.

One difficulty in the way of a better relationship with industry was the position of the deans themselves, suspended uneasily between the values of administration and those of multiple disciplines. These potential mediators were typically struggling to hold together a set of diverging forces and were barely in control. One discussant put it well:

A dean is not really a top manager . . . more a middle manager caught between the faculty and the administration. You have a whip to crack, but you are faced with departmental heads of considerable ferocity. I feel like a lion-tamer surrounded by lions.

The plenary speakers also tried to explain why the visions they described were not being taken up, and why, in Zimmerman's words, 'the universities were always asking for money on trust, like an inferior with his hand extended . . .'. The tenure system and collective bargaining were being used to resist partnership. All an industrialist ever met were moonlighting individual professors and fund-raisers. There was no set of coherent ideas or policies. In Sibley's view, the root of the problem was that there was no credible decision-making capacity within the university, no one able to combine the aims of different disciplines to focus these upon the problems of society, which were multidimensional. Accordingly, the university was caught in a trap. Government was imposing austerity until it saw signs of reform, yet this was only causing universities to retrench around their departmental fortresses. When cuts were demanded, the bridges were the first to go, and each department became more isolated and more defiant.

Gordon McNabb, Associate to the Principal of Queen's University, complained that universities had resisted the strategic grants programme, which encouraged interdisciplinary problem-focused work, organized around an agreed strategic purpose. They still wanted the money to go to individuals 'to do their own thing'. The professoriate was ageing. Its demographics were skewed towards those recruited in the 1960s when funds were sharply increased and the baby boomers had arrived. The spirit of those days lingered. What exacerbated the present impasse was the compartmentalization of the university, kept in a state of fragmentation by the system of peer review which rewarded each member to a discipline for staying within that discipline. Thus a good economist could acknowledge 'externalities' but was not expected to stray beyond the boundaries of his discipline to deal with these.

Interdisciplinary syntheses were frequently rejected by review committees as programmes of research for failing to come up to the standards of purity demanded by the individual disciplines, who regarded the work of neighbouring disciplines with contempt and resisted the 'dilution' of their own approaches. Many interdisciplinary centres in the universities lasted only long enough to be disintegrated by these centrifugal forces which coveted their funds. Promotion was not for solving the problems of industry and society but for augmenting the methods of the discipline itself.[3]

Yet the accusation that corporate sponsorship corrupted disciplines was not supported by available studies. A survey of 12,000 academics in biotech showed that those receiving corporate support performed better on strictly scientific criteria. We overlook the extent to which needed applications give meaning and zest to our work.

Alvin Lee reminded the conference that compartmentalizing and fragmentation killed community. The universities lacked shared social meanings and moral commitments which transcended the use of each discipline as a tool. Were not the values created by Canadians in the international market-place of tomorrow an issue worth commitment? A university system clearly in the forefront of a national campaign to increase productivity and put knowledge into goods and services would never want for funding.

Unfortunately, the academic view of moral commitment was a view from the sidelines, not from the fray itself. Zimmerman complained that industry needed to 'open the minds of the decided' in the universities. The professoriate were fiercely pro-women, anti-South African and anti-smoking and preferred to lecture business people rather than help them. That women deserved greater equality or that apartheid was morally unjustified were obvious moral judgements. How to change these situations without hurting those with legitimate interests in the corporations' future was full of dilemmas and complications.

Not all the plenary speakers felt that partnership with industry would bring the benefits described. Warnings came from Sister Frances Ryan, the editor of the *Catholic New Times*. The academic community had lost touch with its early religious origins and was godless (with a small g). Neutrality and disengagement had taken the place of commitment. To have no purpose of your own is to invite others to use you as an instrument.

As Derek Bok, the president of Harvard, had written recently, a whole generation of students had grown up without the dreams of Martin Luther King, the inspiration of the Kennedies, ideals for human emancipation or dreams of a better world. They had known only divisive Cold War, economic shocks and a return to the ethic of self-advancement, a world shrunken into private ambitions.[4]

It was now being claimed that they would find their salvation in assisting Canadian industry, but what moral commitment or transcendent goals did industry stand for? A menu of careerism, a smorgasbord of private options was no answer. Without shared purposes and moral meanings everything falls to the ground in a culture of self-absorption and narcissism. We have entered an age when many students can't describe their own personal goals and can't explain why they have come to the university. We are 'strip mining' students to gain their marketable skills while junking the rest. But the mere pursuit of affluence can't help the poor, the marginal or the needy. Ironically, it can't even lift our economy. Something altogether finer is needed.

Sister Ryan went on to extol the university as a critical force in society. What made us believe then that industry, as presently constituted, was appropriately designed for its task and needed only our knowledge, facilitation and enthusiasm? Here she was joined by Jo Surich, director of education for the Ontario Federation of Labour. He declared himself a passionate opponent of 'one-dimensional man', the critique made by Herbert Marcuse of American positivism.[5]

According to this view the status quo 'out there' now was elevated to the standing of incontrovertible data and reality, while the ideals, negations and protests latent within ordinary people were of no significance. Social scientists were technicians of the power structure who must not challenge, criticize or question their corporate task-masters. Would that academics knew in what contempt businessmen held them: egg-heads, navel-gazers and persons obsessed with the underbellies of ants. If academics chose to become the creatures of corporations they would fully deserve such disdain.

There was no shortage of academics willing to testify that a minimum wage of 12 cents more per hour would bankrupt the Canadian economy. Jo had to be formally 'consulted' by people designing courses on entrepreneurship. But it was clear from the course content that anything or anyone standing between the entrepreneur and his objective must be broken, labour unions especially.

The university must not propagate a narrow truth. Heidegger became Dean of his university and sold his soul to Hitler and Nazism. If as academics you sell your souls, do not expect to get them back. Heidegger's betrayal was neither forgotten nor forgiven. Today we face the very real prospect that Labor will become the victims of a massive industrial retrenchment, that real wages will deteriorate sharply and that in any 'partnership' you form with industry, working people will be squeezed, partly by force, partly by deteriorating education. Don't ask for your souls back if you participate in that process. There will always be tension between the drive for efficiency and the far broader values of education. What the market values and what people want are not the same. We have to fight for that difference or it will die.

Ferment in the Small Groups

Because the balance of opinion from industry, government and the presidencies of Ontario universities had been in favour of greater partnership, several of the small group discussions were bitter, vehement and resisting. There could be no better indication of how lofty and laudable goals fare among those expected to implement them. I moved from group to group so I can give only a general impression of what was said.

What had completely been overlooked, as several discussants emphasized, was the sheer *power* of business. They held the purse-strings. They would pay for what they wanted and would junk the rest. Industry was in a hurry. It wanted quick results and an immediate and obvious connection between its expenditure and results. Just how long could a university which took initiatives sustain them in the face of people who knew the price of everything and the value of nothing?

The philistinism of business could be seen by their expenditure on R&D, which was half that of several international competitors. What with Canadian social programmes being untouchable, the universities were simply the victims of a general cost squeeze and doctrinal thinking about government as a 'burden' on the economy. They had to be joking. One discussant held up a bumper sticker. 'If you think knowledge is expensive, try ignorance!' The fact was that education was the economy's seed-bed and the politicians in their wisdom had elected to save on seed, because it could be cut back with less immediate clamour.

Nowhere in the presentations was it recalled that the prime mission of a university is to teach undergraduates, and that unsupported by research budgets which allowed teachers to communicate their latest discoveries the whole bridge joining teachers to students was crumbling. If the country was too poor to educate undergraduates, it should admit this, instead of complaining that a seriously eroded educational 'base' was unhelpful to money-makers. Wealth could only be created by well-educated students after they had qualified. To extract additional efforts from chronically under-funded under-staffed universities was like starving the cow you expected to milk. Partnership can only apply to a small *part* of the university, a few graduate departments at best. It first had to fulfil its base mission.

And this should be paid for by tax payers, whose children directly benefit and can complain if they do not. Should it be paid for by commercial pressure groups which seek to reap what they never really sowed in the first place?

Notorious in this respect were the 'matching grant' provisions. Under this rule a university can be given half what it needs from the government to do a job and is expected to 'find' the other half. You can't, as a practical matter, get this from the department which won the grant. That would penalize it for outreach efforts; so you take it from the teaching base of the university and, bit by bit, the fundamentals of education erode.

The distinction between pure and applied knowledge, which it is fashionable nowadays to disparage, remains crucial because it reminds us that pure research is the *source* of what is applied. Block the spring and you will lose everything. We know that Canada's extractive industries are exploiting raw materials millions of years in the making that will be exhausted soon. Do not be surprised if the extractive industries treat universities in the same way – as if there was no tomorrow.

Politicians have been saying for years now that 'universities are badly run' or 'wastefully administered'. Commission after commission has been set up which reported it was not so. But it's an easy and popular thing to say. What is going to suffer is *liberal education*. It is the residue after industrialists have had their pick. It is the pound of flesh cut from near the heart of the university. For what industrialists are interested in are the already strong departments. They were rarely interested in the 'blood circulation' of the university as a whole.

The discussants were also critical of those who had urged the university to take moral stands. It was easy to say but just try it! Faculties consisted of some of the most individualistic, contentious and talkative persons on earth. The difficulty in speaking 'for the university' was like trying to dress you hair at a hair-splitters' convention. Even if there was broad agreement on women's rights and apartheid, there was no agreement on what should be done about these. To fulminate publicly on evils yet have no plan to combat these only brought the university into disrespect. Besides, a dean, with much of his time given over to administration, was a morally compromised person in the eyes of many purists.

The university should teach the processes of moral valuing, not jump to its own conclusions and close off issues. Inquiry should never be seen to end.

As of this moment, the universities were caught between two irreconcilable attitudes on the part of politicians. They claimed that the university was 'free' and what is taught and discovered was none of the government's business and far beyond its ken. Let the 'egg-heads' do what they want. Yet, at the same time, they expected that in exchange for their subsidy they had a right to get from universities what they wanted. It was a 'double-bind' in which academics felt trapped.

At least some of these tensions were directed at the author himself, an academic manqué, a corporate-kept man, doing soft-shoe shuffles for his industrial sponsors. His first book, *Radical Man*, had at least shown some courage in criticizing the reigning orthodoxy,[6] but how horribly had he now subsided into fudging clear critiques of corporate power.

Suitably chastened I retired to let all this sink in and to see what resolvable dilemmas might be hidden in this hornets' nest.

Rhetoric: the Poisoned Fruit

There is something both exciting and appalling in working with academics and politicians instead of business people. The former are in so many ways more articulate, succinct and impressive in what they have to say. Having practiced on captive audiences for years, the way they marshal ideas and express their convictions makes me feel at home.

But, at another level, one begins to realize how polarized the best of rhetoric becomes. To be articulate in the sense of sharpening ideas and communicating them forcefully leads inexorably to *an entrapment within one's own rhetoric*. It is almost as if language was entertaining in proportion to the irreconcilability of the ideas expressed. There is a fatal cleverness about the debates recorded here, which doom some of the best and brightest minds to an eternity of sterile jousting and a total inability to resolve their differences. If, compared with the protagonists here, many business people are 'dull', at least they can think together rather than fence with each other and score points.

One wonders how great a drag on our capacity to create wealth is the Western tradition of *flamboyant individualism* in which the purpose of life is the theatrical presentation of a unique personality, and to be different is far more important than to be reconciled. I had not had such fun at a conference for years – the personal attacks notwithstanding – but had that fun been purchased at the price of a perpetual divide among adversaries?[7] All this I thought to myself. A much shortened account of what I said follows.

The Dilemmas of Partnership

I would like to begin by expanding on what several speakers said about the sheer excitement and challenge of the knowledge revolution. I want to persist in this because visions of what is becoming possible can make the major issues which divide us seem small in comparison. We can transcend our present disputes, I am sure, but only if we have a shared scenario of what our closer partnership could achieve for the university, for industry, for Canada and for the world.

Many of you had angry things to say about industry. So much did I once agree with you that I must be one of the few graduates who, having earned an MBA and a doctorate from the Harvard Business School, proceeded to avoid contact with major corporations for the next fifteen years, working with poor people's organizations and a half-way house for ex-convicts instead. Why have I now returned to business? Some of you had interesting observations on the compromises of middle age. You may be right. But I believe I returned to business because it has changed beyond recognition in the last decade, because it is a more open system for the pursuit of learning than most universities I know of and because its ability to act and then learn from that action is the way people and societies develop.

I am not technically trained and I must be one of the poorest experts on what new technologies have in store for us. But let me tell you about just two developments with which I've been in touch these last three months and judge for yourself what these could do for a partnership between universities, governments and industry.

My friend, Carl Hodges, runs the Environmental Research Center at the University of Arizona. As part of the state's 'arid lands project', Carl's team has isolated two dozen or more halophytes (saltwater grasses and shrubs) from more than a thousand collected throughout the world.

These particular halophytes contain seeds from which vegetable oil can be derived, an oil richer in key nutrients than oils made from olives, safflower seeds or corn. When the oil is extracted, the residue will feed poultry and fish. The hay from the dried grasses will feed cows, horses, camels and donkeys. A high-pressure saltwater spray can leach the surplus salt from the leaves of halophytes to make them edible. The only fresh water required is what the animals need to drink.

There are now experimental farms in Oman and in Mexico with villages that live largely from saltwater agriculture and aquaculture that included talopi-fish, a traditional Chinese delicacy, and water hyacinths, the two being mutually nurturant. I do not have to tell you what saltwater agriculture could do for Africa, much of the Middle East and drought-plagued Third World countries. As you may imagine, there are problems aplenty with the sabotage of early experiments, corrupt local officials, peasants afraid of change, new economic arrangements, reluctant and suspicious corporations – problems enough for academics in several fields.

In a parallel programme, Carl is a prime contractor to the Biosphere project funded by businessman Billie Wood Prince and run by the Institute for Ecotechnics. For the first time, a part of the total ecosystem is to be enclosed within a giant glass biosphere in Arizona, which includes everything from human pioneers to birds, plants, animals and crops. The pioneers have rehearsed several of the major Greek tragedies to give them emotional resilience for the years they will spend in each other's company. The system will be closed to everything but light from the sun and information to discover how the elements within interact.

But there are even more immediate opportunities. Sony and Philips have jointly created a CD-I, otherwise known as a compact interactive disc or optical disc. This is roughly $5\frac{1}{2}$ inches in diameter. Two of these will hold the entire volumes of the *Encyclopaedia Britannica* together with pictures, text, sound and animation (video is also possible but makes the disc far less capacious). With such technology you could explore gallery by gallery the National Museum of Art in

Ottowa or anywhere else in the world, letting the viewer 'walk' down any corridor or around any gallery in the order of choosing, with audio or written commentaries on every picture. You can cross-index every feature in the world of art important to another feature, allowing the learner to follow themes, techniques and developments.

The medical school at Erasmus University in Holland, along with half a dozen 'centres of application of excellence' at the universities of Leiden, Groningen and Amsterdam, are busy working on how these discs could best be used. Virtually every medical disease known to man together with the sounds of faulty ears and lungs can be displayed in full colour and offered to medical students for diagnosis. Symptoms can be fed into a computer encyclopaedia to elicit visual descriptions that either match or don't. The possibilities for home diagnosis, now that the 'boomers' are all ageing together, are boundless. You could enter a dress shop in the late 1990s, punch your measurements into the machine and 'dress yourself' on screen in colours, styles and fits which the factory starts to make the moment you decide.

Surely, there is a psychology, a sociology, an economics, a mathematics, a law, an aesthetics and, yes, a moral dimension to such developments. And I can tell you what, left to itself, industry might do with this technology. When I last inquired, the first mass-market disc was to be *The Life of Frank Sinatra*.[8] So you see, industry might need your help in making choices. . . .

With this vision to bring us together and to draw us on, I would like to return to the dilemmas surfaced by this conference. I have detected three of these, more salient, I believe, and more central than the rest:

1 the enhancement and protection of the university's *basic mission* to teach and develop *'pure' knowledge* versus the need to *apply* its *knowledge* so as to help the whole nation compete economically;
2 the *disciplinary* base of the university versus the *interdisciplinary* nature of most creative solutions;
3 the university as a force for improving the *techniques* and *practices* of wealth creation versus the university as a *moral* and *critical* force within society, questioning its goals, priorities and practices.

Let me take these one by one.

Dilemma 9.1

The enhancement and protection of the university's *basic mission* to teach and develop 'pure' knowledge versus the need to *apply* its knowledge so as to help the whole nation compete economically.

I have 'mapped' this in Dilemma 9.1 with applying knowledge on the vertical axis and the university's basic mission on the horizontal axis. Obviously, we must avoid the extremes – the university strip-mined on the one hand and the still fashionable snobbery of the English-speaking cultures 'education for the independent scholar' on the other.

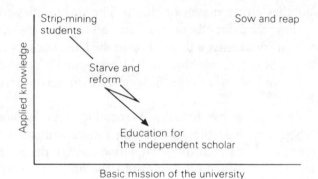

Dilemma   9.1

We cannot afford the latter affectation because knowledge is becoming too complex to be carried in the individual heads of itinerant experts. Knowledge as it grows and grows is necessarily social, the shared property of extended groups and networks.

Still less can Canada, the United States or Britain afford the present adversary relations between education on the one hand and pro-industry governments on the other. The attempt to 'starve into reform' the structure of universities is proving counterproductive. The ideal of reconciliation is that the environment will reap more from the universities if it sows more, and will sow more if it is helped in its reaping. Deans are not without ways of persuasion. A skill shortage is rapidly approaching us and campus recruiters will very soon be cutting each other's throats and bidding up salaries in an attempt to recruit the scarce supply of students in certain disciplines.

Could we not persuade them to pay 'up-front' instead of 'at the end' for skill shortages they might have helped to avoid?

A condition of vigorous recruiting on campus is that the companies who are given privileges and the cooperation of the campus appointments bureau must have contributed something to the supply of qualified students and not just the demand. While state-supported institutions could probably not bar access to the campus, they could do a lot more for companies that gave than for companies that did not, including publishing donor lists to influence students choosing which 'corporate citizen' to work for.

There is a massive increase in in-house corporate education and the notion that universities can get no money for their 'basic mission' of teaching, when many corporations have similar missions, is fanciful. There are dozens of ways of pooling resources and developing parallel curricula.

Any attempt to starve universities into reform is stupid, but so is the habit of fighting back by cutting disproportionately the courses in engineering and administration closest to the government's and to industry's concerns. Could not presidents and deans make agreements with government that every increment of research and knowledge applied to industry's needs be matched by a proportionate amount of funding given the university for its pursuit of knowledge? In this way, a 'virtuous circle' of sowing and reaping, with each increasing together in agreed proportions, could help to develop *both* the basic mission *and* the volume of expert applications.

It is important not to overdo the value of 'pure' knowledge. In the hard sciences, where the speed of a falling body is the same in the laboratory as in the outside world, the university is vital as a place where experimentation can be carefully controlled. But most of the social sciences are not like that. Their subject matter is events *in the wider world* and the notion that such events can be simulated within the university, without serious loss to their significance, is illusory. For better or for worse, the process of application *is part* of sociology, medicine, psychology, economics, law, anthropology and organizational behaviour. There are few truths that can be isolated in these disciplines and their integrities are discoverable, if at all, in the heat of real events, not in monastic seclusion or splendid scholarly isolation. I would benefit these disciplines to test their suppositions in practice.

Dilemma 9.2

The *disciplinary* base of the university versus the *interdisciplinary* base of most creative solutions.

This is a tough one. We have to avoid both extremes. We must avoid single-principle imperialism, the secret aspirations of many disciplines that they will find the independent variable which controls all other variables – not to mention other disciplines – and we must avoid rent-an-expert, a multidisciplinary job shop of technicians vying for corporate favours and willing to give solemn testimony on anything, if paid. This rock and whirlpool are set out in Dilemma 9.2. Equally serious are the disintegrative forces threatening interdisciplinary studies which lie between the horns.

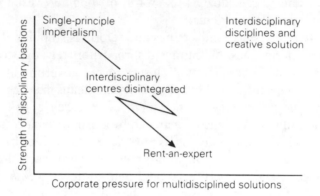

Dilemma 9.2

The answer is to get multiple sponsors for key interdisciplinary centres like MIT's Media Lab, whose watchword is less 'publish or perish' than 'demo or die'.[9] It is funded by IBM, GE, AT&T, Home Box Office, all the major networks, 3M, Polaroid, Kodak, Sony, Hitachi, Mitsubishi, Matsushita, Sanyo and Fujitsu to name a few. Another part of the answer is the *interdisciplinary discipline* of which systems theory, cybernetics, learning theory, organizational development and general semantics are examples.

Instead of staking out a rival piece of territory and professing that genes, or social institutions, or reinforcement, or economic gain or brain physiology 'explain' all other phenomena, systems dynamics allows all variables and all systems to play their part in an interdependent world. The Systems Dynamics Group at MIT, headed by Jay Forrester and Peter Senge, is an example of such 'bridging disciplines', with several outstanding corporations, Hanover and Apple, for example (see chapters 4 and 5), but also Herman Miller, Analog Devices, Ford and Shell as members of an ongoing network.[10]

Such interdisciplinary centres *must be evaluated by the industries they are attempting to serve*, along with other interdisciplinary scholars. If they are left to the mercy of disciplines taken separately, they will never be judged worthy since they have given only part of their time to the discipline which is evaluating them and have abandoned that discipline's imperial mission, an apostasy which is not typically forgiven. Thus it is more important that the Environmental Research Center at the University of Arizona establish saltwater agricultural communities in an ongoing economic system than that plant biologists approve of what they are doing. It is more important that *The Life of Mozart* on compact interactive disc achieves market goals and critical acceptance by music lovers than that the history department agree with the interpretation of Mozart's marriage.

But care must be taken to return to the disciplines what is taken from them. The overheads from interdisciplinary projects should be paid to the disciplines in proportion to the percentage of staff supplied by these disciplines. Unless this is done resentments will fester. People will be prepared to 'reach out' if the platforms they stand on do not collapse as a result, and if they can help to repay those who taught them what they know.

Dilemma 9.3

The university as a force for improving the *techniques* and *practices* of wealth creation versus the university as a *moral* and *critical* force within society, questioning its goals, priorities and practices.

(I had come to this point in my presentation when a faint restlessness began. Those in the back rows especially were looking at their watches, whispering and slipping from the room. Was I losing my grip on the audience? Had I offended or merely bored them? I do not usually lose my audience like this. So I turned up my grandiloquence several degrees in an attempt to keep their attention.)

This brings me to the last dilemma – if you will bear with me a few minutes longer. If we are just the coaches and the mentors of heightened economic performance, then we are reduced to the role of 'corporate kept-men' to use a phrase which one of you coined. If, on the other hand, we simply reject vehemently and utterly the institutions which 80 per cent of working people try to serve, we become enraged spectators on the edge of the economic stage, where the future of Canada is going to be worked out (see Dilemma 9.3).

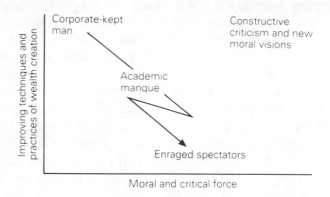

Dilemma   9.3

Many of you said, and wisely, that there was more to life than making money and becoming more efficient and that the university had to engage all of life and not just narrow acquisitive pressure groups. I largely agree with this sentiment. Where I disagree is with some of your premises. Who said that being narrow, acquisitive or efficient was a good way to create wealth? All the stereotypes you have of businessmen as greedy, philistine, ultra-competitive, preoccupied with personal gain, interested only in the short term, anti-intellectual and unconcerned with the plight of working people and the environment, are either untrue or, in so far as they are true, not conducive to creating value for this country.

The creation of value is first and foremost a moral issue of what to make for whom, or what service to offer. It is a question of philosophy, psychology, economics and aesthetics rolled into one. You speak as if we *knew* how to create wealth and that it was a routine, unjust and soul-destroying activity. In truth, we have only political prejudices, the eighteenth-century axioms of a Scottish schoolmaster and the self-serving commentaries of right-wing politicians.

You want a fairer world? How do you know that felt fairness and justice are not the cornerstones of a more creative work-place?[11] The scattered evidence I have seen suggests that this is so. We know that salary differentials are supposed to motivate and, to some extent, they do. But to *what* extent? At what point do those punished by low salaries just want to quit? And, if we made salaries more equal, what is the role of relative equality in maintaining the harmony and cooperation of the work-place? Is it relevant that Japan has a much lower spread between top and bottom salaries than we have? How do you know that the demands of knowledge-intensive businesses are so different from your own ideals?

What makes you think that self-interest and aggression are the chief virtues of business? Did you know that the chief axiom of Japanese business is *amae* or 'indulgent love' among business colleagues?[12] Did you know that Japan gives more of disposable household income to the poorest 20 per cent of its population than any other OECD country?[13]

Frankly, I don't know what values in what proportion create the best products, but I very much doubt if our present system has it figured right. We would not be losing our markets so fast if we knew. Of course, I'd *like* my own values to be the right ones, but I doubt the world will indulge me to that extent. I do suggest it could be the role of the university to find out just what combinations of equality and merit, or competition and cooperation, of toughess and tenderness and egoism and altruism will most enhance the creation of value.

Only *after* we have done this, and the results could surprise us, is it appropriate to complain that the values which enhance the creation of wealth do not include this important value or that one. But I question whether many values will be missing once we learn how to create and innovate. My position is not that values unreflected in the market-place are without importance, but that market forces are like fair winds and tides which we can ride in the direction we wish to go, harnessing their power to what we want.

In an age of information we could buy selectively from corporations who promote and educate their women employees and their minority groups and treat their unions well. We can use buying power to punish dictatorial regimes and reward those trying to reform and democratize. We can patronize the environmentally sensitive and ensure that despoilers of our environment feel our wrath.

It is no coincidence that books like *The 100 Best Companies to Work For* are best-sellers. As the skill shortage bites, corporations must not only attract the best recruits but keep them long enough for continuous learning and educate them for most of their lives. You seem terrified of becoming 'industrialized', when increasing numbers of corporations are having to become 'universitized' in the sense of becoming teaching and learning organizations.

What, for example, should Philips, Sony or Apple do with the technology of compact interactive discs? Isn't this a moral issue as much as a strategic one? We could, of course, make *The Life of Frank Sinatra*, but the spin-offs and the fall-out of this activity would be minor – a few thousand elderly people lost to the nostalgia boom. What if we used the discs to present Canada to the world – its art, its scenery and its culture? What if we used discs to simulate complex types of multimachine manning and flexible manufacturing? Suppose workers could learn in a fraction of the time by making mistakes and losing only phantom thumbs and fingers? Would that not ramify in scores of Canadian factories? Might we not accelerate the learning of school children to an unprecedented extent with Knowledge Navigators, which balance visuo-spatial learning with written and audio materials and which 'interact' with the accumulating knowledge and curiosity of the child?[14]

Nothing dismays me more than your statements that all business wanted was uncritical technicians and lick-spittle loyalists. Canadian industry is challenged by economic systems from the far ends of the earth, which represent a revolution in Western ways of thinking, a sea change and paradigm shift more radical than anything that has gone before. These cultures work *with* their government, postpone their profits, target key technologies, celebrate aestheticism, embrace their unions, merge and acquire only by consent and are reshaping the world economic order by buying simpler manufactured goods from their poorer neighbours, while intensifying the knowledge in their own products.

I don't say they are right, or that we must become like them. I am saying it is open to discussion and to the critical intelligence of the universities. Without your *constructive* criticisms and suggestions – and I stress constructive – Western economies may never know what hit them and many industrialists will feel giddy in a world turned upside down. . . . Thank you very much.

This was said hastily, for the room was now two-thirds empty and I was wondering what I'd done to offend them. Just then a faint cheer broke out from the room beyond the conference hall and an emissary ran into the hall beaming, 'It's just come through on the radio,' he announced. 'The increase in university budgets is to be 5½ per cent.' 'We were expecting 4 per cent', I was told. 'What a relief! Let's have a drink to celebrate.' I took 'Action steps for deans to take' off the wall. It was over.

Notes

1 The case is well made by Bruce Scott in the opening chapter of Bruce Scott and George Lodge, *American Competitiveness*. Boston, Mass.: Harvard Business School Press, 1985.

2 Daniel Bell, *The Coming of Post-Industrial Society*. New York: Basic Books, 1976.

3 All this is familiar stuff for academic survivors of the 1960s; see Theodore Rosak (ed.), *The Dissenting Academy*. New York: Pantheon, 1968.

4 Derek Bok, *Beyond the Ivory Tower*. Cambridge, Mass.: Harvard University Press, 1982, p. 305.

5 Herbert Marcuse, *One-Dimensional Man*. Boston, Mass.: Beacon Press, 1964.

6 Charles M. Hampden-Turner, *Radical Man: Towards a Theory of Psychosocial Development*. New York: Anchor, 1971; London: Duckworth, 1973.

7 The point is made well by Iain L. Mangham, *Organizations as Theatre*, New York: Wiley, 1987.

8 Personal communication with American Interactive Media in Los Angeles.

9 See Stewart Brand, *The Media Lab: Inventing the Future at MIT*, New York: Viking, 1987.

10 The network is officially known as the Program in Systems Thinking and the New Management Style, of which this author is also a member.

11 See Elliot Jaques, *Free Enterprise Fair Employment* (New York: Crane Russak, 1982), especially the research on 'felt fairness' and its correlations with effective operations; see also the last two chapters of James O'Toole, *Vanguard Management*, New York: Doubleday, 1985.

12 See Takie Sugiyama Lebra, *Japanese Patterns of Behavior*. Honolulu, Hawaii: University Press of Hawaii, 1976. The concept is also associated with mutual dependence, a notion quite alien to Western individualism.

13 See European Management Forum, *Annual Report on International Competitiveness*. Geneva, Switzerland: European Management Forum, 1986.

14 These thoughts were encouraged by conversation with Frans Cochius of Philips, until recently the head of Home Interactive Systems.

10

The Hunt for the Unicorn:
a Critique of Pure Profit

The lessons of this book include the notion that any one value or criterion of excellence pursued in isolation is almost bound to steer you into trouble, even catastrophe. We saw in chapter 3, for example, that a runaway division of labour got Thorn into severe difficulties. Labour need not only be divided but integrated. Headlong pursuit of the economies of scale was similarly flawed, as was too much rationality in planning, too harsh or too cosy a relationship with the work-force, and too great an emphasis on increasing turnover.

We saw that even Bill O'Brien's highly integrated and metaphoric concepts like leanness and localism *could be turned into mental spaghetti by a linear mind-set.* Leanness could be maximized, as in the minds of an anorexic girl who starves herself to death. Even creativity can become a cult as we saw at Apple, a definition so 'insanely great' that accountability, cost-consciousness and every other value is slain at the foot of the idol. Moreover, there are always *two* opposed ways of wrecking the ship. You can sacrifice it to something hard, unambiguous, precise, detailed and definite; or to something soft, vague, general, pervasive and indefinite. Nemesis comes in alternative guise, as a compulsive bureaucrat or a mumbo-jumbo mystic.

I suspect most of you will agree with this without too much trouble. Yet in the corner of your minds there will lurk a few absolutes and ultimates, criteria so important that these are, of course, exceptions to what I have been arguing here. One of these reservations is likely to be profitability. All values are relative, you may think, but the need to profit, that is the one pure truth beneath the shifting sands, that is the commercial equivalent of fundamentalist scripture. When all *other* values have been finely balanced, virtuously cycled and transformed into larger meanings, profit will remain 'the bottom line', the ultimate arbiter of the effectiveness of overall strategy. I fear this simply is not so.

I have left to the last chapter my concerns about profit as a moral compass because I needed the force of earlier arguments to assault this last 'bastion of linearity', which will hold out long after the other fortresses have been breached. But we cannot reconcile dilemmas, which, as we have seen, are closely interconnected with each other, if *one* horn among them all remains as a Sacred Unicorn, an imperative beyond question and beyond dispute.

Now no one who leads an organization and plans strategies seriously can doubt that the generating of profits is among those processes which are vital to the survival and expansion of a business. It does not help to stigmatize as greedy an ingredient so important to the learning race and so necessary to its acceleration. Unfortunately, the emphasis on profitability goes much further than this. From being a *necessary* condition for long-term survival, it is often extolled to the point of being a *sufficient* condition, nay the be-all and end-all of economic activity itself, the 'pure essence' to which all other measures dance attendance and to which all other concerns can be distilled.[1]

This attitude seems to have a curious fascination for those schooled in the Puritan ethic, with its yearning for some unambiguous sign of divine favour, something with which to confound bishops, princes and feudal vestiges, whose authority rested upon a vague mystique and an alleged organic place in the great chain of being. Countable, methodical and demonstrable success was the banner of the bourgeois revolution, the yardstick used to belabour political opponents, rooted in the soil of an earlier tradition. Today this attitude is strongest in Britain and the United States, two countries who pioneered the industrial revolution and whose middle classes had to fight rhetorically much harder against an incomprehending and resistant government and against their land-holding classes. Later industrial revolutions in France, Germany, Scandinavia and Japan used 'catch-up' strategies in which government and business and the rural and industrial classes were less ideologically polarized.

The issue then is to what extent are profit and self-interest *ideological slogans* rather than tested means of learning to create wealth? Is the enthronement of the profit motive at the very pinnacle of bourgeois triumphalism the best way of generating wealth or the best way of *defending* that wealth once it has been amassed? A mere glance at Anglo-American politics in this last decade shows that 'the profit motive' has been a political winner, and that unregulated competitiveness well describes the conduct of politicians. But are such values also conducive to generating wealth or have we fatally confused the politics of wealth *retention* with the arts of value *creation*? There are major objections to the 'Unicorn' of pure profit.

1 Profit comes too late to steer by.
2 Motivationally the desire for profit is too narrow to learn from.
3 Profit conflicts with values of equal importance yet higher priority.
4 Putting profitability first makes business strategies too predictable and too easy to defeat.
5 Profiting is a 'text' which needs a 'context' to support it.
6 Profitability is an organic not a mechanical attribute.
7 Profiting may not apply to all the units within a strategic alliance.
8 When imitated by factions and persons within the corporation, profiting becomes suboptimal.
9 It cannot deal with societal and environmental 'addiction'.

Finally, we shall examine the place of profitability in an overall synergy of created values and wealth.

Profitability Comes Too Late to Steer By

The evidence that a company is profitable can, in many cases, come too late for the organization to be steered by those numbers. This is not always so. A restaurant gives you feedback on what customers have ordered and what they enjoyed on the same day that the food was served to them, and within days or hours of the ingredients being purchased. But most businesses are more complex. Friends in Shell estimated that current profits were the consequences of investments made up to thirty years earlier, yet it was hard not to take credit for something initiated before you heard of the company.

If you use present profitability as feedback on the success of *current* operations, the implications could propel you behind foremost into the future. You could have doomed yourself by a decision taken last month and not know it for another ten years or longer. Moreover, present profitability may be the consequence of several hundred decisions taken over the past decades. Knowing which of these decisions contributed more or less to current surpluses is a hopelessly complex calculation. Steering by profit is as difficult as steering a boat by the shape of its wake left three miles astern. It is ludicrously cumbersome and it would take a helicopter to look backwards.

The map coordinates drawn in this book may not have the precision and objectivity of profits, but they are at least contemporaneous. You steer between phenomena to port and starboard and, although their interpretation needs personal judgement, the financial performance, as we saw in chapter 3, will come later. Moreover, the fact of present profitability will not save you from the rocks or whirlpools in your path. Because profits are historical they are realized up to the very second that you are holed and start to sink.

General Motors, in the early 1970s, paid all its senior executives a profit-sharing bonus which they enjoyed right up to the sudden surge in the price of oil and the simultaneous assault of Japanese compacts and subcompacts. Because smaller cars made less profit per unit, GM executives were motivated not to emphasize or defend that end of the market and their destruction was nearly complete. They ran onto the rocks while counting their profits.

Motivationally the Desire for Profit is Too Narrow to Learn From

There are good reasons to suppose that a single-minded emphasis on profit and personal gain could reduce social learning.

Anyone familiar with a nursery knows that clamorous self-concern does not need to be learned. What has to be taught and developed is how to resolve one's own needs with those of others – at first parents and siblings, and then working colleagues, customers, workers, stakeholders and, finally, the inhabitants of distant lands and different cultures.

The crucial capacity is to cross these ever-increasing distances between departments, between technologies, between classes, between suppliers and customers, and between continents. In the world race to achieve such competencies, personal obsessions with what we can gain or grab are very likely to impede our understanding. Indeed, what needs to be emphasized is not gaining, *but contributing in order to gain*. Profit, like happiness, popularity and self-fulfilment, is best gained by *indirection*. If you are all out 'to close a sale' you are likely to run into resistance. Customers realize that you are much less interested in them than in extracting their money.

The reader may smile and reply that 'of course' you must convince customers that you are there to serve them. This is the essence of good sales technique. But my objection remains. Your real motive is one that cannot be authentically communicated without arousing suspicion and dislike. If, in fact, your customers' satisfactions and those of your employees are simply a means to an end to your own profitability, then sooner or later they will grasp this and repay you in kind.

Nor should you expect even a fraction of the loyalty, commitment and concern from those whom you regard as mere instruments of your purpose. Why should they confide in you, risk revealing genuine needs or trust you with their most creative concepts? In short, *you will learn less from them* than you would if you *reconciled* their welfare with your own need to gain therefrom and realized that the fulfilment of creative employees and the satisfaction of customers were *strategic priorities* for those seeking to profit therefrom.

We saw in chapters 4 and 6, where *double-loop* learning was described, that pushing your own position or profit had to be accompanied by a second loop, an invitation to others to inquire into the value of that position, so that it could be corrected and improved as necessary. The profit motive, if pursued narrowly, is likely to weaken further any emphasis on the second loop, the one that allows the environment to modify your conduct. Selling others 'a bill of goods' is not merely of doubtful honesty, it seriously impedes your discovery of what they really want.

For some curious reason, Americans have a love affair with the manipulative ethos. *How to Win Friends and Influence People* through a series of memorized techniques leaves most Europeans cold. America's only home-grown psychology is behaviourism, in which the experimenter, standing outside the subject in every sense of that word, shapes his/her behaviour by schedules of unilateral reinforcement.[2] Huge excitement was generated in the late 1950s by Vance Packard's *The Hidden Persuaders*, the account of a (failed) experiment at subliminal persuasion, in which advertisements were flashed upon the screen for microseconds. The intoxicating prospect of making them want it without them realizing that you have even tried to exert influence was enough to make the book a best-seller.

We find the same affection for lovable rogues in American popular culture, for example *The Music Man*, selling boys bands without the benefit of music, uniforms or instruments, *The Wizard of Oz*, a transformed medicine man, and W. C. Fields in *Never Give a Sucker an Even Break*. In *We're No Angels*, Humphrey Bogart sold empty jars labelled 'sea air', 'country air' and 'all-purpose air'. You unscrew the top and inhale deeply. The sheer hilarity goes on from there.

While it probably does a 'low-tech' economy little harm if Barnum quickens the flow of crowds through his exhibition by a notice saying 'To the Egress', it starts to matter a great deal when products grow in sophistication and become extensions of the human nervous system, like computers, cameras, telephones, fax machines etc. To have the makers and sellers of such products predominantly concerned with their own profits could be counterproductive in the extreme. In Arthur Miller's play *Death of a Salesman*, the myth of self-fulfilling confidence and the salesman's empty optimism were shown to be the ingredients of a tragedy, not comedy. Willy Loman is nearer to the truth than 'Professor' Harold Hill.

But is there any evidence that the drive to profit is being taken too far? The European Management Forum periodically surveys several thousand managers in the world's developed economies to see how they rate themselves, their own country and other economies on such measures as 'reputation for sales push'. By taking various indices from their survey and selecting measures of quality that might reasonably be expected to be in tension with each other,[3] we can estimate whether various values are being maximized or reconciled.

Now the 'sales push' of Americans, the single loop of 'getting them to want it', is likely to be in tension with the *eventual quality of the delivered product*. If Americans push too hard, harder than the quality of the product or service justifies, or push *instead* of improving the product, then this is likely to reduce the credibility of the communicator and the corporation being represented, so that 'sales push' and 'corporate credibility' become dilemmas instead of being reconciled.

Dilemmas 10.1 and 10.2 show just such a problem. We see in 10.1 that in reputation for market push the United States scores 76 out of a possible 100 and is third in the world behind Japan and Korea. But in reputation for product quality, the product which the pushing was all about, the United States scores only 65 out of 100 and is fifteenth in the world, behind Sweden, Denmark, Finland, Italy, West Germany, The Netherlands and others. Moreover, the world pattern is to have a

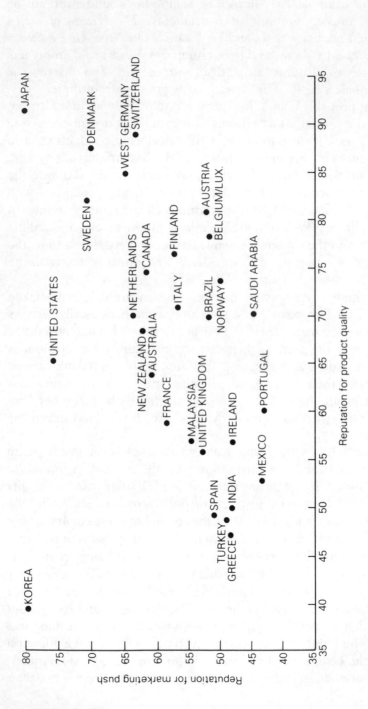

Dilemma 10.1
The numbers represent arbitrary units calibrating the results of the survey.
Source: European Management Forum, 1985

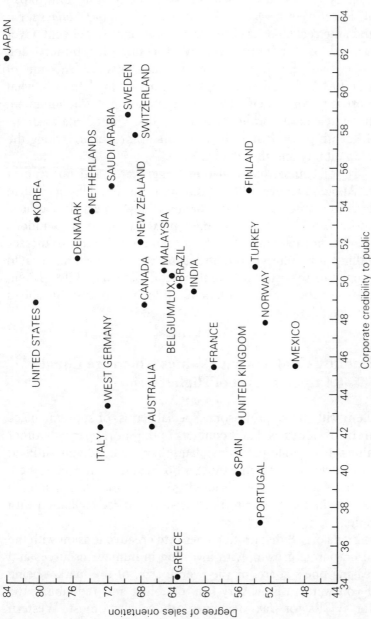

Dilemma 10.2
Source: European Management Forum, 1985

Degree of sales orientation

Corporate credibility to public

JAPAN
KOREA
DENMARK
NETHERLANDS
SAUDI ARABIA
SWEDEN
SWITZERLAND
UNITED STATES
WEST GERMANY
CANADA
NEW ZEALAND
MALAYSIA
BELGIUM/LUX.
BRAZIL
INDIA
FINLAND
ITALY
AUSTRALIA
FRANCE
UNITED KINGDOM
NORWAY
TURKEY
MEXICO
SPAIN
PORTUGAL
GREECE

product somewhat stronger than your push. Switzerland, Denmark, West Germany and Japan are all above 85 in product quality.

It probably increases corporate credibility if you are better than even your own publicity suggests. Dilemma 10.2 shows that, once again, America is near the top in its sales orientation; only Japan exceeds it. But if we ask *how much of what American corporations say is believed*, then the reckoning is clear. She scores only 49 per cent. Over half is wasted as the public simply discounts for puffery and manipulation. So, far from following the Japanese maxim of 'minimum effort and maximum impact' discussed in chapter 8, what we have here is maximum effort with minimum impact, the mountain belly of hype heaving to bring forth mice. The United States drops again to fifteenth place. Britain is worse on all measures, lacking the push, the credibility and the quality.

These are, of course, broad national aggregates and not true of Hotpoint, Apple, Hanover, Dow, ICI and specific US or British corporations encountered in earlier chapters. Dow especially may have learned more from the Japanese than most Japanese corporations have learned from each other. We must examine cultural weaknesses without falling for cultural stereotypes or generalizing the data to every company in that culture. Neither Jeoff Samson, Bill O'Brien, John Sculley nor the various leaders of Multichem put profits ahead of all other considerations.

Profitability Conflicts with Values which are Equally Important yet of Higher Priority

The problem with giving profit some special status, or supreme place in a hierarchy of values, is that it conflicts in the short term with other crucial values. If we hold profit inviolate, then we condemn all illicit intercourse between profit and those who belong in the same bed. Profit is a fruitful lover, not a sacred goddess, and, like a human being, she lives in a state of alternate tension and reconciliation with other people.

We saw in chapter 8 that profit comes into creative tension with the rapidity of corporate growth, with investing in human resources and with increasing one's share, or the overall size, of the market being served. If you want to grow very fast, doubling and redoubling the market for VCRs or fax machines, then what most Western companies pay out in dividends would be better spent on reinvesting in the company for faster growth. Asian companies are better adapted to this strategy than most Western ones because their shareholders want growth, not dividends. Leaders of Western corporations face very real dilemmas in combining these values strategically.

These are very critical questions, as we have seen, and are not solved by simply giving to profitability some higher standing. As we saw in chapter 8, the Japanese culture gives its strongest emphasis to market share and does not celebrate profitability at all. What is publicized is what the corporation has done for customers, as opposed to what it has done for itself and its owners. Market share is not only a more contemporary indicator of success, but it arguably measures the mutuality of suppliers and customers more reliably and more consistently than does profitability. For, while present profitability is usually a sign that value has been delivered to customers in the past, it is no guarantee that this is continuing in the present. Market share measures what has been put into market relationships, while profit measures what has been taken out – with all the perils attendant on taking out too much.

You can be profitable in making carbon paper for some time after the Xerox machine has started to destroy your market or making gas-guzzling cars after the oil price shock has struck, but not for long. The signs that you are in trouble are generally elsewhere, and the profit stream itself may give false comfort. In chapter after chapter we have seen that creating value means 'taking the bull by both its horns' and resolving dilemmas. Consistent with that view we must stop believing in the Sacred Unicorn of profitability. The beast, however beautiful, is a myth.

None of this denies that market share can also be idolized, pursued one dimensionally and end disastrously. What is crucial is how we think – linearly or systematically. If we see either profit or market share as measures of mutuality, we are thinking systemically; if we see these measures as straight lines of rigid rectitude, we are in trouble.

There are important issues of priority. The word is often loosely used in the sense of 'more important'. But priority means *before* or prior; that one value should be put before the other in a strategic sequence is to give it priority. Now, however important profitability may be to the fate of the corporation, it is not usually as effective to put profits *before* growth, *before* investment in human resources and *before* the enlargement of market share as it is to put this afterwards.

This is because taking profits out of an organization will usually slow its growth. The money paid to shareholders cannot be invested in upgrading the skills of employees, and higher margins may limit market share. The reverse sequence is generally more effective. Rapid growth will increase profitability in the longer run. Investing in human resources can make employees more productive, and an increased market share may cause competitors to withdraw and, in any event, can usually be turned to profitability later. It follows that profitability may be *more attainable strategically if it is postponed*, i.e. realized in the longer run rather than the shorter run.

But this is very unlikely to happen if profitability is prized above all else, or is seen as the only conclusive evidence of corporate success. It is this attitude which produces the short-termism for which much of Western industry is blamed and which financial markets are said to demand. It must be stressed that this is an attitude of mind more than a visible result. Long-term strategies, begun years earlier, come to fruition today and tomorrow. The long-term strategic player gets his jam today, *once the virtuous circle is well developed*. Indeed, the long term *includes* many short-term concerns. But the reverse is not true. Managing short term can mean the loss of longer-term objectives. As we might expect then, the United States and Britain, the bastions of profit maximizing, are less able to take long-term views than most other nations (table 10.1).

Putting Profitability First Makes Business Strategies Too Predictable and Too Easy to Defeat

We earlier compared Japanese strategy to judo or karate – will he strike first from the left or from the right? Which way will he swerve when I attack? Will it be more variety of products at the same cost, the same variety at lower cost or, worse still, lower costs and more variety? Will he buy market share and shave profits, or raise margins, make profits and go to the market for more investment and try then for market share? The important thing is to keep one's opponents guessing, most especially about which values will be sought in which order to make the more potent synergy.

If you know what your opponent will do next it is not too difficult to defeat him. The overriding concern of many Western corporations for short-term profits greatly limits their likely moves. If Asians attack

Table 10.1   Extent to which firms take a long-term view

Japan	83.61	1
Sweden	75.64	2
West Germany	74.55	3
New Zealand	72.50	4
Finland	70.48	5
Switzerland	70.24	6
Singapore	66.90	7
Norway	66.67	8
Denmark	66.50	9
Netherlands	66.27	10
South Korea	65.00	11
France	64.26	12
Taiwan	62.35	13
Thailand and Canada	60.00	14
Malaysia	59.39	16
Belgium/Luxembourg	59.29	17
Australia	59.21	18
United States	57.53	19
Italy	56.96	20
Ireland	54.67	21
United Kingdom	54.59	22
India	54.43	23
Austria	52.73	24
Mexico	52.67	25
Turkey	50.59	26
Brazil	50.00	27
Hong Kong	47.50	28
Spain	44.50	29
Portugal	43.12	30
Greece	38.57	31

Source: European Management Forum, 1986

the market at its broadest and take market share among the lower-priced popular lines, most Western corporations will obligingly retrench around a few profitable up-market niches where they can hold their margins.

You can easily defeat a profit-maximizer by the simple expedient of taking the profit out of a particular product for several years and *outwaiting the opposition*. Unable to pay the dividends expected, and more conscious of any decline in the share price, the Western corporation will withdraw.

This situation is particularly serious when Asians have several reasons for still making a product and we are looking only at the profitability of that particular unit. For example, a medical imaging technology may be the basis of a dozen more envisaged products. Its production and development may be teaching 2,000 employees valuable skills of development, production and assembly. Its capacity to detect tumours may save an estimated 60,000 cancer patients a year and save on far more expensive treatments. The more reasons there are for making it as well as possible, the more its price can be forced down temporarily until the Western supplier gives up.

Yet we in the West may be narrowing our attention as our competitors broaden their own. Those in retreat become preoccupied and anxious about the very profits they are losing by being narrow in the first place. When Asian inroads into Western markets began to bite seriously in the late 1970s and early 1980s, Western voters rushed to elect the advocates of profit and *laissez-faire* in Britain, the United States, Canada, Holland and West Germany. The attack on our markets led to a creedal crisis, which led in turn to a reaffirmation of that creed. We were being punished for our dalliance with the mixed economy, for not letting business be as profitable and self-interested as it wished.[4] We must return to Victorian values!

But if the right-wing is wrong, so is the left. Indeed, the tragedy of Western wealth creation is that left and right on the political spectrum have split the solution between them and each extols a part, not in itself viable. Profit is neither good or bad in itself. Rather it is strategically ineffective unless woven into a larger configuration of reconciled values. It is not profits or people but both, not merit or participation but both, not competition or cooperation but both. The danger is that, under pressure, we shall fall back on profits, merit and competition as eternal verities and tear ourselves asunder.[5]

The effect of having one unicorn in our midst, *one* value whose pure extension cannot be questioned, is that this idolization spreads to other values and dilemmas. Consider Michael Porter's famous bifurcation between the low-cost generic strategy and the strategy that seeks a premium product with an abnormally high return. The attempt to do both is specifically warned against. Muddy the otherwise clear issue and you will fall between stools.[6]

Porter is right, of course, *but only if one thinks short term about how to make profits quickly*. The shortage of time makes an either–or choice necessary. One absolute, the need to profit now, makes a second choice between absolutes necessary – either a low-cost generic strategy or a premium product. Unicorns beget more unicorns, while bulls beget bulls.

But suppose we were willing to postpone profitability? This makes the dilemma resolvable. A company makes an original and excellent product, yet offers it at an extremely economical cost, slashing its own margins. This will effectively deter other entrants to this market, who will probably doubt their own capacities to achieve so much for so little evident reward. The result will be that, after several years of low or non-existent profits but rising market share, the Asian competitor will find itself supreme. In contrast, after five years of profiting hugely from its patent, the Western firm finds itself besieged by low-cost imitators. The better strategy is surely the first, although it requires the submerging of any emphasis on 'the bottom line' for several years.

Many readers may react to this argument by emphasizing that profitability should be long term not short term. The bottom line should be extended in time! But this is a rout disguised as a tactical retreat. We live here and now, in the short term. Either profits are to be maximized or this objective is going to be qualified by other considerations. If qualified it loses its status as fundamentalist dogma. If we must forgo profits now to recoup them later, to what criteria should our allegiance be transferred? What should we do now to make our strategic moves less stereotyped and less predictable?

Profiting is a Text Needing the Support of a Context

From chapter 6 onwards we have seen the text and context interweave. Profit-making figures against a ground which is in contrast with it, standing out from that background. Profiting then is a text within a context. It follows that any profit orientation needs a contrasting orientation to make it work effectively. Societies have sectors which are for profit and not for profit, but ideally the latter will support the former. For example, a good health service shores up employees in their work, allowing them to take greater risks because a major source of avoidable insecurity has been taken care of. A very high standard of public education makes private enterprise considerably more prosperous, since all children, regardless of economic circumstance, are given the opportunities they need. A private enterprise economy grows in public soil and the nutrients, irrigation and care of that soil are priceless advantages, yet do not compete in the same manner as the plants themselves. As Lester Thurow has pointed out, competition for profit between US automobile companies was literally underwrought by the National Highways Defense Act. Private vehicles compete on public roads.[7]

This much is obvious, but the dilemma between profiting and supporting is found within the corporation as well. We saw in chapter 3, for example, that the service department of Hotpoint could not become a profit centre lest it started profiting from the correctable faults in products made by the rest of the company. It was there to support the profit-making activity of others, and this is true of many parts of the corporation. Most especially is it true of the highest reaches of top management at Hotpoint, Apple, Hanover, Dow, AKZO, ICI, Shell and others. These persons act as coaches, mentors, score-keepers and cheer-leaders for the profit-making activities of their companies, *but their own roles are largely nurturant and supportive*, giving aid, advice, encouragement and rewards to their front-line troops. They do not think first or foremost how they can use their high status to win from the rest of the company. They cooperate so that *others* may better compete, think so that others may better act, reflect so that others may better practise.

The danger with profit orientation is that no one will be willing to play these more supportive roles, or symbolize the learning which makes profiting possible. Support is especially important in recessions. It is estimated that Britain lost around a quarter of its manufacturing capacity in the 1979–83 recession. These companies could not profit so they should die, right? They should release their resource for more profitable use by better managers. Perhaps. Certainly the performance of the surviving manufacturers has been impressive as we might expect from such culling of the weak. But today there may be simply too few producers, with the result that any increase in demand sucks in imports and pushes the trade gap further into deficit. More support for the profit-making sector in its earlier troubles might have been wise. Profiting gets its *resilience* from support by other values. It is too brittle to go it alone.

Profitability is an Organic Not a Mechanical Attribute

The case for profitability as a supreme arbiter is based on a mistaken metaphor. The corporation is conceived of as a machine in something akin to a demolition derby with competing machines. Losers are junked and their unusable parts cannibalized by other, more successful, competitors. In this way machines and drivers improve with losers feeding resources to winners. The assumption is that these 'losing' bits and pieces can be reassembled quickly and easily into winning combinations by better managers. Despite some waste and destruction in the demolition process, there would be far more waste if the less able were not pushed off the track. Profitability is the sum of each contestant's strength, speed and skill.

But if we conceive of companies as social organisms which have grown over ten or twenty years, then destruction takes on aspects of trauma and death.[8] Their parts may be less valuable than the living creatures from which they were stripped. Years of growth and learning may be irreversibly lost by one bad decision. Unprofitability may have been temporary, a growing pain, but disintegration is for ever. When the recession ends, the plant will not recover, and it may take decades or more to grow its replacement. In the organic metaphor, profitability is but one important sign of healthy growth, but is its temporary absence sufficient to condemn the company? Not if we wish to expand rapidly after the recessions are over, not if the complex learning of networks is to be preserved, not if we want resilient corporations.

Profiting may Not be Applicable to All Units Within a Strategic Alliance

A seventh objection to profit maximization is that it may not be applicable to all products and services in a particular collaborating network. What about an investment bank which makes little or no profit yet lends money to a key national industry which, enhanced by its low cost of capital, becomes a world-class competitor, eliminating several rivals? The bank did not maximize profits, yet the organization, taken as a whole strategic alliance, won valuable markets.

The same issue applies to products that 'give birth', like first, second, third, fourth and fifth generation computers or microchips. The question is less whether one particular generation is profitable, taken as a single range of products, but what their making contributes to the next generation and the next. The experience learned through volume development and production becomes the basis of moving to the next level. It might be worth forgoing profits on stages one, two or three if the consequence was to out-run and out-learn competitors so that all subsequent stages belonged to that company.

This issue comes down to the question of who is competing with whom. Is each bank, each supplier, each subcontractor out for itself, or can a more effective combination of these be regarded as a strategic entity, a supra-company? Now that airlines are joining with other airlines and with hotel chains, car rentals and travel agents, which is the entity that must profit and by how much?

Likewise, if the Japanese government leases its robots at a loss, that could still make every factory that employs these robots and turns them in for the latest models more competitive than they would otherwise have been. The problem with the profitability criterion is that we are never sure to what units it should be applied, nor how wide is the strategic alliance which, taken as a whole, needs to be profitable in how long a time-span. English-speaking countries are not generally sympathetic to the idea that one unit might be content to sacrifice its local income for the benefit of the larger whole, yet alliances formed with such sacrifices may be unbeatable as a combination, with profits *returning* to those who only appeared to give them away through the success of the whole alliance.

When Imitated by Factions or Persons Within the Corporation Profit Orientation becomes Suboptimal

Our eighth objection to profit maximization as a strategy, and the self-interest which is its rationale, is that an organization's employees are likely to model their own behaviour on that idealized by their firm. If the corporation is all out for itself, why should not each employee, each department, each function, each faction and each union place its own perceived interests above those of other groups, including customers, shareholders and the community? In such a value system people will work together only when they can directly gain by doing so, but will scurry down the rigging at the first sign that the ship may not be seaworthy or if a more attractive craft comes alongside.

Why should a corporation invest in its human resources and in the future learning of its employees if each individual promptly takes that training to the highest bidder? British and American corporations make lower 'invisible' investments in their people because they fear to pay twice, once to raise the competence of employees and again to prevent their selling that advantage to a rival corporation.[9] Self-interest, which is qualified neither by gratitude nor loyalty to the firm, is clearly suboptimal. Yet, firms themselves extol the value that undoes them.

For accelerated corporate learning of the kind that can win the learning race has to be much more than the knowledge carried around within single heads. Knowledge is becoming so complex that only stable human networks can encompass it. The more subtle and difficult the communication, the closer human relationships need to be, and the more damaging to the larger system does narrow self-interest become.[10] Turnover rates of 25 per cent per annum or higher are catastrophic. No one will wait for their profits because they will be long gone from the corporation and care only about gains which can be made during a brief occupancy. Profit maximization as an ethic atomizes the organization into adversarial pieces. It has become our Achilles' heel and we may never learn, because to want profit too much is to overlook its necessary preconditions.

Profit Motives Cannot Deal with Societal and Environmental 'Addictions'

In practice the free market is severely limited in key areas. We do not encourage trade in addictive non-medical drugs, or in babies, or in certain kinds of porn. Just as the human body can crave more and more of a drug that is actually poisoning it, so a society can crave lethal weapons, cadavers, or human organs which, if freely traded, would inflict social damage.

We saw at the end of chapter 6 that the environment could become addicted to chemicals, especially pesticides. It can take more and more of these to hold an explosion of pests in check, especially when natural predators fall prey to the toxins and the genes of insects become immune. In all such cases the market fails to work and for the same underlying reason. *The personal short-term gain experienced by the microcosm combines to create a catastrophic longer-term deficit for the macrocosm.* Each farmer needs to keep his pests at bay more effectively than competitors, yet this very contest could poison the whole environment they share. Each 'fix' for the drug addict brings pleasure, but the accumulation brings death. The fact that customers may be desperate for drugs or pesticides and cannot face life without these does not mean that a wise society should allow them to be supplied.

Again this is *not* an argument against profit as an ingredient within a developing economy, but only an argument against regarding profit as an unqualified good, not to be interfered with or qualified by meddlesome persons. The fact is that any country that targets pollution control technologies today, before the demand is heavy, will probably enjoy a handsome stream of profits into the next century when, very predictably, we all start to choke and the horrendous warnings will multiply. We will make these profits in the future by taking a broader view of creating wealth and value in the present, by seeing that the ultimate customer is the environment itself, that in evolutionary survival 'the unit' which survives is people *plus* their environment.[11] The limitation of profit as currently conceived is that it strips the profiting person away from his or her environment and allows the first to 'gain' notionally at the expense of the second.

The Place of Profitability in a Configuration of Values

Profitability is *one* crucial ingredient in a strategic synthesis of values designed to create wealth as broadly defined. It is similar to yeast in its capacity to make a combination of ingredients rise. We should be neither ashamed of profit nor exultant at its making. It is a far better description of a successful economy than it is a prescription for what to form strategies about.

If the real race is to learn, and if the competition will be won by those who create the most valuable configurations of knowledge in the shortest time, then profits are needed to pay 'the school fees', to sponsor the next generation of learners and the next. They are clearly a mundane necessity – but an inspiration? Business is on the verge of a virtual renaissance which will make the ethos of early philistine industrialists and the doctrines of Grantham grocers' daughters into vestiges of the past. To reduce these extensive skeins of knowledge to measures of more or less money paid to persons not even present in the organization and not, for the most part, known as individuals with recognizable faces is to reduce a culture to an abstraction and a community to a set of accounts. This will produce not only a diminution in the energy and creativity with which we work but a loss in the potential of all of us to find meanings in our lives. The hunt for the unicorn is a doomed quest, for no pure unambiguous essence of business virtue exists. We are like jugglers with more and more balls in the air who will drop them all if we get fixated on one.[12]

Throughout this book we have found two meanings within commonly used terms. We separated values and we joined them in chapter 1. We learned before we acted and after we acted in chapter 2. We discovered people coming up to standards and standards coming up to people in two kinds of learning in chapters 4 and 6. We distinguished the unit value of products from their integral value in chapters 6 and 8 and contrasted efficiency with effectiveness in chapter 7. There are two kinds of profitability as well. There is profit as private gain and profit as a somewhat rough guide to mutual satisfaction between the corporation and its stakeholders. It is the latter which has kept the West far ahead of statist economies. An imperfect feedback loop is better by leagues than no feedback loop at all. Yet multiple feedbacks are more effective still. Profit as one element of multiple measures of what is valuable is the way forward strategically.

Notes

1 Jay Ogilvy in *Many Dimensional Man* (New York: Oxford University Press, 1977) makes the point that we are a monotheistic culture, unlike the Ancient Greeks and contemporary Japan. We try to distill and to reduce the many into one, hence 'one nation under God', *e pluribus unum* etc.

2 See B. F. Skinner, *Beyond Freedom and Dignity*. New York: Random House, 1964.

3 European Management Forum, *Annual Report on International Competitiveness*. Geneva: European Management Forum.

4 This point was made by George Lodge in *The American Disease* (New York: Knopf, 1984) and in his contribution to George C. Lodge and Ezra F. Vogel (eds), *Ideology and National Competitiveness* (Boston: Harvard Business School Press, 1987).

5 See Charles M. Hampden-Turner, 'The Trap of Ideology', in *Gentlemen and Tradesmen: The Values of Economic Catastrophe*. London: Routledge and Kegan Paul, 1983, ch. 10, p. 182.

6 Michael F. Porter, *Competitive Strategy: Techniques for Analyzing Industries and Competitors*. New York: Free Press, 1980, ch. 2.

7 Lester C. Thurow, *The Zero Sum Solution*. New York: Simon and Schuster, 1985, p. 172.

8 This idea is taken from Gareth Morgan, *Images of Organization*, Beverly Hills, Calif.: Sage, 1986.

9 Ronald Dore makes much of this in *Taking Japan Seriously*. Stanford, Calif.: Stanford University Press, 1987.

10 The point is made by Bill Ouchi, *Theory Z: How American Business can Meet the Japanese Challenge* (Reading, Mass.: Addison-Wesley, 1981); see especially his concept of 'clan culture'. See also 'the team as entrepreneur' in Robert Reich, *Tales of a New America* (New York: Times, 1987, ch. 8).

11 This insight is Gregory Bateson's; see *Steps to an Ecology of Mind*. New York: Ballantine, 1975.

12 The metaphor is taken from discussions with managers at Hanover Insurance reported to me by Peter Senge.

Bibliography

Abegglen, James C. and Stalk Jr, George, *Kaisha: The Japanese Corporation*. New York: Basic Books, 1985.

Argyris, Chris, *Inner Contradictions of Rigorous Research*. New York: Academic Press, 1980.

Argyris, Chris, *Strategy, Change and Defensive Routines*. Boston, Mass.: Pitman, 1983.

Argyris, Chris (with Putman, R. and Smith, D. M.), *Action Science*. San Francisco, Calif.: Josscy-Bass, 1985.

Argyris, Chris, 'Skilled Incompetence', *Harvard Business Review*, September/October 1986.

Argyris, Chris and Schon, Donald A., *Organizational Learning: A Theory of Action Perspective*. Reading, Mass.: Addison-Wesley, 1978.

Argyris, Chris and Schon, Donald A., 'Reciprocal Integrity', presented at the Symposium on Functioning of Executive Integrity, Case Western Reserve, October 1986 (mimeo).

Argyris, Chris and Schon, Donald A., 'Rigor or Relevance? Normal Science and Action Science Compared', Harvard University and MIT, September 1988 (mimeo).

Axelrod, Robert, *The Evolution of Cooperation*. New York: Basic Books, 1984.

Baden-Fuller, C., Nicolaides, P. and Stopford, John, 'National or Global?' *Centre for Business Strategy Working Paper No. 28*. London, June 1987.

Bateson, Gregory, *Steps to an Ecology of Mind*. New York: Ballantine, 1975.

Beer, Stafford, *The Brain of the Firm*. New York: Wiley, 1981.

Bell, Daniel, *The Coming of Post-Industrial Society*. New York: Basic Books, 1976.

Bennis, Warren and Nanus, Burt, *Leaders: The Strategies for Taking Charge*. New York: Harper and Row, 1985.

Berlin, Isaiah, *Two Concepts of Liberty*. Oxford: Clarendon, 1958.

Berlin, Isaiah, *The Hedgehog and the Fox*. New York: Mentor, 1965.

Blake, Robert R. and Mouton, Jane S., *The Managerial Grid*. Houston, Tex.: Gulf Publishing, 1965.

Boisot, Max, 'Intangible Factors in Japanese Corporate Strategy', *Atlantic Papers*. Paris, 1983.

Bok, Derek, *Beyond the Ivory Tower*. Cambridge, Mass.: Harvard University Press, 1982.

Bolman, Lee G. and Deal, Terrence E., *Modern Approaches to Understanding and Managing Organizations*. San Francisco, Calif.: Jossey-Bass, 1984.

Brand, Stewart, *The Media Lab: Inventing the Future at MIT*. New York: Viking, 1987.

Burns, James MacGregor, *Leadership*. New York: Harper and Row, 1978.

Burns, Thomas and Stalker, G. M., *The Management of Innovation*. London: Tavistock, 1966.

Campbell, Joseph (ed.), *The Portable Jung*. New York: Viking, 1971.

Carlyle, Thomas, 'Signs of the Times 1829', in *Thomas Carlyle Selected Writings*. Harmondsworth: Penguin, 1971.

Christopher, Robert C., *The Japanese Mind*. London: Pan Books, 1984.

Cohen, Stephen and Zysman, John, *Manufacturing Matters*. New York: Basic Books, 1987.

Corning, Peter A., *The Synergism Hypothesis: A Theory of Progressive Evolution*. New York: McGraw-Hill, 1983.

Corning, Peter A. and Corning, Susan, *Winning with Synergy*. New York: Harper and Row, 1986.

Dore, Ronald, *Taking Japan Seriously*. Stanford, Calif.: Stanford University Press, 1987.

Emery, Fred and Trist, Eric, *Towards a Social Ecology*. London: Plenun, 1973.

European Management Forum, *Annual Report on International Competitiveness*. Geneva: European Management Forum.

Forrester, Jay W. and Senge, Peter M., 'Tests for Building Confidence in Systems Dynamics Models', *TIMS Studies in Management Sciences*, No. 14, 1980.

Gaffrey, Rachel, 'Systems Thinking in Business: An Interview with Peter Senge', *Revision*, 7(2), 1984.

Gallwey, Tim, *The Inner Game of Tennis*. New York: Doubleday, 1974.

de Geus, A. P., 'Planning as Learning', *Harvard Business Review*, March/April 1988.

Goold, Michael and Campbell, Andrew, *Strategic Styles*. Oxford: Basil Blackwell, 1988.

Gouldner, Alvin, 'Metaphysical Pathos and the Theory of Bureaucracy', *American Political Science Review*, 49, 1955, pp. 496–507.

Green, Sebastian, 'The Hotpoint Story', *London Business School Case Studies*, No. 3, 1987.

Halal, William E., *The New Capitalism*. New York: Wiley, 1986.

Halberstam, David, *The Reckoning*. New York: Avon, 1986.

Hampden-Turner, Charles M., *Radical Man: Towards a Theory of Psychosocial Development*. London: Duckworth, 1973.

Hampden-Turner, Charles M., *Maps of the Mind*. New York: Macmillan, 1981.

Hampden-Turner, Charles M., *Gentlemen and Tradesmen: the Values of Economic Catastrophe*. London: Routledge and Kegan Paul, 1983.

Hampden-Turner, Charles M., 'Approaching Dilemmas', *Shell Guides to Planning*, No. 3, 1985.

Hampden-Turner, Charles M. and Baden-Fuller, Charles, 'Strategy and Dilemma', *Centre for Business Strategy Working Paper No. 51*, London, 1988.

Hampden-Turner, Charles M. and Carlisle, Franklin, *Lifestyle Marketing*. Menlo Park, Calif.: SRI International Leading Edge Publications, VALS program, 1986.

Hedley, Barry, 'Strategy and the Business Portfolio', *Journal of Long-Range Planning*, February 1977.

Jaques, Elliot, *Free Enterprise Fair Employment*. New York: Crane Russak, 1982.

Jaques, Elliot, *The Form of Time*. New York: Crane Russak, 1982.

Jaques, Elliot, *Requisite Organization: The CEO's Guide to Creative Structure and Leadership*. Arlington, Va.: Cason Hall, 1989.

Kanter, Rosabeth Moss, *The Change Masters*. London: Allen and Unwin, 1984.

Kauffman, Draper L., *Systems 1: An Introduction to Systems Thinking*. Minneapolis, Minn.: Future Systems, 1980.

Keifer, Charles F. and Senge, Peter M., 'Metanoic Organization', in John D. Adams (ed.), *Transforming Work*. Alexandria, Va.: Miles River Press, 1984.

Kotter, John P. and Lawrence, Paul R., *Mayors in Action*. New York: Wiley, 1974.

Lawler, Edward E., *High Involvement Management*. San Francisco, Calif.: Jossey-Bass, 1986.

Lawrence, Paul R. and Lorsch, Jay W., *Organization and Environment*. Boston, Mass.: Harvard Division of Research, 1967.

Lebra, Takie Sugiyama, *Japanese Patterns of Behavior*. Honolulu, Hawaii: University Press of Hawaii, 1976.

Lessem, Ronnie, *The Roots of Excellence*. London: Fontana, 1985.

Lodge, George C., *The American Disease*. New York: Knopf, 1984.

Lodge, George C. and Vogel, Ezra F. (eds), *Ideology and National Competitiveness*. Boston, Mass.: Harvard Business School Press, 1987.

Mangham, Iain L., *Organizations as Theatre*. New York: Wiley, 1987.

Marcuse, Herbert, *One-Dimensional Man*. Boston, Mass.: Beacon Press, 1964.

Maslow, Abraham, *Motivation and Personality*. New York: Harper and Row, 1954.

McCarthy, Eugene N. and Kilpatrick, James K., *A Political Bestiary*. Illustrated by Jeff MacNelly. New York: McGraw-Hill, 1978.

McGregor, Douglas, *The Human Side of the Enterprise*. New York: McGraw-Hill, 1960.

Michael, Donald N., *On Learning to Plan and Planning to Learn*. San Francisco, Calif.: Jossey-Bass, 1973.

Mintzberg, Henry, 'The Manager's Job: Folklore or Fact', *Harvard Business Review*, July/August 1975.

Mintzberg, Henry, 'Planning on the Left Side, Managing on the Right', *Harvard Business Review*, July/August 1976.

Mintzberg, Henry, 'Crafting Strategy', *Harvard Business Review*, March/April 1987, pp. 66–75.

Mintzberg, Henry, 'Opening up the Definition of Strategy', in J. M. Quinn, H. Mintzberg and R. M. James (eds), *The Strategy Process*, Engelwood Cliffs, N.J.: Prentice Hall, 1987.

Mittroff, Iain, *Business NOT as Usual*. San Francisco, Calif.: Jossey-Bass, 1987.

Morgan, Gareth, *Images of Organization*, Beverly Hills, Calif.: Sage, 1986.

Morgan, Gareth, *Riding the Waves of Change*. San Francisco, Calif.: Jossey-Bass, 1988.

Myers, Norman (ed.), *GAIA: An Atlas of Planet Management*. New York: Anchor Press, Doubleday, 1984.

O'Brien, Bill, *Hanover Booklets*; see especially 'Leanness', 'Localness', 'Openness', 'Advanced Maturity', 'The Customer', 'Building a Merit Environment'. Hanover Insurance, 100 North Parkway, Worcester, Mass. 01605.

Ogilvy, Jay, *Many Dimensional Man*. New York: Oxford University Press, 1977.

O'Toole, James, *Vanguard Management*. New York: Doubleday, 1985.

Ouchi, William, *Theory Z: How American Business can Meet the Japanese Challenge*. Reading, Mass.: Addison-Wesley, 1981.

Pascale, R. T. and Athos, A. G., *The Art of Japanese Management*. New York: Simon and Schuster, 1981.

Peters, Tom and Waterman, Robert H., *In Search of Excellence*. New York: Harper and Row, 1982.

Porter, Michael E., *Competitive Strategy: Techniques for Analyzing Industries and Competitors*. New York: Free Press, 1980.

Porter, Michael E. (ed.), *Competition in Global Industries*. Boston, Mass.: Harvard Business School Press, 1986.

Postle, Denis, *Catastrophe Theory*. London: Fontana, 1980.

Quinn, James Brian, 'Logical Incrementalism', *Sloan Management Review*, (20), Fall 1978.

Quinn, James Brian, Mintzberg, Henry and James, Robert M., *The Strategy Process*. Englewood Cliffs, N.J.: Prentice Hall, 1988.

Quinn, Robert E., *Beyond Rational Management*. San Francisco, Calif.: Jossey-Bass, 1988.

Rapaport, Anatol, *Strategy and Conscience*. Boston, Mass.: Houghton Mifflin, 1963.

Reich, Robert B., *The Next American Frontier*. New York: Times, 1983.

Reich, Robert B., *Tales of a New America*. New York: Times, 1987.

Roethlisberger, Fritz and Dixon, William, *Management and the Worker*. Cambridge, Mass.: Harvard University Press, 1937.

Rosak, Theodore (ed.), *The Dissenting Academy*. New York: Pantheon, 1968.

Schein, Edgar H., *Organization, Culture and Leadership*. San Francisco, Calif.: Jossey-Bass, 1985.

Schon, Donald A., *Beyond the Stable State*. New York: Randon House, 1971.

Schon, Donald A., 'Creative Metaphor: A Perspective on Problem Setting in Social Policy', in A. Ortny (ed.), *Metaphor and Thought*. Cambridge: Cambridge University Press, 1979.

Schon, Donald A., *The Reflective Practitioner*. New York: Basic Books, 1982.

Scott, Bruce R. and Lodge, George C. (eds), *American Competitiveness*. Boston, Mass.: Harvard Business School Press, 1985.

Sculley, John, *Odyssey: From Pepsi to Apple*. New York: Harper and Row, 1987.

Senge, Peter M., 'Catalyzing Systems Thinking within Organizations', in F. Massarik (ed.), *Advances in Organization Development. Report of the Program in Systems Thinking and the New Management Style*. Cambridge, Mass.: MIT Press, 1987.

Skinner, B. F., *Beyond Freedom and Dignity*. New York: Random House, 1964.

Smith, Diana M., 'Intervention into Conflict: A Critical Study of Exemplary Practitioners', Thesis Proposal, Harvard University. Available from Mass Action Design Associates, Newton, 1987.

Stata Ray, 'Organizational Learning – The Key to Management Innovation', *Sloan Management Review*, (63), Spring 1989.

Takeuchi, H. and Porter, Michael E., 'Three Roles of International Marketing in Global Strategy', in Michael E. Porter (ed.), *Competition in Global Industries*. Boston, Mass.: Harvard Business School Press, 1987.

Thurow, Lester C., *The Zero Sum Society*. New York: McGraw-Hill, 1980.

Thurow, Lester C. (ed.), *The Management Challenge: Japanese Views*. Cambridge, Mass.: MIT Press, 1985.

Thurow, Lester C., *The Zero Sum Solution*. New York: Simon and Schuster, 1985.

Toffler, Alvin, *Future Shock*. New York: Bantam, 1970.

Toffler, Alvin, *The Third Wave*. New York: Bantam, 1980.

Vogel, Ezra, *Japan as No 1*. New York: Harper and Row, 1979.

Vogel, Ezra, *Comeback: Building the Resurgence of American Business*. New York: Simon and Schuster, 1985.

Watzlawick, Paul, Beavin, J. H. and Jackson, D. D., *Pragmatics of Human Communication*. New York: W. W. Norton, 1967.

Weisskopj, Walter, *Alienation and Economics*. New York: Dutton, 1971.

Wolf, Marvin J., *The Japanese Conspiracy*. New York: Empire Books, 1983.

Wood, Graig, 'The Hotpoint Story, 1921–1981', Master's Thesis, Warwick University, 1983 (mimeo).

Index